I0146760

Yearnings in the Meantime

DISLOCATIONS

General Editors: August Carbonella, *Memorial University of Newfoundland,* Don Kalb, *University of Utrecht* & *Central European University,* Linda Green, *University of Arizona*

The immense dislocations and suffering caused by neoliberal globalization, the retreat of the welfare state in the last decades of the twentieth century, and the heightened military imperialism at the turn of the twenty-first century have raised urgent questions about the temporal and spatial dimensions of power. Through stimulating critical perspectives and new and cross-disciplinary frameworks that reflect recent innovations in the social and human sciences, this series provides a forum for politically engaged, ethnographically informed, and theoretically incisive responses.

YEARNINGS IN THE MEANTIME

'Normal Lives' and the State in a
Sarajevo Apartment Complex

Stef Jansen

berghahn
NEW YORK · OXFORD
www.berghahnbooks.com

First published in 2015 by
Berghahn Books
www.berghahnbooks.com

© 2015, 2018 Stef Jansen
First paperback edition published in 2018

All rights reserved.
Except for the quotation of short passages
for the purposes of criticism and review, no part of this book
may be reproduced in any form or by any means, electronic or
mechanical, including photocopying, recording, or any information
storage and retrieval system now known or to be invented,
without written permission of the publisher.

Library of Congress Cataloging-in-Publication Data

Jansen, Stef.
Yearnings in the meantime: 'normal lives' and the state in a Sarajevo
apartment complex / Stef Jansen. -- First Edition.
    pages cm. -- (Dislocations; Volume 15)
Includes bibliographical references and index.
ISBN 978-1-78238-650-6 (hardback: alk. paper) -- ISBN 978-1-78238-651-3
(ebook)
1. Sarajevo (Bosnia and Herzegovina)--Social conditions--21st century.
2. Ethnology--Bosnia and Herzegovina--Sarajevo. 3. Yugoslav War,
1991-1995--Bosnia and Herzegovina--Sarajevo. I. Title.
HN639.S37J36 2015
306.0949742--dc23

2015003140

British Library Cataloguing in Publication Data
A catalogue record for this book is available from the British Library

ISBN 978-1-78238-650-6 (hardback)
ISBN 978-1-78533-821-2 (paperback)
ISBN 978-1-78238-651-3 (ebook)

CONTENTS

Part I: Figuring 'Normal Lives'

Part II: Diagnosing Daytonitis

Part III: Living With Daytonitis

ILLUSTRATIONS

PREFACE

I never see the dawn, said Marco, his voice rattling in his throat, that I don't
say to myself perhaps... perhaps today.

—John Dos Passos, *Manhattan Transfer*

While I am revising this manuscript for publication in the winter of
2014, something special is happening in Bosnia and Herzegovina.
A sudden revolt has rocked a series of towns and its reverberations
continue in protests and citizen plenums. Key demands concern
social justice. Most of the fury is directed at the inequality between
'politicians' and 'ordinary people', the privileges enjoyed by a corrupt, criminal ruling caste organised through political parties and the
privatisation process that has cemented these. Many of the demands
revolve around the need to establish a fair and functional 'system'
that will finally allow people in Bosnia and Herzegovina to 'move
forward from the dead point' and live 'normal lives'. This is the first
time since the early 1990s that the country sees such attempts to formulate the beginnings – however fledgling – of a more or less univer-
salist political agenda on redistribution – one that does not focus on
constitutional and territorial issues of recognition and representation
through an identitarian prism. Within hours of the first demonstrations, friends were telling me I would need to add a third part to the
epilogue in this book.

I have not written this epilogue, partly because I am too busy on
the street protests and in the plenum in Sarajevo. Priorities... In this
preface I therefore merely flag the possibility that this entire book on
'normal lives' and 'the state' in Bosnia and Herzegovina has itself,
totally unexpectedly, become a preface. Hindsight will show if this
is indeed the case and if the Meantime may be reaching its long-
yearned-for end.

ACKNOWLEDGEMENTS

I am grateful to the people in Dobrinja who unselfishly agreed to make time for what many no doubt perceived as a confirmation of their fateful exposure to a foreign gaze and some perhaps also as yet another pointless research exercise by an intrusive outsider. To those who cooperated only reluctantly, because they have long known that the key challenge in Bosnia and Herzegovina (BiH) is not to identify problems, but to solve them, I say: I hope this book includes a fair representation of the reasons for this understandable reluctance. Special thanks for valuable research assistance go to Melina Sadiković, whose dedication to better understanding, a better Sarajevo, a better BiH and a better world, not only helped overcome the reluctance of many interlocutors but also my own creeping doubts as to whether it was even worth trying. Other Sarajevans who kept me going, perhaps without being aware of their significance for this project, include Almir Bašović, Draško Luković and Nermina Mujagić. I also want to extend heartfelt thanks to the Čelebičić 'tribe' for making me feel welcome in their warm and non-judgmental embrace. Conversations with all those people – about social theory, about music, about human relations, about novels, about politics, about football, about justice, about exasperation with and commitment to life in Bosnia and Herzegovina – are my lifelines in Sarajevo. With regard to my research, I also want to thank them for never saying 'ta ć' ti to ba? [why bother, mate?] and thus saving me from the ever-present risk of being sucked into Sarajevo mass hypnosis (see www.youtube.com/watch?v=f797eI3pMeI).

The ideas in this book have also been shaped in sustained dialogue with a group of researchers at the University of Manchester writing doctoral dissertations on questions of statecraft, temporality and engagements with the future in the post-Yugoslav states: Čarna Brković, Deana Jovanović, Goran Dokić, Ivan Rajković and Vanja Čelebičić. It has been a true privilege to work with such gifted and committed people; I continue to learn from them. For constructive engagements I also thank participants at conferences, seminars and lectures where I have presented earlier versions of the arguments contained in this book. Amongst others whose critical interventions as well as support have helped me considerably, I want to thank Dunja Njaradi, Jan Grill, Larisa Kurtović, Jessica Greenberg, Andrew Gilbert, Elissa Helms, Staffan Löfving, Madeleine Reeves, Sarah Green, Keir Martin, Soumhya Venkatesan and Michelle Obeid. The latter, Čarna Brković and Vanja Čelebičić (who I also thank for generously allowing me to include her photographs and preparing them for publication) provided constructive critical comments on the draft manuscript. So did Ivana Spasić, who I thank for over fifteen years (and counting) of impassioned dialogue, fascinated as we are by shared social scientific puzzles and/or life questions, but also for helping me to steer a course through the swamp of positionality as someone from Here ('The Centre') who is There ('The Semiperiphery').

I need all the help I can get with this, because this book was entirely written in Sarajevo. More often than not my Here is actually There. The most important person to make it so, and to help me navigate this, is Nejra Nuna Čengić, who has also been the key dialogue partner in the making of the book. Without her continuous contributions, I am afraid to say, the book would perhaps have been completed much earlier. Yet in that case it would have been of much poorer quality. Alternatively, it might not have seen the light of day at all – for a major theme in this work, the exasperated sense of 'pattering in place', applies not only to a structure of feeling amongst Sarajevans, but also to many of my own experiences in this city, including those of writing this book. If anyone knows this, Nuna does. Therefore, my greatest gratitude goes to her: for the support, inspiration, conversations and critical interventions that shaped the entire process of writing, and, no less importantly, for everything else besides.

Large parts of the 2008–10 research for this book were financially supported by the British Academy (grant 'Transformations of home, hope and the state in Bosnia-Herzegovina') and by the Leverhulme Trust (grant 'Transforming borders: a comparative anthropology of post-Yugoslav home'). I thank them for their preparedness, still rare today, to invest in a project on Bosnia and Herzegovina that does not inscribe itself in the identitarian categories of 'ethnic conflict' and/or the normative ones of the 'transitional justice' industry. Likewise, I thank the people at Berghahn Books, including Molly Mosher, an excellent anonymous copy editor, the editors of the *Dislocations* series and three anonymous peer reviewers, all of whom restored my belief that intellectual rigour and humane efficiency can go together in academic publishing.

The notion of 'gridding', introduced in chapter 2, and some of the data from and arguments on Dobrinja schools in chapter 3 appeared previously in an article entitled 'Hope for/against the state: gridding in a besieged Sarajevo suburb', in *Ethnos* (2014, 79[2]: 238–60). Parts of the arguments and materials in chapter 5 were published as 'On not moving well enough: temporal reasoning in Sarajevo yearnings for "normal lives"', in *Current Anthropology* (2014, S9: S74–S84).

INTRODUCTION
[or, Towards an Anthropology of Shared Concerns]

In the summer of 2009, I made an unexpected appearance in a Sarajevo newspaper. Illustrated by a photo capturing me in overacting teaching mode in front of a group of course participants, an article reported on that year's Regional Peace Academy under the title 'Far from normal life'.[1] Throughout my work in Bosnia and Herzegovina (BiH)[2] since 2000, and in Serbia and Croatia before that, references to 'normal lives' have been ubiquitous and, without exception, positive. During my 2008–10 ethnographic research for this book in Sarajevo, this emic term again emerged as a signpost for a particularly important shared concern. On the one hand, in a forward-looking sense, it was the most common way in which people phrased their hopes and fears for the future: 'We just want a normal life'. To say this was to remove any need for explanation of what that life would look like – it was just normal – and the word 'just' denoted the perceived modesty of this desire, sharply set off against present conditions, which were believed not to allow the fulfilment of even such humble expectations. On the other hand, in a backward-looking sense, I found 'normal' to be a very common term to appraise previous lives in Yugoslav BiH. This again suggested self-explanatory consensus and modest criteria of evaluation, converging in an affirmation of the comparative superiority of conditions 'before' with regard to their facilitation of 'normal lives'.

A booklet produced at the tenth anniversary of the 1995 Dayton Peace Agreement, which brought an end to almost four years of military violence in BiH (Helsinški parlament građana 2005), provides a sensitive insight into just how widely shared this concern was. Based on five hundred short street interviews across the country, it conveys the stark sense of entrapment that prevailed. Asked what they expected for their future, the vast majority of interviewees indicated strong limitations both in terms of what they felt they could expect and in terms of the social reach of their hopes. Apart from the many who said they did not expect anything at all as long as the political situation did not change, most mentioned hopes for health, employment, education and family continuity. Many said they hoped to 'earn their pensions' and the most frequent reply transferred hopes to the next generation. Very few respondents formulated any hopes beyond their households. 'Normal lives' functioned as a very common object of yearning and as an indicator of the modesty of normative standards. Yet few felt that such lives were about to appear on the horizon. Indeed, the sense of lack of improvement in their predicaments, diagnosed as intimately related to the (geo)political stagnation and dysfunctionality of Dayton BiH, was itself a key pattern.[3] If anything, the sense that one was not going anywhere had intensified during my research a few years later. In the booklet, when asked what he most frequently talked about with people, a forty-year-old hairdresser summarised the core of many ordinary conversations and public interventions during my research: he mostly talked, he said, about 'when things will improve' [*kada će ovo na bolje*: litt. when will this (move) towards better].

Based on research in an apartment complex in the outskirts of Sarajevo, this book is an attempt to ethnographically pry open such yearnings for 'normal lives' (a term I use exclusively in descriptive fashion) and the political reasonings they entailed. I focus on the embedding of life trajectories in the political ordering of sociality because 'normal lives' were widely believed to require 'a normal state'. Charting a narrative course through experiences of city transport, schooling, building maintenance, clientelism, war and geopolitics, this book shall time and again return to the questions raised by seemingly self-explanatory statements that one had once lived a 'normal life' and that all one wanted was to live a 'normal life' – nothing more and, importantly, nothing less, than that.

Shared Concerns: 'Normal Lives' and the State in Dobrinja

Most Sarajevans live in the city's post-Second World War settlements, of which the furthest outlying apartment complex is called Dobrinja. Dobrinja was built on agricultural land, in planned phases from the late 1970s onwards. While it contains a section with detached private houses, also relatively recent but known as *mahala* (a term more commonly used for hillside city quarters surrounding the Ottoman-era *čaršija* – the commercial centre), most of the settlement consists of planned apartment blocks, relatively low-rise due to the proximity of BiH's main airport. A part of Dobrinja was erected as a press village for the 1984 Olympic Winter Games and the last prewar buildings were completed shortly before the 1992–95 war. During and after my research, this apartment complex was expanding again. The prewar construction of Dobrinja had unfolded within Yugoslav self-management socialism, financed mainly by so-called socialist giants, large socially owned firms that allocated inheritable tenancy rights to workers who paid contributions into special funds. The 1991 census found no absolute majority of any national grouping amongst Dobrinja's inhabitants, who were reputed to be relatively well educated and to have a predominantly middle-income profile.[4] Solidarity housing policies reserved some flats for lower-income households. Most of Dobrinja's prewar population of over thirty-two thousand consisted of young households with children who had come from other parts of Sarajevo.

During the 1992–95 war (see Narrative Glossary below), Dobrinja was almost entirely encircled by Serbian nationalist forces, who also took full control over the easternmost section of the settlement. Later, I explore how this proximity to the siege line and the ensuing isolation from the rest of the city during the first months of the violence – a kind of siege within the siege – informed a specific war experience.

FIGURE 0.1. The logo of the 1984 Olympic Winter Games on a central Dobrinja apartment block (photo by Vanja Čelebičić, 2014)

At the time of my research, damage in Dobrinja remained extensive and visible. Due to wartime shelling, leaking roofs posed a widespread problem. Many buildings had been reconstructed, often at least partly with foreign humanitarian aid, but some flats were still uninhabitable. In the flat above the one where I lived, for example, outer walls had been repaired but its inside was bare concrete. Immediately beyond this building, the so-called Inter-Entity Boundary Line – dividing Dayton BiH into its two war-produced entities – ran through the easternmost section of the apartment complex. Hence, while living in one entity, the Federation of BiH, I looked out over the other: Republika Srpska.[5]

It is from this vantage point in the outskirts of the Sarajevo agglomeration that I embarked on my ethnographic study. I lived in Dobrinja from February to August 2008 and from February to June 2010, with shorter visits before, in between and after.[6] So, who did I live amongst in Dobrinja, and how did these Dobrinjci live? I now sketch some aggregate patterns, to be elaborated upon throughout the book.

Who lived in Dobrinja? Amongst the scarce available figures for this apartment complex, the most exact ones are election results. In 2008 (local) and 2010 (general) elections, SDP (Socijaldemokratska partija) – a party with a less ethnonationally defined programme than other main parties – attracted by far the largest proportion of votes

FIGURE 0.2. A Dobrinja building several years after reconstruction (photo by Vanja Čelebičić, 2010)

here. This relative electoral dominance of the successor party to the Yugoslav League of Communists, then in opposition in most of BiH's numerous parliaments, was particularly notable amongst people with longstanding residence in Dobrinja, who are at the centre of this book. Further, in terms of population statistics, adding up the 2007 records of the four local communes in Dobrinja we arrive at a total of 24,589 inhabitants, of which over 53 per cent were women. Compared to the prewar situation, the total population of Dobrinja, as that of Sarajevo and BiH as a whole, had thus dropped dramatically. The nationality composition also changed strongly due to in- and out-migration. In the absence of a census, no confirmed figures existed but those that did circulate suggested that, despite the prewar and wartime exodus of most people declaring Serbian nationality (some of whom moved to the settlement's eastern outskirts), Dobrinja's population still remained less nationally homogenised than that of many other places in BiH. On the basis of 2007 figures from local communes, we reach these proportions: 77 per cent Bosniaks, 12 per cent Serbs, 8 per cent Croats and 3 per cent Others. I have been unable to find out how these percentages were reached and, if they involved a survey, how questions were phrased. Moreover, the secretary responsible for keeping them told me herself that population records had never been systematically updated. She suspected all figures – not just those concerning nationality – were roughly missing their targets by a third, but she did not hazard a guess in which direction. As we shall see in this book, such poor legibility of the population was of concern not only to state administrators, from whom this was to be expected, but also to many others.

The lack of reliable statistics was reflected in all other government organs whose mandate covered Dobrinja: those of the municipality of Novi grad, the City of Sarajevo, the Canton of Sarajevo, the Federation of BiH, the state of BiH and the in-country EU supervisory agencies. This is therefore a good point at which to apologise for the sense of bewilderment that readers may experience due to my dense references to BiH's labyrinthine administrative–territorial structure in the early parts of this book. A rational, pyramidical organigram of BiH's government apparatus as stipulated in the Dayton constitution would have served as a more conventional and easier overture, but instead of starting out with such a 'view from nowhere', I will provide this only in chapter 4. Until then I attempt to introduce the reader to BiH statecraft in ways that reflect my ethnographic findings as closely as possible. If 'the state' failed to establish a high degree of legibility of the population, people in BiH, in turn, found that the state remained opaque from their perspective.[7] Yet at the same time its categories were ever present. In the course of this book I aim to bring the institutional sites of statecraft in BiH into view in the manner in which (and insofar as) they emerged in the pursuits of Dobrinjci to attain 'normal lives'. More often than not they will therefore appear as undifferentiated parts of a confusing, muddled and always incomplete mirage that hovers over yearnings for 'normal lives'. Conveying initial disorientation and even lasting bewilderment, I am afraid, is a necessary dimension of my approach. No one in Dobrinja had an organigram of Dayton BiH on the wall and no one consulted one before trying to sort out a pension, reporting a burglary, attempting to avoid a tax payment or applying for a building permit. At this stage, I thus plead for patience and ask the reader to take me on my word that the frustration of virtual wandering through an incomprehensible statescape has its merits in terms of ethnographic evocation. People in Dobrinja know the feeling all too well.

Refraining from an initial organigram, let me instead offer an initial approach to the question of *how* people in Dobrinja lived on aggregate. This overview – not based on ethnography, but not quite a view from nowhere either – is assembled from 2007–08 figures sourced from local communes in Dobrinja, from Novi grad municipality and from Dayton BiH's dispersed offices for statistics.[8] Again, due to the poor reliability of official statistics, large grains of salt are in order. Dobrinja belongs to Novi grad municipality, one of the most populous in BiH with some one hundred and twenty thousand inhabitants (ca. 10 per cent down from 1991), including ca. twenty thousand displaced persons. The only Sarajevo municipality, and one of a few in BiH with a positive natality/mortality balance, it inherited one of the largest numbers (36,500) of socially owned flats in the country, about 90 per cent of which had been privatised by 2007. Most had been 'bought' for certificates by the tenancy rights holders (and many had then sold them on). Although Novi grad was ranked as one of the relatively more prosperous municipalities in BiH, only around 16 per cent of its inhabitants were officially employed. Their registered average monthly net wage was 807 convertible marks (KM; €412) versus just over 925 KM (€472) across the Canton of Sarajevo and 740 KM (€378) across the Federation of BiH.[9] Many employees also received a (federal) average of 262 KM (€134) for meals and transport. Fourteen per cent of the population of Novi grad was registered as unemployed, but only a fraction received any benefits on this basis (ca. 300 KM [€153] for a period of three months to a maximum of two years). More than 6,500 people lived in households of war-disabled persons or fallen soldiers. Many of them received some (non means-tested) war-related allowances, especially for war disability (at 100 per cent disability, 805 KM [€411]) or as families of fallen soldiers. While much lower allowances existed for the category of civilian victims of war (at 100 per cent disability, 300 KM [€153]), these were only paid out to some with the highest percentages of disability and were very hard to obtain. These and other war-related payments were also widely perceived as a major tool of clientelism by political party structures: many people received nothing, some received only small amounts and the lion's share was paid out to a small, well-off category. Finally, Novi grad housed around twenty thousand pensioners (ca. 16 per cent of the population). In 2007, the average monthly pension across the Federation was 340 KM (€173) and half of all pensioners received the minimal pension: 282 KM (€144). Other (means-tested) welfare payments were extremely difficult to obtain and varied from a few dozen KM, for most beneficiaries, to maximum a few hundred KM for a select few.

There are different ways to form an idea of the relative value of these figures. First, we can juxtapose them with the last official amount (2007) for a four-member household 'basket' for nutrition and hygiene: 528 KM (€270). While it would be tough to fulfil monthly needs of only food, drink and toiletries with this sum, note that this official basket does not cover even the most modest standards of 'normal lives': housing, utilities, clothing, health care, education, transport, and so on. Figures for an alternative, so-called 'syndical' household basket that circulated in those days hovered around 1,500 KM (€767). By any measure, then, BiH counted one of the largest proportions of people living under or around the poverty line in Europe, as was regularly pointed out in the media. This brings us to the second way to assess the above income figures in relative terms. On a global scale, clearly, people in BiH were on aggregate not amongst the poorest. Despite a widespread rhetoric of 'struggle for survival', relatively few were hungry. Yet, as in other post-Yugoslav states, the main points of reference were Western European standards and recollections of lives in the Socialist Federal Republic of Yugoslavia (SFRY). In that respect, as we shall see throughout this book, almost all my interlocutors assessed their current lives in terms of a dramatic downturn. Under the authority of the League of Communists, Yugoslav workers' self-management had revolved around a 'mixed' system of planning and market mechanisms, embodied in the specific decentralised form of 'social ownership' (for a critical analysis, see Woodward 1995). Regardless of many discrepancies between the rhetoric and the practice of Yugoslav socialism, which they rarely dwelled on, Dobrinjci with longstanding residence in the apartment complex retained a notion of previous 'normal lives' in positive contrast with their current predicaments. As we shall see with regard to a variety of issues throughout the book, they recalled lives that had been relatively predictable: their flow had been securely gridded in the institutions of Yugoslav socialist self-management, which bore all the hallmarks of a twentieth-century developmentalist project. All but two of my interlocutors had originally moved into their flats through workplace-centred housing allocation policies and become owners after the war. In the late Yugoslav period, marked by considerable unemployment rates and inflation (again, almost never mentioned), at least one member of each of those households – and often more than one – had been permanently employed in a firm or institution that had provided them not only with a modern flat, but also, in almost all cases, with higher wages (even in absolute terms) than they could earn today, when prices were much higher. Add to this a wider and more inclusive range of free services in social protection, health care, education and leisure, and it is clear that the exasperation with current lives must be understood in relation to recollections of previous ones.[10] As we shall see, this is true not only for living standards, broadly understood, but also for the core topic of this book: the relationship between yearnings for 'normal lives' and the spatiotemporal ordering processes of statecraft.

It was with these emic conceptions of 'normal lives' in mind that I embarked on an ethnographic study of statecraft in BiH. Initially, inspired by a flourishing ethnography of people's everyday encounters with state agencies – their 'sightings of the state' (Corbridge et al. 2005: 9) – I planned to trace interactions in specific interfaces of public provision: education, pensions and health care. My focus was to be on neighbourliness and inequality. In that way, I wanted to reconstruct people's hopes and fears with regard to statecraft in this apartment complex, from its inception in late socialist Yugoslav BiH, over its fate during war, to the situation in Dayton BiH. I did work in local schools but I soon reconfigured my project. For one thing, public city transport unexpectedly emerged as a productive interface for observational ethnographic study, allowing me to work through 'episodes' of heightened engagement with statecraft (Wedeen 1999a). Moreover, I realised that a focus on 'sightings' failed to grasp a crucial dimension of the social life of the state in Dobrinja. With regard to statecraft, namely, a much more striking pattern emerged: the state featured as a central category in my interlocutors' attempts to reason through their predicament in Dayton BiH, but rather than to actual sightings, they insistently drew my attention to their *desire* for sightings. They wished to see the state and be seen by it. A projected 'normal state' was at the heart of their yearnings for 'normal lives'.

To deepen insights into this dimension of lives in Dayton BiH, I expanded on my participant observation by including forty in-depth interviews on everyday practices, concerns and expectations with regard to life trajectories and statecraft in Dobrinja from its initial construction in Yugoslav BiH to the present.[11] Apart from a willingness to participate, interviewees therefore shared one characteristic: they had all moved to this settlement in the 1970s or 1980s. Almost all of them had resided there during the war years too, although a few had spent short periods elsewhere. While forty interviewees cannot support any claims to statistical representativeness, I purposively included people of different profiles along lines of gender, age, occupation, wealth, (ethno)nationality, religious practice and party membership. I chose such a broad sweep of interlocutors in order to investigate concerns that were shared by different categories of people in Dobrinja. Let me now discuss this against the background of widely circulating portraits of Sarajevo.

Beyond 'Trivision'

A mosque! A Serbian orthodox church! A catholic cathedral! A synagogue! And all that in close proximity right in the centre of one European capital city! I can see all four buildings through the laundry that hangs out to dry on the sixth-floor communal front terrace of the building where I am writing this. Exhilaration at this architectural embodiment of cultural–religious diversity is a favourite way of introducing guests to Sarajevo in tourist publications, media and literary descriptions. In BiH, where religious heritage is the main marker of nationality categories, each of these iconic Ottoman or Habsburg era places of Abrahamic worship is associated with a different national grouping of the city's population: Bosniaks (until 1993 known as Bosnian Muslims), Serbs, Croats and Jews. Due to Sarajevo's widely broadcast fate in the 1990s war, it is often a concern with such national diversity that channels the outside gaze onto the city. Whether phrased as a measure of multiculturalism, tolerance, coexistence, hybridity or cosmopolitanism, some commentators lament the relative demise of that diversity, while others marvel at its relative persistence and at the way in which Sarajevans negotiate it.

During my research, a 'groupist' notion of nationality (Brubaker 2002) was crucial to political debates in and around BiH as a categorical logic and as an institutionalised vector of representation. Such considerations have historically always played an important role in the government of the BiH polity as part of larger formations (Bougarel 1996b). Yet, in Dayton BiH, with largely nationally homogenised populations in its various subpolities, national groupism had been intensified and to a large extent territorialised. A joke that did the rounds in Dayton BiH illustrated this. A journalist asks a Bosnian to comment on the political situation in his country. He scratches his head and replies: 'Mmmm ... I don't know what to say, I am in three minds about this [*Troumim se*]'. Like in English, the more common phrase refers to being in *two* minds [*dvoumiti se*] and the joke hinges on mocking a structural feature of Dayton BiH: the organisation of everything 'by three'. This threeway mode of vision and division ('trivision'?) is the driving logic of the Dayton 'ethnopolis' (Mujkić 2007), governed through a constitutionally cemented, foreign-enforced consociation of three nationally defined 'constituent peoples': Bosniaks, Croats and Serbs.

In Dayton BiH political institutions and in the mediascape – itself largely divided in three – cleronationalist entrepreneurs eagerly reached for the constitutional trump card of 'vital national interests'. On aggregate, nationalist rhetoric could mobilise many people for electoral purposes and, more importantly in my view, demobilise alternative politics (see Gagnon 2004). BiH's capital city was not free of any of this. Yet while war-related inward and outward migrations had drastically reduced face-to-face national–identitarian diversity in everyday lives, I found that many longstanding Dobrinjci routinely refused to inscribe themselves in this matrix. Politically, they often articulated this through affiliation with inclusive BiH citizenship. It was thus partly in reaction to the institutionalised 'national order of things' (Malkki 1994) that many Sarajevans had become skilled celebrators of their city's multiculturality. While there was often considerable ambiguity in this discursive formation centred on Bosnianness rather than on any of the three 'constituent peoples', it is still worth pointing out a contrast. In Banja Luka, the main city in Republika Srpska, which saw no military conflict but was taken right away by Serbian nationalist forces in 1992, many catholic churches and all sixteen mosques were destroyed (Galijaš 2011: 245–54). In besieged Sarajevo the four places of worship mentioned above – and all other ones in the city – remained standing.

Having said that, I contend that a focus on identitarian questions, important as they are, fails to account for very important dimensions of life in Sarajevo or, for that matter, BiH. Ultimately, a lament of the demise of Sarajevan multiculturalism and an insistence on its persistence are two sides of the same coin. Likewise, an 'orthodox' focus on differences between people affiliated with nationality groupings and a 'heterodox' one on fluid, hybrid positionings that bridge those differences both remain within the identitarian *doxa* of Dayton BiH (Bourdieu 1982: 133). In both approaches, a unidimensional emphasis on questions of (ethno)national 'culture' makes its inhabitants appear predominantly, or even exclusively, in the identitarian register institutionalised in the Dayton configuration and consolidated in much foreign media reporting. This is so regardless of whether they feature, in realist–essentialist terms, as representatives of one of BiH's three 'peoples' (Hayden 2007), or, in hybrid terms, as individuals who position themselves 'subversively' across or outside of such categories (Markowitz 2010). In both cases, identity categories are privileged as the relevant matrix of understanding life in BiH and Dayton 'trivision' is reproduced.

In contrast, this book aims to contribute to the collective efforts of ethnographers who have studied social practices as they unfold in postwar, postsocialist Dayton BiH without a priori privileging the identitarian matrix.[12] We all found that many people in BiH did worry, one way or another, about nationality questions, but that this did not always and everywhere predominate in their dealings with opportunities and difficulties, in their hopes and fears for the future. My investigation of people's concerns as they emerge from everyday routines and from their own attempts to reason their way through their predicament in Dobrinja does therefore not presume any primacy of the identitarian register. The main reason for this is empirical: identitarian groupism simply did not emerge as particularly prominent from my encounters. I did not construct my questions in terms of its categories and my Dobrinja interlocutors themselves did not foreground them in their reasonings about 'normal lives' and the role of statecraft therein. More generally, my study simply does not foreground questions of what people are (or, rather, what they say they are, because ethnographic arguments on what *is* necessarily ground their truth claims at least partly in a performative–communicative moment that is frequently glossed over in culturalist and ontologist literature).

Rather than highlighting any identitarian concerns they might well have had, my interlocutors guided my interest towards their social locations (Green 2005). Following their lead, my argument revolves around where and when their lives unfolded, how they understood this and how they felt this conditioned what they were able to do or not. In their reasonings about such questions, my Dobrinja interlocutors attributed a central place to the state. How then, given the institutionalised ubiquity of Dayton trivision, could those reasonings develop relatively obliviously to issues of national identification? To understand this, I suggest an analytical distinction between the state*hood of* BiH and state*craft in* BiH. Questions of the state*hood of* BiH revolve around what the state is, claims to be, and should be. In Dayton BiH, contestations here mainly concerned the legitimacy of the very existence of a BiH polity and its administrative–territorial anatomy. These disputes often focused on questions of sovereignty and representation in identitarian terms (whether (ethno)national or 'civic'-supranational). This book shifts the analytical lens to other questions. My interlocutors, namely, systematically foregrounded reasonings about state*craft in* BiH. With this latter term I refer to questions of what the state does, claims to do, and should do. Here, I will show, key concerns revolved around the provision of material conditions and temporal structures for the unfolding of 'normal lives'.

Clearly this is an analytical distinction. Epistemologically, questions of what the state is are intimately related to those of what it does and the distinction does not necessarily emerge empirically as an either/or choice. One and the same person can of course be deeply concerned with issues of both what I call statehood and what I call statecraft, and he or she may not differentiate between the registers that I analytically separate here. In my earlier work with minority returnees in northeast BiH (e.g., Jansen 2008a) they often emerged as part of one and the same issue in everyday reasonings. For example, many problems that Bosniak returnees in Republika Srpska encountered in terms of health care and educational provision were directly implicated in disputes on the legitimacy of the national–territorial anatomy of BiH. Here, questions of what state institutions were doing, claimed to be doing and should be doing could not really be detached from questions of what they were, claimed to be and should be. Concerns with statecraft in BiH (e.g., should there be a school or a medical centre in this or that village? Which repairs were required for it to be functional? How many people should be employed to secure health and education provisions? etc.) tended to be informed by and sucked into conflicts on the legitimacy of statehood of BiH (e.g., should BiH exist? Should Republika Srpska exist? How much autonomy should the entities have? Which government organs should control education and health policy?). In the process, identitarian categories invariably moved to a central position.

While less sharply so, this tendency will emerge as relevant in the course of my study of Dobrinja too. Like in Belgium, where I grew up, a crucial strategy of political manoeuvring by competing politicians consisted of invoking the (il)legitimacy of configurations of statehood in order to deflect responsibilities with regard to statecraft. Let me explain how this worked in Dayton BiH in a simplified manner. Surveys, media reports, ethnographic studies and even the most cursory, random conversations with Bosnians across the country showed that most people wanted jobs, proper health care, a stop to crooked privatisation and other corruption, a fairer distribution of resources, quality education, a functioning administration, an effective judicial apparatus, and so on. They were exasperated with a state that was not doing what they felt it should be doing. These concerns they shared. Many, of course, were also keen to express their dissatisfaction with what the state was and should be, in terms of national representation, territorial organisation and the legitimacy of BiH as a polity itself. Here, starkly different positions existed, often along lines of national identification. Popular preoccupations thus foregrounded complaints about inadequate statecraft, many of which were shared, and anxieties about statehood, many of which were opposed to each other. Yet the former were rarely successfully politically articulated: in the strategies of domestic and foreign functionaries, disputes on the statehood of BiH overshadowed shared concerns regarding what the state was doing and should be doing. As we shall see, the overall structure of such manoeuvring was that 'all roads led to Dayton', that is, to entrenched divisions on the legitimacy of BiH as a polity. In that way, again not unlike the situation in Belgium, the ruling caste could put concerns with statecraft on standby. This, I suggest, was not a neutral, innocent phenomenon, but a political intervention in itself.

And so is my response, embodied in the analytical approach in this book. Key to my study of Dobrinja yearnings for 'normal lives' and the state is that there was no necessary correlation between one particular take on the statehood of BiH and one particular position on statecraft in BiH. A concern with legibility, functionality, discipline, predictability, provision, and so on (i.e., with what the state was doing or should be doing) could be combined with any one position on what the state of BiH was or should be. Different people across the country could, and did, foreground the need for proper public health care, city transport and efficient administration and combine this with any particular view on the (il)legitimacy of BiH as a polity.

Were my Dobrinja interlocutors preoccupied with questions of legitimacy of Dayton BiH's national–territorial anatomy? Certainly. Did
their concerns about what the state was doing and should be doing
often shift to worries about what it was and should be? Yes, and this
book shows how this occurred. Yet a key political intervention of my
study is that it works against the tendency to *automatically* slip from
discussions of statecraft straight into discussions of statehood. Analytically distinguishing between them I purposively slow down the
interpretative process and pause to investigate, first and foremost,
what we could call the 'first degree' of the concerns with the state
that I encountered in Dobrinja: reasonings about statecraft in BiH.
In this book I attempt to treat concerns with statecraft primarily as
concerns in themselves, only then tracing how they were implicated
in questions of BiH statehood. Significantly, this allows us to discern
a degree of sameness in the preoccupations of people across post-
Yugoslav former frontlines. Research in Republika Srpska (Brković
2012a) and in Serbia (Greenberg 2010, 2011; Simić 2009; Spasić 2013)
during the same decade has uncovered reasonings about statecraft
that are remarkably similar to the ones described in this book. Many
of the concerns I foreground were thus shared across entity and state
borders. Yet, at the time of writing, within BiH, the Dayton institutional framework – with its privileging of questions of statehood in
the identitarian register – rendered it unlikely for such concerns to be
self-consciously articulated as 'shared'. For now, they appeared as
parallel at best.

What then did people in Dobrinja do during my research period?
Well, usually they were not voting in elections, waving flags, attending religious services or singing anthems – all of which would in many
cases likely be charged by identitarian divisions in Dayton BiH. Most
of the time, they worked or they sought work, they attended classes
at school or university, they slept, they talked on the phone or com-
municated over the internet, they cooked, they ate, they played, they
shopped, they shovelled snow, they watched football, they queued
at post offices, they chatted over coffee. In Dobrinja, many also spent
much time waiting for buses. If this all sounds pretty 'normal', a key
pattern that emerged from my observations and conversations was a
worry that 'normal lives' were unattainable in Dayton BiH. Part one of
this book, entitled 'Figuring "normal lives"', ethnographically pries
open this shared concern, proposing ways to capture the workings of
the emic term 'normal lives' in anthropological terms. Chapter 1 situ-
ates my analysis of 'normal lives' through critical engagement with
writings on normality, hope and temporal reasoning. Starting from

FIGURE 0.3. A central street of Dobrinja, a key site for shops, services and the *korzo* [evening stroll] (photo by Vanja Čelebičić, 2010)

FIGURE 0.4. The small stream *Dobrinja*, which runs through the middle of the settlement, another favourite for a stroll (photo by Vanja Čelebičić, 2014)

worries that life was anything but 'normal', it explains my decision to follow my interlocutors in approaching questions of normality in terms of lives, and my choice of the notion of 'yearning' over that of 'hope'. Deploying ethnographic material on prewar, wartime and postwar engagements with city transport, chapter 2 explains how Dobrinjci reasoned that any approximation of 'normal lives' would require an ordering framework. To analytically grasp this I introduce the concept of 'gridding', allowing me to embed the long periods spent waiting for buses in a form of meta-waiting for the movement statecraft was supposed to entail. In critical dialogue with a libertarian paradigm in the anthropology of the state, chapter 3 develops this further through an analysis of Dobrinja wartime schooling and other forms of self-organised upward and outward griddings as collective attempts to recalibrate the abnormality of lives under siege, with a focus on its temporal dimensions.

Gdje To Ima?

Since yearning and its temporality emerged as a core theme in my research, I ended up with a less developed focus on practices within and around state agencies than initially intended. Having defended a privileging of 'what people do' in the previous section, I concede this regretfully, but I also wish to offer a justification. What if people continually impress on an ethnographer that most things they do are removed from what they consider 'normal lives'? What if they systematically relate this to their particular spatiotemporal location in Dayton BiH, which, they insist, renders any 'doing' extremely difficult and condemns them to 'waiting' instead? And what if this 'waiting' is so all-encompassing and unspecified as to be closer to 'yearning'? These specificities, combined with a purposively broad sweep in my selection of interlocutors, made the shared concern with 'normal lives' accessible to me less through action and more through (non-)verbal communication. It was in rants and laments, in sighs and silences, that 'normal lives', and, therefore, as we shall see, statecraft took centre stage.

Like many others in the post-Yugoslav states, people in Dobrinja complained a lot and most felt they had a lot to complain about. Around kitchen tables and at bus stops, in cafés and on markets, in workplaces and in schools, people expressed worries about food prices, utility bills, health care, pensions, clientelism, unemployment, schooling, safety, city transport, and so on. Many such shared concerns could not be identified as specific to BiH but Dobrinjci themselves nevertheless frequently insisted on their uniqueness.[13] 'Our' achievements and our problems were then presented as off the scale of any comparison. Our mountains and our rivers were more beautiful, our diaspora children beat all others at maths in the U.S., our coffee was tastier, our fruit juicier, our humour more humorous, and our socialising more social. A naïve foreigner may wonder 'more beautiful, smarter, tastier, juicer, funnier and more social than *what* exactly?', but I never had the courage to ask this heretic question. Above all, I read in these statements a desire to regain a dignified place on the world map, threatened and deformed by experiences of the last two decades. Importantly, by the same exceptionalist token, whatever was wrong with our country was also declared to be much more wrong than it could possibly be anywhere else. In Dayton BiH, to crown such exasperated declarations that something in the country was incomparably wonderful or hopeless, speakers often leant back, raised their voice, hands and possibly eyebrows, and theatrically exclaimed: *Pa gdje to ima!?* This rhetorical question literally means 'Well where does that exist?', and the implicit answer was that, surely, 'that' could not possibly exist anywhere else but here and now.

A phrase containing this answer also circulated widely as a tool of exceptionalist self-description: *To nigdje nema!* [That doesn't exist anywhere (else)!]. Yet clearly, the exclamation *Pa gdje to ima!?* elicited no substantive replies. Indeed, it did not allow them, as I learned when I jokingly started responding to friends with: 'Well … for example in Belgium …' Still, the question of location in *Pa gdje to ima!?* did reflect a pattern in people's trawling for answers to the question of what hindered their pursuit of 'normal lives'. My Dobrinja interlocutors overwhelmingly did this through evocation of Dayton BiH as an 'abnormal' spatiotemporal constellation. Generally, this exceptionalist mode did not imply that they considered people in BiH to be inherently unique. In fact, their insistence that they simply desired to live 'normal lives' positioned them as not very exceptional at all—again indicating a desire to regain a dignified place in a wider world. What they identified as exceptional was that their spatiotemporal location constituted a predicament in itself (see Čelebičić 2013). So it was their living-in-Dayton-BiH, they argued, that prevented them from living 'normal lives'. Note that this does not simply evoke topography ('BiH') but also a historical conjuncture ('Dayton'). In terms of the 'where', they impressed on me that Dayton BiH's position in the European Union's (EU) semiperiphery was yet another permutation of

centuries of Bosnian in-betweenness. As for the 'when', most felt that
Dayton BiH defied any solid qualification as 'postwar', which itself
complicated the formulation of reasonings about any 'pre-' dimension. Lives in Dayton BiH were thus considered lives in the 'meantime'. This Meantime, a term I will capitalise from now on, forms the
foil against which the yearnings for 'normal lives' I explore in this
book must be understood. *Pa gdje to ima!?* then, is an all-encompassing reference to a spatiotemporal location that afflicts one's life and
that of one's co-citizens. I call this affliction 'Daytonitis'.

I did not coin the term Daytonitis to draw attention to people's
use of medical metaphors or to their coping or resistance strategies
relying on such metaphors or on medical treatment.[14] Nor will I pose
as a doctor offering a medical report of Dayton BiH through the
structural–functionalist image of society as body. Instead, I mobilise
some terms from biomedical pathology to make sense of how my
interlocutors themselves made sense of their predicament. Dobrinjci
routinely launched what we could call political pathologies. If the
Ancient Greek παθος [pathos] means 'pain', 'suffering', but also
'experience', and λογια [logia] denotes the 'study of', but also 'an
account of', these pathologies amounted to studies of suffering that
were at once accounts of experience. Clearly, people in Dobrinja did
not live by reason alone. They mobilised many different knowledge
practices to make sense of their predicament, including, for example,
religion, magic, art and, indeed, medicine. Yet in this book I am
particularly interested in how they diagnosed it, in political terms.
Derived from δια [dia: through] and γιγνωσκειν [gignoskein: to
learn], 'διαγνωσκειν' [diagignoskein] means 'to discern, to know
thoroughly'. I focus on the way my interlocutors tried to 'take apart'
their predicament through political reasoning. This is partly a consequence of my chosen approach but it also reflects the way such
reasoning predominated in their interactions with me and with each
other in my presence. Everyday life in Sarajevo was characterised
by the hyperproduction of talk about politics, focused mainly on the
discussion of 'symptoms'. Derived from συμπτωμα [symptoma: ac-
cident, misfortune, that which befalls], in medicine a symptom is a
departure from normal function or feeling as noticed by a patient.
It is subjectively felt and can therefore only be captured indirectly.
Part two of this book, entitled 'Diagnosing Daytonitis' presents emic
Dobrinja diagnoses of the affliction I call Daytonitis around two 'constitutional symptoms' – systemic effects of an affliction that affect the
entire body rather than a specific part or organ – that were seen to
make 'normal lives' impossible.

Chapter 4 focuses on a symptom that was – in initial diagnoses at least – considered largely internal to Dayton BiH: the lack of a system. This involved a peculiar interplay of structural and moral dimensions. Structurally, the problem was identified as a marked absence of the state in some ways that coexisted with its exaggerated presence in other ways. This resulted in difficulties with locating its gridding capacity and a pervasive sense of abandonment. In the moral dimension, laments on values having been 'messed up' by the war and its aftermath existed in tension with lingering suspicions that there might be more longstanding problems with people in BiH themselves. Yet in the accounts of my interlocutors, the ways in which Daytonitis beset their pursuit for 'normal lives' did not emerge merely as a matter internal to BiH. Therefore, chapter 5 zooms in on the related constitutional symptom of spatiotemporal entrapment. This concerns spatial entrapment in the EU's 'immediate outside', and exposure to a monitoring outside gaze in a semiprotectorate where everything was experienced as being in suspension. In the Dayton Meantime, the exclamation went, 'we are pattering in place'. Reasoning on statecraft was thus often temporal reasoning and this chapter foregrounds this temporal dimension of entrapment, investigating the normative value of forward movement in people's yearnings for 'normal lives' on BiH's projected 'Road into Europe'.

Part three of this book, entitled 'Living with Daytonitis' traces how people in Dobrinja politically engaged with the spatiotemporal affliction of Daytonitis that beset them. It highlights the difficulty in the Dayton Meantime of engaging in any politics beyond party realpolitik due to the fraught interplay between concerns with statecraft in BiH and the statehood of BiH. Taking a considerable step back from the ethnographic material and working with notions of hegemony, fantasy and conviviality, chapter 6 discusses the role of complicity in the persistence of domination by a ruling caste despite massive dissatisfaction. The book ends with an epilogue that revisits its main arguments in the light of two events in Sarajevo during its writing: a sudden winter emergency in 2012 and an equally sudden protest in early summer 2013.

Pathology and Coevality

I am aware that my use of the register of affliction and biomedicine carries a risk. Is this a case of yet another Balkanist othering by a westerner through the language of pathology? Is this an ethnocentric proposal to measure BiH politics by Weberian ideal–typical standards of stateness, for example, or to assess the normality of 'normal lives'? No, it is not. It is not *my* analysis that introduces the register of pathology into how Dobrinjci reason through their predicament. Instead, this occurs on their initiative. As Ssorin-Chaikov (2003: 9) has argued in his study of the state in Siberia, 'discourses of failure [of the state] highlight ... a social life of its functionality by dispersing "the state" as a subject of conversation in the minute texture of everyday routine'. Dobrinja perceptions of the failure of statecraft, then, are legitimate objects of analysis: a qualification of Dayton BiH as 'abnormal' is probably the lowest common denominator of all domestic assessments from any possible position in the political landscape. Due to their Eurocentric and linear tendencies, such normative diagnoses are generally treated with suspicion in anthropology. I take them seriously precisely in order to avoid ethnocentrism and patronising. Notably, my interlocutors did not consider westerners to be innocent bystanders in the creation and maintenance of their predicament. My position as someone born, raised and employed in Western Europe often came into play precisely because people in Dobrinja themselves devised accounts that related the symptoms of their unsatisfactory situation to their living-in-Dayton-BiH. This is why I call the affliction they thus discerned 'Daytonitis'.

This is also why I place a strong emphasis on coevality. I employ the term 'shared concerns' to highlight preoccupations that were widespread amongst my interlocutors. Yet, in addition, it indexes an awareness about my own positioning. Even long after I tried to draw the proverbial line under my 'research period' in Dobrinja, my life in Sarajevo – now in the city centre – led me to reflect particularly intensively on coevality and on my commitment to an anthropology that explicitly takes it into account. I continually wish to flag how my Dobrinja interlocutors and I shared a particular historical conjuncture. And this brings me back to the fact that this book does not focus on identitarian questions. In Dobrinja, I did not feel labelled most strongly because, as someone from Western Europe, I was 'culturally different' (although sometimes, in some ways, also that). More often and more strongly, my specific positioning shaped up around the ways in which people associate me with a 'Centre' in a geopolitical constellation that their concerns with 'normal lives' and the state evoked. In Dayton BiH, most reasoning about the state occurred under the looming presence of what was summarised in the notion of *stranci* [foreigners], the collective label for the in-country foreign intervention agencies, their personnel and their superiors in (mostly) western capitals. Although I was never employed by or affiliated to any of those agencies, my presence always carried the sign of the *stranac*. In my coeval approach, I want to systematically acknowledge this: we shared this historical conjuncture.

In this situation, I could have tried to revalorise the cultural, perhaps even ontological differences between my interlocutors and the western me. Instead, my research confronted me time and again with people impressing on me that they were not quite that different from me. Diagnosing Daytonitis, many insisted that – much more than in cultural difference – the roots of their problems could be found in categorical subordination (Ferguson 2006) as it was articulated in the historical conjuncture we shared. Interested in the importance of both the 'where' and the 'when' in their reasoning about the state, this has led me to place a greater emphasis on the workings of time. In this way I hope to unearth the significance of temporality from under the identitarian noise that tends to foreground more spatially conceived patterns of cultural difference (Fabian 1983; Buck-Morss 2000). As we saw in the discussion of the exclamation *Pa gdje to ima?*, I follow my interlocutors to conceive of the specificity of their predicament less as an expression of a transmitted system of meanings and more as one provoked by spatiotemporal location. The key to my analysis of the yearnings for 'normal lives' in this book, then, is less that they are Bosnian yearnings and more that they are Dayton BiH yearnings.

I thus foreground the experience of lives in the Dayton Meantime against which such yearnings can be understood. To a degree, I aim to detect what could be called the rules of the game; yet here 'the game' is not focused on the reproduction of an existing social configuration but rather on the evocation of a not-yet existing one and, to a certain extent, of one that does not exist anymore. More importantly, however, I want to convey the 'feel for the game' and people's engagement with and investment in the value of the game itself, which Bourdieu calls *illusio* (2003: 147). I aim to show what mattered to my interlocutors' practice and how it mattered: in what ways shared concerns were indeed shared and of concern. I thus try to make sense of the ways in which people tried to make (political) sense of their situation. The emphasis here is on trying, both for Dobrinjci and for me. Like Ferguson in his study of decline in Zambia, I found that, often, 'greater ethnographic knowledge revealed only that, in the end, matters were as unclear to "the locals" as they were to me' (1999: 208). This did not stop Ferguson from pursuing insights and nor did it prevent me from trying to reason my way though the reasonings of people in Dobrinja in the period from 2008 to 2010.

A NARRATIVE GLOSSARY OF THE WAR
OVER SARAJEVO

[This narrative glossary has been quarantined in a box so that readers familiar with BiH might skip it and so that others may easily consult it again while progressing through the book.]

Even for the purposes of this book, this necessarily elliptic attempt to introduce some key terms of the 1992–95 war and the Dayton Peace Agreement in narrative form is only one amongst many possible ones. Yet I do not wish to hide behind an awareness of the selective, constructed nature of historiography to shelter from criticism; until proven wrong by counterargument, I am prepared to stand by what I recount here as a credible narrative of what actually happened. Other important things happened too and other patterns could be highlighted. The question is not whether to be selective – that cannot be avoided – but on which grounds to be so. My guiding principle is practical: what do readers have to know to follow the book's argument? I therefore focus on Sarajevo – without claiming that its siege is representative of the entire war in BiH. Yet, it would be naïve to think I could start from a blank slate. Readings of the war that employ a straightforward national matrix already dominate amongst English-speaking audiences. To contextualise the relatively low intensity presence of nationality questions in this book, I therefore pay a disproportionate amount of attention to them in this box. This is a paradox I cannot escape.

1990s elections in the Socialist Federal Republic of Yugoslavia (SFRY) were organised separately in its six republics. In BiH they yielded 36 per cent of the votes for the Bosnian Muslim nationalist Stranka demokratske akcije [Party of Democratic Action, SDA], 30 per cent for the Serbian nationalist Srpska demokratska stranka [Serbian Democratic Party, SDS] and 18 per cent for the Croatian nationalist Hrvatska demokratska zajednica [Croatian Democratic Community, HDZ], with the remaining votes going mainly to nationally undifferentiated reformed communist parties. As a consequence, SDA, SDS and HDZ carried out a threeway division of government positions (see e.g., Anđelić 2003; Bougarel

1996a; Burg and Shoup 1999; Ćurak 2004; Mujkić 2007; Pejanović 2002; Vlaisavljević 2006). Operating with parallel rhetorics of religious revival, free market economics and increased national self-determination as the route to full democracy, and keen to get rid of 'the communists', they thus entered into a *marriage de raison* in which they started the threeway division of people, territory, institutions, arms, capital and most everything else. Yet the very existence of a BiH polity and its status within a Yugoslav (con) federation – its statehood – was disputed within BiH, in Croatia and Serbia, and amongst important players in the so-called international community. In late 1991 and early 1992, in close coordination with the governments of what they considered to be their mother states, SDS and HDZ proclaimed their separate national polities within BiH. SDA favoured a unitary, independent Bosnia and Herzegovina.

Even during their initial cohabitation, focusing on the elimination of non-nationalist alternatives, those parties introduced a military dimension into the struggle between their statemaking projects. With war already raging in Croatia, well before the major clashes in BiH itself, SDS, HDZ and SDA set up parallel structures and formed militias through their local branches and through religious institutional networks. Taking advantage of the decentralised SFRY security setup, each of them soon gained control over police and Territorial Defence infrastructure in areas they dominated. The overwhelming logistical dominance of SDS in the prewar period and in the early phases of the war followed from its position vis-à-vis the now Serbian-dominated Jugoslovenska narodna armija [Yugoslav People's Army, JNA] and from the work of agents sent by the Serbian government. It was also through local SDS chapters that JNA distributed weapons amongst Bosnian Serbs in the lead up to war, while many other people bought them through informal channels. Public mobilisation calling for a non-military, non-nationalist resolution in several BiH towns was ultimately ineffective.

In the spring of 1992, with militia-manned barricades appearing and disappearing, a referendum was held on whether to declare BiH a sovereign state within the borders of the Yugoslav Socialist Republic of Bosnia and Herzegovina established in the Second World War. With SDA and HDZ, each for reasons of their own, arguing in favour, this proposal received the support of 62.68 per cent of the total electorate. This equalled almost the entire turnout. In line with SDS calls, a majority of Bosnian Serbs did not take part in the poll but many in the territories it controlled had voted earlier, in November 1991, in a separate plebiscite, to remain within what was left of Yugoslavia, now dominated by the Milošević government of Serbia. On the basis of the referendum outcome, the Sarajevo-based BiH government (now formally abandoned by SDS and later gradually so by HDZ) proclaimed independence. The Republic of BiH (RBiH) was soon widely recognised internationally (most EU states and the U.S. did so on 6 April 1992) but it could not establish a minimally effective presence over its entire territory. Most of northern and eastern BiH, including parts of Sarajevo, were swiftly proclaimed 'Serbian' in coordinated operations by paramilitary units and the army that was soon to be Vojska Republike Srpske [Army of Republika Srpska, VRS], the formation that, in coordination between SDS and the government of Serbia (then officially: Federal Republic of Yugoslavia), 'inherited' most JNA equipment in BiH. It was in this preemptive strike that most lives were lost and that ethnic cleansing was at its most intensive. Meanwhile, the HDZ-dominated Hrvatsko vijeće odbrane [Croatian Defence Council, HVO], in close cross-border collaboration with Hrvatska vojska [Croatian Army, HV] and paramilitary units, established its own 'Croatian' territories. This left only a small proportion of BiH under control of the Territorial Defence units, small self-organised formations, (special) police forces and SDA militias that would soon merge into Armija Republike Bosne i Hercegovine [Army of the Republic of Bosnia–Herzegovina, ARBiH]. Most of Sarajevo, and of Dobrinja, fell into this category. Surrounding territory was taken by VRS, thus closing the siege. The airport to the south was relinquished to UN forces, whose paradoxically nonintervening intervention became a central factor in the war over BiH. All armies later turned to mobilisation of able-bodied men of military age.

Over time, each of these three armies came to stand, both in the eyes of many of the people it was supposed to defend and in the eyes of many others, for a national grouping. Yet this process was never unambiguous. VRS and HVO had non-Serbs and non-Croats in their ranks, but in small numbers and operating under Serbian and Croatian flags and towards specifically nationally defined war aims. The national dimension was thus a programmatic dimension of their self-representation. In contrast, in places such as Sarajevo and Tuzla ARBiH did retain a degree of inclusivism in terms of personnel and war aims, true to its programmatic commitment to a united BiH. Yet while emphasising its devotion to a multinational Sarajevo, SDA also propagated the national–religious renaissance of Bosnian Muslims, whom they called Bosniaks from 1993 onwards. SDA introduced nationalist policies, encouraging people to identify as Bosniaks, to display Islamic piety and to claim entitlements on that basis. In besieged Sarajevo it became harder not to identify along national lines, and, for those who could display loyalty to the Bosniak nation (i.e., those whose names indicated Muslim heritage), it became more attractive to do so. A related but not totally overlapping factor consisted of demographic shifts: displaced Bosniaks arrived and many people moved out. The majority of Dobrinja Serbs and Croats were amongst the latter – with many leaving before the military violence broke out. Many Serbs moved into nearby parts of Sarajevo controlled by VRS. In the central parts of Sarajevo, besieged by VRS and subject to relentless shelling and sniper fire, shifts in the nationality structure of the population (in terms of variety and in terms of intensity of identification), increasing moves towards Islamisation and the reliance on paramilitary units and (other) gangs who singled out remaining Serbs for particularly harsh mistreatment caused SDA-controlled ARBiH to increasingly resemble the image that its opponents attributed to it: a Bosniak nationalist force.

Yet if the population of besieged Sarajevo housed a rapidly increasing majority of people who identified as Bosniaks, alongside this identification, over and above it, or instead of it, many expressed loyalty to a civic BiH polity. This was (and is) often dismissed by HDZ and SDS as a perfidious smokescreen hiding aggressive Bosniak nationalist attempts to install an Islamic state through what is called 'majorisation' – since the census category of 'Bosniaks' (then 'Muslims') comprised a relative majority in the last census in 1991. While this may be correct for some in wartime Sarajevo, it is important to understand that for many others this loyalty to BiH lay less in national identification as Bosniaks and more in a war-produced shared fate of living in besieged territory held by ARBiH, for a long period the weakest of the three main military formations. This, of course, should also be understood in a context where VRS forces based in what they called 'Serbian' Sarajevo aimed shells and sniper fire at the city precisely because they considered it to be 'Muslim' Sarajevo.

War-related displacement along the continuum from violent expulsion to pre or postwar self-evacuation nationally unmixed the BiH population to a large degree. Operations of ethnic cleansing – the expulsion of people of undesired nationality from certain territories with physical force or under threat of it – became an integral part of the war. The claim of having suffered such expulsion also became a political tool: nationalist discourses in BiH refer to all war-related displacement of 'their' people as 'ethnic cleansing'. In this view, for example, all Serbs who left Dobrinja have been 'ethnically cleansed' too. Violence was used against SDS sympathisers and the fight against 'fifth columnists' involved targeted discrimination, including physical mistreatment, of some Serbs who remained in Dobrinja. Yet it is also true that many of those who left did so in evacuations coordinated secretly by SDS before it closed its siege – a siege, let us reiterate, that was organised explicitly under the sign of the Serbian nationalist cause. Others stayed: an estimated ten thousand persons with Serbian national backgrounds shared the bomb shelters, the hunger and the cold of besieged Sarajevo (ICG 1998: 3), and some occupied positions of responsibility in the wartime government structures and in ARBiH.

Through various forms of war-related displacement, with varying degrees of decision making, over two million Bosnians, about half the population, fled their prewar place of residence during the 1990s. The Istraživačko-dokumentacioni centar (IDC) – taking in people of all national backgrounds and relying on testimonies as well as identification records of human remains and statistical analysis – identified just under one hundred thousand dead or missing and did not expect this number to rise much further (2013). Around forty per cent of those war dead were reported to be civilians. IDC death toll calculations are disproportionally high for people identified (presumably by name) as Bosniaks, particularly amongst civilian victims, over 80 per cent of whom have been identified as such. Figures also display peaks in certain areas and in certain periods where VRS military dominance was overwhelming. We can thus deduce that, in national terms, 'Bosniaks' were most likely to be murdered (regardless of their self-identification) and 'Serbs' were most likely to murder them (under Serbian flags and in an explicit mission to establish a Serbian state). In the Sarajevo region – including the VRS-held areas – IDC figures peak in the first months of the war and present a total of about 5,600 killed or missing civilians and about 8,000 soldiers (of whom over 70 per cent were from ARBiH ranks). In both cases a very large majority of those people were identified as Bosniaks. Across BiH, civilian dead make up about one-fifth of all victims identified as Serbs and about two-fifths amongst Croats, while amongst Bosniaks they outnumber the total of military victims.

The U.S.-brokered 1995 Dayton Agreement that brought an end to the military violence consolidated the division of BiH into two Entities: the Federacija Bosne i Hercegovine ('The Federation', initially often called the Muslimansko–Hrvatska Federacija [Muslim–Croatian Federation]) and Republika Srpska. It also installed a small district around Brčko in northern BiH and stipulated a mandate for in-country foreign supervision and troops. The Federation was itself decentralised into Cantons with largely nationally homogenised populations, dominated by either AR-BiH-SDA or by HVO-HDZ. Unmixing was further cemented by the postwar evacuation (largely organised by SDS) of Serbs from VRS-held Sarajevo territories now transferred to the Federation. Many of them were allocated houses in eastern BiH from which Bosniaks had been expelled. Others stayed closer to Sarajevo. HDZ engaged in similar endeavours in western BiH. With some exceptions, unmixed, nationalised polities had thus become fact. The 1991 census saw 50 per cent of Sarajevans declaring their nationality as 'Muslim'. Due to disproportionate outmigration by Serbs and Croats and immigration by Bosniaks, the postwar proportion of Sarajevans with 'Muslim' socioreligious heritage is thought to have risen to 80–90 per cent (note that, at the time of writing, no census data for Dayton BiH exist and that territorial boundaries have changed). With their reductionist focus on questions of (ethnonational) 'being' and their self-interested adherence to Dayton trivision, Bosniak, Croatian and Serbian nationalist entrepreneurs take this to mean that up to 90 per cent of Sarajevans *are* Bosniaks/Muslims. Yet like the Dayton constitution – an annex to the Peace Agreement – such interpretations ignore non-ethnonational self-identification and, most importantly, questions of degrees of loyalty and affiliation (Jansen 2005b).

In Dayton, Dobrinja was almost entirely allocated to Canton Sarajevo, in the Federation, but a small area remained disputed. A foreign arbitration process in 2001 fixed the boundary just inside the settlement, leaving only the easternmost edge in Republika Srpska (Jansen 2013a).

Notes

1. 'Daleko od normalnog života', *Oslobođenje*, 28 July 2009, 8. Unless otherwise indicated, all translations from Bosnian—Serbian–Croatian,German and French are mine.
2. I use the acronym 'BiH' (for Bosna i Hercegovina), widely used locally, sometimes pronounced /bix/, and sometimes /bɛ i xa/. As an adjective referring to this country, including all its inhabitants, I employ 'BiH' or 'Bosnian' (short for Bosnian and Herzegovinian). 'Bosniak', on the other hand, refers to the nationality category known previously as 'Bosnian Muslims'.
3. The BiH constitution was an annex to this Agreement, signed on a U.S. airforce base in Dayton, Ohio. 'Dayton' (sometimes 'Dejton') was used as a noun and in adjectival form [*daytonsko*, sometimes *dejtonsko*].
4. Following dominant, if not unanimous, tendencies in local use, I employ the term 'national' where referring to 'ethnonational' or 'ethnic' issues.
5. After the war Dobrinja thus remained effectively divided, like the state of BiH it was part of (Jansen 2013a). Yet for clarity's sake this book will use the label 'Dobrinja' exclusively for the territory allocated to the Federation of BiH. The eastern edge of the settlement that now belonged to Republika Srpska will be referred to as *Istočno Sarajevo* [East Sarajevo]. Likewise, I employ the label *Dobrinjci* solely for inhabitants of the 'Federal' part of Dobrinja. Note also that, while some inhabitants did also express belonging to Dobrinja, I simply use this term to make the text readable. This book is not a community study of Dobrinja, but an ethnography of yearnings for 'normal lives'. It is *with* Dobrinjci – i.e., *from* Dobrinja – that I reach out into (desired) encompassments of 'normal lives'.
6. Since July 2010, I have continued to spend well over half of my time in Sarajevo, now living in the city centre.
7. To keep the text readable, I will use the term state hereinafter without inverted commas.
8. www.novigradsarajevo.ba; *Mjesečni statistički pregled Federacije BiH August* 2008; *Statistički Bilten za Mjesec Juli* 2008.
9. All wages and allowances mentioned in this book are expressed in net monthly amounts.
10. My engagement with Yugoslav socialist self-management and with its dynamics of statecraft will be channelled mainly through the recollections of my interlocutors themselves: a wilfully 'presentist' methodology for an ethnographic contribution.
11. Thirty of these were recorded, with permission. Half of all semi-structured interviews were conducted by Melina Sadiković. With regard to the core themes of 'normal lives' and the state, there were few noticeable systematic differences between the interviews conducted by this female Dobrinja resident on the one hand and by my male Western

European self on the other. In both cases, most interviewees tended to occupy a pedagogical position, seeking to educate an imagined audience that was presumed to be
relatively ignorant of their fate.

12. I refer to such work in the course of my arguments. An example is the only edited
collection of ethnographic texts on postwar BiH in English (Bougarel, Duijzings and
Helms 2007).

13. Central to the legitimacy claims of socialist Yugoslavia in ideological terms, such
self-proclaimed exceptionalism was common in popular parlance across its successor states. In the postwar period, no doubt, it was further conditioned by the sense
of humiliating entrapment and abjection (Jansen 2009), which, in Sarajevo, took on
particular significance due to the experience of siege.

14. For an investigation of postwar, postsocialist BiH through the ethnographic prism of
healing, see Jašarević 2012.

PART I

FIGURING 'NORMAL LIVES'

Chapter 1

'NORMAL LIVES'

[or, Towards an Anthropology of Yearning]

in which, in dialogue with anthropological writings on normality and hope, we are acquainted with ubiquitous, backward- and forward-looking evocations of 'normal lives' as a prism on a particular historical conjuncture in BiH – the Dayton Meantime – placing such yearnings, and the regime of temporal reasoning in which they exist, at the centre of this study

'Normality' and Anthropologies of Upheaval

There is a tendency in anthropology to approach phenomena from a direction that intuitively seems to be opposed to them, thus providing a diagnostic perspective. Many studies of home concentrate on the experiences of displaced people and writings on health often focus on those of sick ones. Similarly, the issue of 'normality' – sometimes glossed as 'normalcy' or 'the normal' – often emerges in studies of what is considered 'abnormal'. For example, anthropologists write about practices labelled primitive or uncivilised as a way to uncover standards of 'normal' development and civilisation. Often they do this in order to unveil the arbitrary nature of such standards as well as their imposition for purposes of control and exploitation. Foucault's genealogies of modern notions of madness, criminality and sexuality have provided us with an array of additional conceptual tools to analyse much broader phenomena of 'normalisation', from discipline, over biopolitics, to the figure of 'docile bodies'. In sum, social scientific uses of the term 'normal' usually entail critique, explaining the process of 'normalisation' that is its condition of existence. Taking into account the connotation of 'ordinary', 'mundane', 'quotidian' and 'usual' that 'the normal' carries in popular parlance in many languages, it is therefore no surprise that many anthropological writings on 'normality' emerge from research on radical upheaval. I now briefly discuss this in relation to two forms of upheaval that predominate in the literature: war and postsocialist transformation.

Studies of political violence emphasise the remarkable malleability of notions of 'normality', testifying to people's resilience and adaptability in extreme conditions. For example, work on the protracted war in Mozambique (Lubkemann 2008) and on the second Palestinian intifada (Allen 2008; Kelly 2008) documents people's capacity to become accustomed to conditions of violence through routinisation. Reclassifying the 'abnormal' as 'normal', the extraordinary is then made ordinary, the unpredictable predictable. Stressing the largely nondiscursive character of this routinisation, Allen states that 'the process of taming violence … is expressed in the capacity to stop noticing, or at least stop noticing all the time' (2008: 476). Partly this is possible because for many people, much of the time, protracted political violence is encountered through boredom and frustration, rather than through blood and battle (Kelly 2008: 353; see also Allen 2008: 473; Lubkemann 2008: 14).

Interrogating assumptions of peaceful 'normality' versus violent 'abnormality', such studies thus highlight the significance of routines. Jean-Klein (2001) has shown how, in the first intifada, an effort to suspend many 'normal' activities that marked families' lives, particularly rites of passage, was a strategy of Palestinian resistance to mark and condemn the 'abnormality' of the conditions of Israeli occupation. In the second intifada, however, the significance of routines shifted: their stubborn continuation now became the order of the day. Politically, this show of resilience in the face of Israeli Army attempts to disrupt 'normal' activities and expectations was framed as a resistant strategy called *sumûd* [steadfastness, stoicism]. Yet both Allen and Kelly point out that their West Bank interlocutors' commitment to routines was sometimes nothing more than a way of 'getting by as an everyday embodied, material practice' (Allen 2008: 473). Noting that this cannot be grasped as a dichotomous question of either resistance or accommodation, Kelly explains that the immediate concern of most Palestinians was to live a semblance of 'ordinary lives'.[1] People thus endlessly queued, waited, underwent checks and made detours to get to work or to school. The 'sense of the ordinary' that Kelly's Palestinians strove to reproduce was mainly configured around expectations of normative life trajectories. As Das has argued regarding the aftermath of violence in India's Partition and after

Indira Gandhi's assassination, life was recovered not through 'some grand gestures in the realm of the transcendent but through a descent into the ordinary' (2007: 7).

These studies insist that, while fear is crucial to understand life in violent conditions, a focus on spectacular suffering or struggle is insufficient. They demonstrate the value of ethnographic research into how people caught in violence may attempt to pursue life projects that extend beyond it, without presenting romanticising narratives of the against-all-odds 'normality' of plucky people under extreme duress. In war much is undone, but much is done and redone too; it is a 'productive and generative … transformative social condition' (Lubkemann 2008: 36), which is not to imply that what is done is good, let alone heroic. Indeed, Kelly goes as far as to explicitly focus 'on the apparently boring' (2008: 353). These anthropologists thus share a refusal to reduce people's lives in wartime to stripped-down existence entirely determined by the totalising dehumanisation of 'abnormal' violence that has destroyed an unproblematised 'normality' associated with peace. Instead they document how, in war too, people act pretty much as people. That is not necessarily a consolation.

Lubkemann argues that in Mozambique war was not 'an "event" that suspend[ed] "normal" social processes, but [it had] instead become *the* normal – in the sense of "expected" – context for the unfolding of social life' (2008: 1). This far-reaching taming of violence into the ordinary raises a question: were war conditions considered 'normal' – expected – for an undetermined period? Or were they seen as such for the time being – and therefore in principle 'abnormal', but routinised precisely through a temporary suspension of 'normal' standards of evaluation and expectation? The latter pattern emerges from Kelly's study during the second intifada, where the prevalence of boredom was inherently related to the fact that many saw the violence, at least initially, as temporary (2008: 364). Kelly notes that there were in fact two senses of the ordinary at work, in tension with each other: one that empirically described the typical and the mundane, including a normalising of the abnormal (which he calls the 'is'), and one that normatively prescribed an ideal (the 'ought') (ibid.: 366). While violent disruption could never be ruled out, making the routinisation of 'abnormality' a precarious achievement at best, the intifada thus sparked 'constant speculation on the nature of ordinary life' (ibid.). This, Kelly shows, emerged from pervasive frustration with the impossibility of realising or even properly planning different lives. If the 'descent into the ordinary' congealed around the practical expectations of normative life trajectories, the notion of the 'ordinary' thus allowed the articulation of more distant aspirations around the 'ought' too. It is able, Kelly argues:

> to bring together hopes and desires, on the one hand, with direct experiences, on the other. It allows intangible aspirations to be rooted in concrete practices, and the hard reality of everyday life to be imagined in some other way. ... As such, the search for the ordinary is shot through with a residual hope that it still may be possible, but a fear that it might not. (ibid.)

This engagement with questions of 'ordinariness' in terms of life projects, experiences and aspirations, and with the tensions between the 'is' and the 'ought', resonates with the findings of another body of anthropological writing on questions of 'normality': studies of post-socialist transformations. Most of this work, focusing on the former Soviet Bloc, reads emic discourses of 'normality' as denoting a desire for renewed belonging to a universe referred to as Europe or The West. In studies on Hungary (Fehérváry 2002), Poland (Galbraith 2003), Latvia (Plakans 2009) and Estonia (Rausing 2002), this orientation towards European/Western 'normality' is shown to include an urge for spatial reintegration into the 'normal' western–capitalist realm versus the 'abnormal' eastern–communist one, folded into a desire for temporal reinsertion into 'normal' western–capitalist dynamics once set in motion but considered to have been interrupted by 'abnormal' eastern–communist processes until 1990. These authors point out that their interlocutors considered this return to the 'normal' path of development both necessary and legitimately deserved – indeed, the experiential gap between that normative self-evidence and actually existing difficulties of everyday life was often a major source of frustration, which itself was blamed on the legacy of 'abnormal' socialism.

Within this framework, studies in postsocialist states have addressed 'normality' predominantly by tracing a 'descent into the ordinary' through a focus on access to consumer goods and aspirations associated with western middle classes. As Fehérváry's summarises:

> Throughout the post-Soviet region, ... uses of 'normal' ... refer to objects, services and standards of living which are clearly extraordinary in their local context – and yet are imagined to be part of 'average' lifestyles in Western Europe or the United States. ... a 'discourse of the normal' indexes a profound adjustment of identity set in motion by the sudden geopolitical shift of these countries from Soviet satellite to aspiring members of a reconfigured 'Europe' ... These longings are most evident in the realm of the material .... (2002: 370)

Like in Kelly's study, the notion of 'normality' is thus shown to allow the articulation of practical life pursuits, here focused on consumption, in terms of distant desires and aspirations. Again, it is frustration with the 'abnormal' that sparks this. Here, the normative dimension is more clearly configured as forward movement and 'the abnormal', in the form of legacies of socialism, is seen to slow down progress. In a study in Romania, Hartman (2007) has focused on the temporality implied in this normativity. While The West/Europe was a key reference in his interlocutors' self-positionings as being in transition to 'normality', this did not involve a straightforward notion of development towards western-style liberal-democratic capitalism. The present continued to be experienced as 'abnormal', 'pre-normal transition time' of contradictory practices and moralities, but the contours of (future) normality were left undefined (ibid.: 188). In that way, 'normality' functioned as a projected flawless state of 'living decently', suspended in the future. Hartman, after Žižek, labels it 'the utopian object of impossible Fullness' (ibid.: 200).

Keeping hold of Lubkemann's point on the routinisation of the 'abnormal' into the 'normal', Kelly's elaboration on the tension between the 'ordinary' as the 'is' and as the 'ought', and Hartman's conceptualisation of 'normality' as a utopian object of aspiration, let us now explore these questions in a setting marked by both war and postsocialist transformations, including envisaged incorporation into the EU: the post-Yugoslav states.

'Normality' in the Post-Yugoslav States: The 'Was', the 'Is' and the 'Ought'

Wartime research in Sarajevo (Maček 2009), in Dubrovnik, Croatia (Povrzanović Frykman 2002) and in refugee camps (Gilliland, Špoljar-Vržina and Rudan 1995) has traced people's determined efforts to negotiate 'normality' through the continuation of everyday activities. My own postwar research in Serbia, Croatia and BiH likewise found that wartime was reconstructed as a period in which people tried to tame 'abnormality' by a commitment to routines. In later chapters, I will discuss this stubborn insistence on 'normality' in both practices and aspirations with examples of public transport and schooling. For now, I relate it to the question of suspension discussed above: instead of routinisation, people in the post-Yugoslav states tended to retain a strong distinction between war conditions and 'normality'. War was usually cast as normality's ultimate counterpoint. Of course, people did to a degree get used to war conditions and they incorporated the threat of violence into their practices: during war, normality was thus 'negotiated', even 'imitated' (Maček 2009: 62). After all, any sense of normality had been shown to be fragile due the 'poisonous knowledge' of the war experience (Das 2007: 77). Yet research shows that most people dealt with this radical doubt about conditions they had previously largely taken for granted, brought about by sudden experiences of loss, precisely through a sustained effort to purify the 'normal' from the 'abnormal'. And key to this was keeping war out of the category of the normal. They decidedly did not 'stop noticing'. Especially in BiH, forced reconsiderations of the self-evidence of 'normality' itself mainly strengthened the intensity with which most clung to it as a standard.

Since the terminology of 'normality' is also widely used in the post-Yugoslav states to denote 'sanity', many recollections of the war period contain positive references to this or that individual having managed to 'stay normal', thereby distancing her or him from the 'abnormal' war situation. The evocation of 'normality' as a value standard features prominently in a series of ethnographic studies in post-Yugoslav Serbia (e.g., Greenberg 2011; Jansen 2005a; Simić 2009) and BiH (e.g., Bartulović 2013; Helms 2007, 2010; Jansen 2006a, 2008a, 2009, 2010; Jansen and Helms 2009; Jouhanneau 2013; Kurtović 2012; Povrzanović Frykman 2008, 2012; Stefansson 2010). These writings document the maintenance of a distinction between the descriptive 'is' and the normative 'ought', with the register of 'normality' reserved for the latter. Yet, what we find here is not only a normative aspiration for the future: in its references to the 'ought', post-Yugoslav discourses of 'normality' also enlist the 'was'.

This 'was' is absent from Kelly's study of negotiations of ordinariness: many of his Palestinian interlocutors did not have much actual 'ordinariness' to recall, for no period of sufficient stability had graced their lifetime (2008: 365). In studies of postsocialist transformations in the post-Soviet Bloc the 'was' is also detached from 'normality': in fact, here the socialist past is posited as the 'abnormal' that needs to be overcome by a return to Europe, but which keeps raising its ugly head. Research in the post-Yugoslav states provides substantially different insights, showing previous everyday lives to be a central positive source for the evocation of 'normality' for very broad layers of the population.[2] In my research in Serbia, Croatia and BiH, the phrase I most commonly encountered to appraise life experiences in socialist Yugoslavia was *normalan život* [a normal life]. It was overwhelmingly deployed in positive contrast with one's current predicament. For example, in my ethnographic study of homemaking in northeast BiH in 2000–01, many displaced persons evaluated potential return negatively, referring to the lack of perspectives for a 'normal life' (Jansen 2008a). When asked what kind of life would qualify as such, answers almost unanimously evoked previous lives. The 'ought' was thus opposed to the 'is' but intimately related to the 'was'.

This contrast with findings in post-Soviet settings is partly a product of diverging pasts under the banner of socialism. Officially, Yugoslav socialism was proclaimed to be 'nonaligned', i.e., not part of either the U.S. or the Soviet Bloc, and engaged in the progressive development of workers' self-management. More important for current normative judgments is the recollection of differences in terms of everyday experience. In the post-Yugoslav states, consumption did not emerge in concerns with 'normality' in the same way as it did in studies in post-Soviet settings (but see, e.g., Erdei 2012; Simić 2009). It did appear, but predominantly in terms of which goods, services and experiences had previously been *more* accessible than now (see Patterson 2011). Crucially, evocations of 'normal lives' embedded such access in much broader expectations. Writing on Serbia, Greenberg has argued that defining 'normality' mainly in terms of consumption obscures the existential depth of the notion, which was shaped partly precisely through a radical confrontation with the fragility of material worth brought about by war-induced hyperinflation (2011: 94). This awareness was even stronger in BiH, where most of the post-Yugoslav devastation took place. Regarding remembered lived experience, people often first of all sought to liberate me – a Western European – of any notion I was believed to hold that their previous lives had been anything like those in the Soviet Bloc. Indeed, in retrospective evaluations of everyday lives, parallels were most often ignored, allowing the articulation of a remembered superior position in 'everyday geopolitical' terms, where living standards were twinned with a sense of worth symbolised by cross-border mobility and global recognition (Jansen 2009).

While actual differences between remembered lives in different socialist states explain much of the contrasts between anthropological treatments of 'normality' in those states, I want to avoid entrenching Yugoslav exceptionalism. Instead, my focus on 'normality' is meant to counteract regionalising patterns within scholarship – including in terms of research funding and publication opportunities – that treat the post-Yugoslav states as a separate Balkan field of expertise, appropriate for the study of postwar reconstruction, nationalism and reconciliation, but less acceptable as sites in which to address post-Cold War change (Gilbert et al. 2008). I suggest that people in the post-Yugoslav states found post-1990 changes particularly difficult to grasp precisely because the impact of military violence articulated so intimately with that of post-Cold War transformations. Directly related to that, there was an acute sense of being under scrutiny: as I experienced all too frequently at my own expense, many people, even those who strongly favoured 'Euro–Atlantic integration', resented being subjected to the judging gaze of 'The West'. This was itself experienced as 'abnormal', and it further put the gap between one's life and 'normality' on show for powerful others to evaluate and reward or punish (see Greenberg 2010). In Dayton BiH, this gaze included the in-country presence of foreign intervention agencies. Yet rather than treating these specificities as mere markers of difference from other postsocialist contexts, I aim to develop them into insightful prisms onto general questions of 'normality' in particular historical conjunctures.

The 'Lives' in 'Normal Lives'

This book disentangles the widespread functioning in Dayton BiH of the emic notion of 'normal life' as an almost entirely consensual label in both a backward-looking and a forward-looking sense: a 'normal life' described what one had lived before the 1990s (the 'was') and it evoked an aspiration for the future (the 'ought'). In both its past- and future-oriented modalities, it was vague – indeed, this was what made consensus possible. Reflecting findings in other contexts of war and postsocialist transformations, 'normal life' emerged most frequently as an issue when discussing its absence in current 'abnormal' conditions that were felt to have started with the war and had so far failed to disappear. In terms of the 'is', then, it appeared as a case of 'is not'. Relative consensus also prevailed amongst the BiH population that 'politics' was to blame for this predicament, but disagreements existed on which politicians were primarily to blame, and particularly entrenched divisions persisted on what to do about it.

Departing from most existing studies, I have decided not to speak of 'normality' but to follow my interlocutors in approaching 'normality' in terms of lives – the ways in which they remembered they had lived, in which they lived now, and in which they hoped or feared to live tomorrow. To position my study, let me now briefly elaborate on five interrelated implications of this conceptualisation.

Firstly, congruent with the emphasis of writings on negotiations of the 'normal' in violent conditions, thinking in terms of 'lives' directs the spotlight to people's practices (Das 2007). In my Dobrinja research, references to 'normal lives' evoked anything from being able to walk the streets safely (contrasted with war and with postwar crime), over permanent access to electricity and running water (interrupted during wartime, reinstalled for most afterwards), rights to employment, housing and health care (reduced by post-socialist transformations), to holidays on the Adriatic coast (now unaffordable for many). I do not assess the veracity of the representations of the past this entails: undoubtedly, seaside holidays, stable employment and even electricity were not equally accessible to all Bosnians in Yugoslav times. What is important is that, with regard to this past dimension in evocations of 'normal lives', people relied mainly on recollections of mundane practices. Only occasionally did references to 'normal lives' address socialism as an ideology, workers' self-management as a system, the SFRY as a multinational polity, or a categorical Yugoslav (or any other) 'identity'. In Dobrinja, it was a desire to maintain, or, more often, to reestablish some degree of continuity with the practices of remembered everyday lives that remained central to many people's hopes and fears for the future.

A second corollary of conceiving of normality in terms of 'lives' is that it alerts us to the embedding of concerns with security, living standards, equality, freedom, enjoyment and dignity in worries about moral values. This dimension has also been highlighted in studies in former Soviet Bloc states, especially with regard to socioeconomic inequality and lawlessness, but also in terms of love relationships. Patico (2009), for example, found Russian women complaining of a shortage of appropriate homegrown men for 'normal' relationships. In post-Yugoslav Serbia, Greenberg (2011: 95) recounts how students linked the reluctance of people to invest in relationships to a lack of predictability and prospects, that is, to a lack of 'normality'. 'Normal', she explains, 'serves as a diagnostic category for shifting social, political and economic relations, and the kind of agentive possibilities that emerge in those contexts' (ibid.: 89). I found a concern with values to be rife in Dobrinja too, and any engagement with 'normal lives' was therefore a continuous exercise of positioning and negotiation.

A third implication of conceptualising the 'normal' in terms of 'lives' is that it foregrounds structures of temporality, here associated with modern living. As Foucault has argued in his work on the rise of the disciplinary society, if place was central to the exercise of power in feudal times, in 'modern society' the focus shifted to control of people's time, and specifically maximum extraction of time to render their bodies docile and productive (1994: 80). The notion of 'normal lives' allows us to approach this question from the other direction: what happens when 'modern' rhythms and trajectories that govern lives are suddenly suspended? In Serbia, Greenberg found that much vaunted normality was understood to include a 'kind of predictability that would allow [one] to follow-through on commitments made to oneself and others', to establish routines that 'entailed an ability to render one's desires or personal commitments into an actionable truth' (2011: 93). Possibilities to live particular lives were seen to be intimately related to temporal structure. In Dayton BiH, I found that evocations of 'normal lives' tended to refer copiously to one's endangered yet legitimate entitlement to school one's children and to earn a pension, both of which were constructed around ordered, staged progress. I will analyse this within a wider normative discourse of a society where one may reasonably expect to 'move forward'. Foregrounding the emic notion of 'normal lives', I place this temporal dimension at the centre of the investigation.

Fourthly, speaking of 'normal lives' highlights the anchoring of individual and household concerns within ordering frameworks – which I shall refer to as 'grids' – especially through evocations of statecraft. Even if often focused on households and immediate surroundings, Dobrinja references to 'normal lives' systematically indexed a social configuration in which structures of expectations were ordered in an institutional manner.[3] Evocations of 'normal lives' did thus not only highlight tensions between familiarity and normativity, but also between freedom and normalisation (Foucault 1975, 2010). The wartime disintegration of grids was considered to have 'bared' (Agamben 1998) previous 'normal lives', and without calibration by institutional frameworks no predictability could be imagined that would render them possible again. While there is no historical necessity for grids to be state related, the 'language of stateness' (Hansen and Stepputat 2001: 5) was central to Dobrinja evocations of 'normal lives'.

A final implication of conceptualising 'normality' around lives is that my tracing of the 'descent into the ordinary' resonates with Kelly's foregrounding of the 'boring'. Do not expect stories of spectacular wartime suffering, resistance or revolutionary struggles. The nonspectacular, frustratingly unchanging predicament of living in the Dayton Meantime featured centrally in how people tried to make political sense of their lives. Moreover, in a forward-looking sense, 'normal lives' were supposed to be boring too, at least in the sense of predictability. Asked where he would ideally like to live, a young Palestinian told Kelly he would pick Sweden, because 'nothing ever happens there'. He hoped, Kelly explains, 'to live in an "ordinary state", where life was benevolently mundane' (2008: 365). The same line of argument, with the same country of choice, was very common in Dayton BiH.

Hope Suspended between Past and Future

Having made a case for conceptualising normality in terms of lives, the question emerges as to how to approach a phenomenon as elusive as 'normal lives', even after specifying my interest in terms of temporality and grids of statecraft. In Dayton BiH, everyone said that current life was not normal, and was not about to become normal any time soon.[4] The shared concern with 'normal lives' could therefore not be studied empirically through a description of people's routines (the 'is'). How can the presentist methodology of ethnography approach 'normal lives' in a situation where they appear only as an absence, as the affectively overcharged object of evocations of what 'was' and what 'ought to be'? One route would be to focus on memories of 'normal lives'. I will investigate this backward-looking dimension but always in conjunction with its future-oriented counterpart. Addressing the latter is a greater challenge due to the traditional anthropological privileging of the 'past in the present', itself partly a consequence of our ethnographic methodology, which starts from what we can observe, and we can only observe what is. 'What is' includes traces of 'what was' and in anthropology this is reflected in a preoccupation with the past at the expense of the 'future in the present' (e.g., Malkki 2001: 325–27; Munn 1992: 116). This book folds itself into anthropological writings that seek to overcome this imbalance.

'The future in the present' has recently become a focal point in anthropology and related disciplines, with much recent work converging around the notion of hope. In the scholarly literature, this term is used in a bewildering variety of ways[5] but has a common denominator in its reference to a future orientation that is positively affectively charged: a degree, however small or hesitant, of expectant optimism. Many authors are concerned with the very possibility of hope in the context of current political and theoretical developments (e.g., Harvey 2000). Generally, the presumption prevails that, under the right conditions, hope is a good thing – that most people would rather have more of it than less and that an increase in hope would make the world a better place rather than a worse one. Ultimately, even as part of arguments that hope can paralyse (Crapanzano 2003: 18), this is what is seen to distinguish it from other orientations towards the future, such as fear, fatalism, avoidance or disorientation. I now position my research in relation to three trends in academic work on hope. In this section I scrutinise arguments under the rubric of 'hope' that call for a temporal reorientation of our analysis to the future in order to grasp 'possibilities'. In the next two sections, I turn to work on regimes of temporal reasoning and economies of hope, respectively.

Insofar as it is based on the empirical analysis of people's hopes, much of the burgeoning interest in hope tends to converge around specific examples, such as the possibilities afforded by new bioscience technologies (e.g., Novas 2006; Anderson 2007). It thus often runs parallel with what is presented as an epochal shift in the world, and particularly in capitalism's mobilisation of 'the resource of forethought' (Thrift 2006: 284–87) and the valuation of immaterial or affective labour as a prospecting for the yet to come (Hardt and Negri 2000). Some authors seek to capture such concerns in a Deleuzian register, foregrounding emergence, becoming and indeterminacy (e.g., Anderson 2006). This emphasis, in turn, sometimes reflects a programmatic choice by scholars seeking to establish the value of their 'open-ended' understandings against what they consider to be historicist, determinist or otherwise 'closed' analyses that fail to grasp a host of 'possibilities'.

References to 'normal lives' in Dobrinja were mostly structured around a fraught desire for reinsertion into some form of forward movement along linear temporality, much like the one associated with modernism. The backward- and forward-oriented evocations of 'normal lives' I encountered did not therefore fire my optimism about people's creativity in the face of disillusions with modernist utopias; neither did they suggest dramatic shifts in temporal orientations, with which a Deleuzian terminology of hope would allow me to catch up. In some cases, I find, the preference for Deleuzian conceptualisations entails a disturbing tendency to project openness to indeterminacy onto the people studied for reasons internal to epistemological positionings within the academic field of anthropology. Biehl and Locke (2010), for example, call for such a reorientation of anthropology. Yet rather than providing a study of people's engagements with 'possibilities', it is their commitment to Deleuzian thinking itself that leads them to summon up some selective examples that portray Sarajevans as embracing emergent alternative futures.[6] In empirical terms, two points seems to escape such Deleuzian manifestoes. Firstly, indeterminacy also allows for catastrophic possibilities, so people are not necessarily keen on it, perhaps especially after having suffered heavy losses. Secondly, the lack of direction inherent in indeterminacy may be experienced as a lack of any movement at all and therefore not as a sign of bountiful possible futures but of stagnation, with nothing particularly likely to 'emerge' or 'become'. If the current situation is considered to be the result of dramatic loss, that itself may be a frightening prospect.

A somewhat more rigorous approach characterises Miyazaki's proposal (2004, 2006, 2010) to conceptualise hope as a method. Seeking to 'replicate' the hope embodied in activities and dreams of financial traders in Japan and compensation claims of Suvavou people in Fiji as specific instances of knowledge practices, Miyazaki addresses the work of hope in anthropology, philosophy and critical social theory. He places his efforts in the tradition of calls by Benjamin, Rorty and especially Bloch for a temporal reorientation of knowledge from a contemplative one to a prospective one. His book *The Method of Hope*, Miyazaki states, is 'not so much a study of the hope of others as an effort to recapture that hope (Fijians' as well as Bloch's) as a method for anthropology' (2004: 25). The reference to philosopher Bloch is a recurrent one in the literature. Bloch's *Principle of Hope* (1986) offers a kind of unsystematic encyclopaedia of a broad range of human activity, affect and thought, such as myth, dreaming, pleasure, technology, travel, art, and so on. In each one of them, Bloch seeks to let a thousand flowers bloom to uncover hope from under the mere 'ideological': a forward-dawning; an anticipatory not-yet-conscious containing unrealised surplus meaning that prefigures the future (ibid.: 116). For those patient enough to wade through it, Bloch offers much inspiration: his is a radically dynamic, materialist, anti-positivist and anti-historicist approach that draws attention to the category of possibility.

Strikingly, Miyazaki leaves undiscussed the fact that Bloch explicitly posits Marxism as the real expression of hope, 'struggling on behalf of "concrete" as opposed to "abstract" Utopia', and embodying 'real' as opposed to 'ideological possibility' (ibid.: 479–81). To say that Bloch 'abandon[s] the notion of a predetermined end' (Miyazaki 2004: 15) thus glosses over the tension between his insistence on indeterminacy and his classification of all 'forward dawnings of the not-yet' as prior reflections of a known *Good Novum*. As Miyazaki himself illustrates, and as any ethnography would have to acknowledge, there are many different forms of hope, often un-related to the political making of a better world. Sucking them all into one kind of hope, as Bloch does, we end up with paradoxical evocations of indeterminacy and teleology. Yet, as Gekle (1998: 56) argues, if we drop Bloch's teleological postulation of an objective Novum and if we take seriously a multiplicity of hopes (including ones that we find undesirable) on their own terms, hope appears less as a principle and more as an affect or a disposition. This is precisely what Miyazaki wants to avoid. Instead, he proposes we replicate instances of hope that we study into 'hope for anthropology'. I per-sonally find it difficult to see how anthropologists – as opposed to, say, Christian theologians, who have extensively engaged with *The Principle of Hope* – can fully subscribe to Bloch's exercise of temporal reorientation without reproducing his teleology. Bloch's philosophy is grounded in explicit normative positionings in terms of his own hope, which implies a different starting point from that of most eth-nographers. This is noticeable in Miyazaki's turn to hope as a method too, yet, unlike Bloch, who does not hide his Marxist commitments, he remains vague about his hopes 'for anthropology'. Indeed, how does one hope for anthropology? Which particular understandings of anthropology are involved here? Whose anthropology is this? As for his hopes for the world, Miyazaki calls on us to 'redefine radically and imaginatively the constitution of critique' (2006: 165). He rejects lamentations of the loss of hope, aligning himself with commentators who instead embrace ambivalence and loss of direction (Miyazaki 2010). Ultimately then, while he is critical of it, Miyazaki's work resonates here with writings that speak of hope within a Deleuzian register, foregrounding emergence, becoming and indeterminacy.

I too favour an analytical perspective that is alert to possibilities, to 'the not-yet' – but the promotion of a particular knowledge practice (or a 'method') is not my main concern here. At the core of this book is not my 'hope for anthropology', but what Miyazaki calls 'the hope of others'. Where he rejects this as his object of analysis, I focus on the hopes embodied in evocations of 'normal lives' by people in Dobrinja in 2008–10. It is fair to say that, to a degree, I did cherish a timid hope to find hope in Dobrinja and to 'replicate' it in my work – not 'for an-thropology', but for (this part of) 'the world' and, thereby, for myself. Yet, along the way, I struggled to find an appropriate place in my argument for hope as it is conceptualised in most of the literature. In fact, if I was to write this study in the key of 'hope', my ethnographic material would lead me to a book on hopelessness, particularly in terms of 'social hope' (Rorty 1999).

The exercise of seeking to document the 'hope of others' while also wishing to contribute to a 'reorientation of knowledge' in anthropology drew my attention to the ways in which people in Dayton BiH structured the actual *possibility* of hope as a positive, expectant orientation to the future. What did my interlocutors consider to be the conditions of possibility for hope? And to what extent did the Dayton BiH Meantime provide those? If I found hope, so conceived, to be in short supply, I was struck by persistent longings for hope. People seemed to be waiting to be able to start hoping, but the length of the wait made it increasingly difficult for them to believe that there would be anything at the end of it. This resonates with Crapanzano's portrayal of white people in 1980s South Africa who were 'caught in the structure of waiting' (1985) and found 'refuge … in this sustained and indefinable waiting. They were removed; they were not responsible' (Crapanzano 2003: 18). Yet, if the latter were expecting the end of Apartheid – a prospect they generally dreaded – people's projections in Dayton BiH indexed something more positive, but less definable, at least alongside catastrophic scenarios of renewed war or total economic breakdown. Generally, a kind of abstention from hope prevailed, as if, having set up the contours of possible hope around 'normal lives', people were unable to formulate any hopes beyond very short-term and very long-term ones at all. Even the hopes they did cherish rarely ventured beyond their immediate households. Projected 'normal lives' were thus suspended between, on the one hand, narrow, straightforward reproduction of patterns known from past lives, and, on the other, something as vast and vague as Hartman's conceptualisation of normality as a 'utopian project of impossible fullness' (2007).

Regimes of Temporal Reasoning

Much classic anthropological work that explicitly takes people's dealings with futures as its object – for example, studies of cargo cults, divination, witchcraft or millenarianism – focuses on the persistent relevance of custom, magic or religion. Likewise, writings on collective political future-oriented activity – for example, the study of indigenous campaigns against dam-building projects – often reaffirm the importance of the past rather than exploring engagements with the future per se. I find this reluctance to deal with what we could call more 'secular' future orientations disconcerting. As ethnographers, we know that people engage with the future in many ways and we seem to be particularly well placed to contribute to understandings of how they hope, fear, desire, aspire, long, expect, anticipate, avoid and plan. One reason why anthropologists have often shied away from analysing mundane forward-oriented practices may be that they are often considered the terrain of other scholars. For Appadurai (2004: 60), this is a consequence of a skewed definition of the discipline's core concept – culture – which, he says, has unnecessarily led to the abandoning of the analysis of 'plans, hopes, goals, targets ..., wants, needs, expectations, calculation' to economics and development studies. In response, Appadurai seeks to actualise the latent ability of the culture concept to encompass orientations to the future, in particular by conceiving of the 'capacity to aspire' as an interactive, social 'cultural capacity'. In people's immediate wants, he argues, we can read 'horizons', or 'intermediate and higher-order normative contexts' (ibid.: 68).

Although Appadurai proceeds on the basis of a sophisticated conceptualisation of culture, embedded in a critique of 'the terms of recognition' and in numerous disclaimers, in my view his culture concept still jeopardises his desire to place 'futurity, rather than pastness, at the heart of our thinking about culture' (ibid.: 83). In Bloch's terminology, we could say that the retrospective, contemplative temporality of his analysis thus remains opposite to the prospective temporality of the object of his analysis: aspiration. My work in the post-Yugoslav states has made me wary about both the analytical value of the culture concept for my research – even more so if I wish to foreground the future – and the critical potential of anthropological interventions internal to the politics of recognition. I am not committed to Appadurai's project to save 'aspirations' as an object of anthropological analysis by 'repatriat[ing] them into the domain of culture' (ibid.: 67). Nor do I hope to reinvigorate the culture concept – itself a main reason for anthropology's predominant orientation towards the past – as our discipline's prime piece of intellectual property. I do share his interest in the ways in which 'intermediate and higher-order normative contexts' constitute conditions of possibility for particular aspirations, but rather than conceptualising them in terms of a particular (Sarajevan? Bosnian? Balkan?) 'culture', I am most interested in how temporal reasoning shapes up in particular historical conjunctures. Against culturalist representations of people in BiH as caught in timeless cycles of Balkan violence, as prisoners of a Yugoslav socialist past, or even as off-modern subalterns, I thus conceptualise my research around concerns with the future explicitly conceived of as embedded in a geopolitical conjuncture. I investigate how aspirations in the Dayton BiH Meantime shape up cn the intersection of both histories cf hope (i.e., futures one once had, both thwarted and fulfilled) and projected normative future paths. I found inspiration for this approach in recent anthropological wr_tings on time and the future as well as in Bourdieu's early work. I now deal with both in turn.

Writing about the contemporary U.S., Guyer (2007) tentatively draws out tendencies in what Appadurai would call 'intermediate and higher-order normative contexts', which she refers to as 'temporal framings', 'prevailing templates', 'a public culture of temporality', or, after Bourdieu, 'generative schemata'. Guyer detects a shift that privileges the faraway future and the immediate present at the expense of the 'near future'. Chapter 5 ethnographically addresses this issue. Here, I expand Guyer's focus on prevalent modes of temporal reasoning to take in both forward- and backward-looking dimensions of the evocations of 'normal lives' I encountered. My research guided me increasingly to questions concerning the possibility to articulate and act upon certain kinds of hope. I am especially interested in how this is related to a prevailing regime of temporal reasoning – how a particular historical conjuncture entails a particular horizon of expectation (Kosseleck 1985: 273). How does this shape up on the intersection of sedimentations of past modes of expecting, (mis)remembered from previous lives, and of futures that are projected (or lack thereof) in the present?

We thus arrive at questions of the production, accumulation and distribution of hope. Using the metaphor of map reading, Appadurai conceives of the capacity to aspire as, 'a navigational capacity which is nurtured by the possibility of real world conjectures and refutations' (2004: 69). The 'metacapacity' to aspire, he says, is 'not evenly distributed in any society ... the better off you are (in terms of power, dignity and material resources), the more likely you are to be conscious of the links between the more and less immediate objects of aspiration' (ibid.: 68). While Appadurai mentions practice theory only in a negative light, this call for an economy of hope resonates strongly with the work of Bourdieu. So, on another level, do Guyer's (1997) and Ferguson's (1999, 2006) writings, focusing less on the distribution of particular forms of temporal reasoning in a specific social configuration and more on how they come to prevail in particular historical conjunctures. In order to emphasise their relative regularity and (geo)political production and maintenance, I will speak of 'regimes of temporal reasoning'. Let us now delve a little deeper into the economy of hope.

A Political Economy of Hope and Entrapment

Instead of expanding the concept of culture to incorporate economics, Bourdieu broadens the terms of 'economy' to incorporate patterns often associated with culture, and presumably noneconomical.
While this approach runs through his oeuvre, for our purposes here
I will focus on his early studies of 'temporal dispositions' in Algeria
(Bourdieu 1979: 2). Focusing on a period of imposed transformation,
Bourdieu highlights the tensions between temporal dispositions
associated with precapitalist Kabyle peasant life and the modernising
universe imported by French colonisation. In the former, he argues,
'temporal consciousness' was organised around 'simple reproduction
and cyclical time' (ibid.: 8). Centred on a sense of honour, this made
'a virtue of necessity' by 'adjusting one's hopes to the objective prob-
abilities' (ibid.: 16). The Kabyle peasant economy was 'rhythmically
structured' by a 'mythico-ritual calendar', which functioned both as
a principle that organised temporal succession and as an integrating force that harmonised conduct, thus ensuring predictability and
cohesion, for 'the social order is first of all a rhythm, a tempo' (ibid.:
27–28).

At the time of Bourdieu's research around 1960, many Kabyle
moved to the cities and became 'subproletarians' on the margins of the
'modern sector'. Yet they did not straightforwardly shift to 'modern'
temporal consciousness, built around calculation and forecasting.
In an early example of what he later called the 'hysteresis effect',
Bourdieu shows how different dispositions coexisted, 'as if these societies were not contemporary with themselves' (ibid.: 5). Bourdieu
and his collaborators found that, as one ascended socioeconomic
scales, hopes for oneself and for one's children were more 'realistic'
(i.e., corresponding to objective conditions) and more 'rational' (i.e.,
more calculated). Those Kabyle who had gained regular employment
in the 'modern sector' could count on the kind of minimal security
that facilitates such aspirations and planning – 'a life-plan' (ibid.: 62).

> This realistic aiming at the future (*l'avenir*) is only accessible to those who
> have the means to confront the present and to look for ways of beginning to
> implement their hopes, instead of giving way to resigned surrender or to the
> magical impatience of those who are too crushed by the present to be able to
> look to anything other than a utopian future (*un futur*), an immediate, magical
> negation of the present. (ibid.: 63)

The latter, Bourdieu argues, was the predicament of most Kabyle
ex-peasants. They abandoned their villages but continued to evaluate

the casual, unskilled labour in which they engaged in terms of a tra-
ditionalist village ethos. Implicitly knowledgeable about their material conditions of existence and of the gap between their subjective
hopes and objective chances, they were 'condemned ... to despair',
leaving open only 'escape into daydreams and fatalistic resignation'
(ibid.: 62). Subproletarians were bereft of the predictability that came
with the temporal structures of both regular paid employment and
peasant traditions and thus lacked a hold on the present that would
allow reasoning about the near future. In Appadurai's words: in the
given social configuration, they were disadvantaged in terms of the
(meta)capacity to aspire. The main concrete aspiration for most was
to find a 'genuine occupation', ideally in the civil service, which was
perceived as providing 'minimum guarantees against arbitrariness
and, above all, ... security, defined not so much by the amount of
the wages as by their regularity' (ibid.: 71). This, Bourdieu argues,
also explains the 'conservatism' of those who did have such regular
jobs, because they had 'everything to lose': they were at 'the peak of
a *negative career*, the one which leads towards a relapse into the sub-
proletariat' (ibid.: 62).

　While I am uncomfortable with Bourdieu's homogenised notions
of tradition and modernity, his approach is inspirational for my BiH
study for at least three reasons. First, he approaches temporality as
a matter of practice through reasoning (Adkins 2011). Second, he
highlights how social ordering and cohesion rely on predictability,
rhythms and trajectories in what he later called 'temporal structures' (Bourdieu 1990: 183). Third, he shows how the production
and distribution of temporal dispositions are themselves social processes, where unequal positionings facilitate particular dispositions.
Through an analysis of regimes of temporal reasoning in particular
social constellations in particular historical conjunctures, a political
economy of hope thus seeks to understand what and how people can
and do hope at a given point in time and space. As Hage points out:
'We need to look at what kind of hope a society encourages rather
than simply whether it gives people hope or not' (2002: 152).

　Bourdieu's work focuses on inequalities arising from a clash
between two regimes of temporal reasoning in a colonial process of
modernising transformation. Coming from the other end, Ferguson
(1999) traces people's creative responses when a previously prevalent
modernist temporal template becomes asynchronous with their experiences. His ethnography of 'abjection' on the Zambian copperbelt
(ibid.) and his writings on postcolonial Africa more generally (2006)
demonstrate how a regime of temporal reasoning may continue to

inform orientations after the demise of its condition of existence. Others highlight the possibilities opened up by new regimes of temporal reasoning, for example in patients' activism to steer bioscience by replicating its own hopeful future orientation (Novas 2006). Increasingly, anthropologists draw attention to the global hierarchies involved, for example, in people's attempts to produce particular household futures under neoliberalising policies (e.g., Han 2011), in their projection of hopes onto particular places in experiences of (non-)movement (e.g., Jansen and Löfving 2008; Mar 2005), and in their investments in particular regimes of temporal reasoning underlying modernity and development (e.g., Rofel 1999).

This brings us to one further key element of my approach to hope: the role of movement and entrapment. This dimension has been developed in Hage's writings on the current historical conjuncture in Australia. Hage sees neoliberal capitalism as involving a particularly uneven distribution of the ability to give meaning to life, to assert one's worth as a human being and to gain recognition for it (2003: 9–18). Following Bourdieu, he argues that some people have less chances to 'accumulate being' than others (ibid.: 15–16). Crucially, after Pascal and Spinoza, he argues that hope is not just about a particular status (e.g., having a certain amount of wealth) but that it also entails questions of future-oriented movement (Hage 2002; 2009). This sense that one is 'going somewhere' is a social capacity, enhanced by sociality, and its greatest enemy is 'stuckedness' (Hage 2009: 97). Worries about losing jobs due to precariousness of tenure then become more prominent than exact income levels. A key category of the population in Australia, Hage says, is constituted by people who feel they are losing the share of hope they once enjoyed: they resent that they are 'not going anywhere' anymore while others – for example, immigrants – seem, comparatively, to be 'going somewhere' (2003: 9).

Dayton Meantime:
Contours of a Regime of Temporal Reasoning

This book suggests that this sense of 'not moving well enough' (Hage 2009: 99) can be felt to characterise an entire polity at a specific historical conjuncture. Here I want to link this back to questions of normality, with the aid of Navaro-Yashin's work on the nonrecognised Turkish Republic of Northern Cyprus (TRNC), where 'life is kept on hold' (2003: 121). Navaro-Yashin positions her reflections explicitly 'against the grain of … normalizing representations of "the political" in anthropology' (ibid.: 107). In a classic defamiliarising anthropological move, she focuses on an 'abnormal' context precisely because it estranges and thus sheds a light on presumably 'normal' conditions. Navaro-Yashin calls on us to 'depict those expressions of emergency and desolation in what could otherwise have been studied as "the culture" or "social structure" of Turkish-Cypriots, rationalizing a situation that is historically contingent' (ibid.: 120). While people, in order to exist in such contexts, are required to routinise the abnormal, she argues that 'linear metaphors for the life cycle do not apply' in the TRNC (ibid.: 110). Furthering 'the pretense (or ideology) of "normal everyday life"', she states, would play into the hands of the Northern Cypriot government (ibid.: 109).

Navaro-Yashin's rejection of everyday life as an analytical rubric is, in my reading, first and foremost an expression of a resolute anti-culturalism that we have in common. She argues that: '[A]n ethnography of a context in limbo ... requires that we center "disruption" in our analyses ... since it is central to the lived experiences of our informants. ... The frozen time, the time interval, has become the consciousness of temporality' (ibid.: 121). Yet while in the TRNC this might require us to 'perceive what is between the lines, ... to work on what appears to pass unnoticed' (ibid.: 120), in Dobrinja I did not need to dig between the lines to unearth submerged or suppressed patterns of disruption. Ubiquitous exasperation with the 'abnormality' of current lives and concomitant evocations of 'normal lives' in which one would 'move well enough' implied that the focus on disruption was very much part of Dobrinjci's own reasonings. Like Navaro-Yashin, then, I aim to 'sense the political' in a social configuration considered abnormal and 'on hold', and, like her, I will place concerns with the state at the centre of my analysis. Yet, partly for the ethnographic reasons spelled out here, and partly because I favour clearer boundaries around what can and what cannot be counted as ethnographic 'sensing' (see Jansen 2013a), I approach this precisely through close attention to the ways in which my interlocutors themselves refused to 'normalise the abnormal'.

In this book, then, I do not pursue a focus on the relative distribution of hope within a single social configuration, although various positionings in terms of class, gender, age, ethnicity and education clearly did provide unequal access to articulate hope and to act upon it. Instead, I aim to disentangle the everyday geopolitics of hope in Dobrinja in a particular conjuncture. Through evocations of 'normal lives' I investigate a set of conditions, or at least a perception of sharing such conditions ('Daytonitis'), which my interlocutors saw as hindering the articulation of hope. This includes an analysis of experiences of decline after self-proclaimed modernism, here Yugoslav socialist developmentalism. In Dobrinja, I will argue, 'abjection' (Ferguson 1999) took a particular form due to the articulation of postsocialist transformations with postwar reconstruction. Since there was almost universal agreement that things had not improved enough since the end of the military violence, people conveyed a sense of life after the disappointment of hope. This inchoate sense of collective entrapment in the Dayton BiH Meantime, alongside exposure to continuous (equally inchoate) exhortations to move forward on the 'Road into Europe', is at the heart of my analysis.

Due to the lack of an articulated political language to handle life in the Meantime – to understand it, to criticise it, let alone to articulate alternatives in terms of 'social hope' (Čengić 2008) – such concerns emerged mainly in eruptions of fury and in continuous dissatisfaction with 'politics'. The vast majority of my interlocutors in Dobrinja (and, in different ways, EU officials) felt that a 'functioning state' was a prerequisite for any movement in BiH, and therefore, for the movement of 'normal lives' itself to unfold. Here, my research uncovered an acute sense of abandonment. Yet, at the same time a multitude of municipal, cantonal, entity, state and supra-state bodies were seen to govern one's life in all kinds of unnecessary and annoying ways, thus leading to simultaneous resentment at what those authorities did, and, at least as much, about what they were not doing. Ethnographically, then, I found no excitement at the flourishing of multiple 'emergent' possibilities and no celebration of indeterminacy. It may not be within the boundaries of academic etiquette, but a juxtaposition of two expressions that circulated widely in Dayton BiH sums it up nicely: here we have a historical conjuncture where one could simultaneously complain that 'nobody fucks us five per cent' [*niko nas ne jebe pet posto*] and that 'everyone fucks us' [*svi nas jebu*]. And, in the Dayton Meantime, in this highly gendered imagery – implying neglect in the first phrase and domination in the second – the sexually uninterested 'nobody' and the sexually voracious 'everybody' could be located pretty much anywhere from the local post office to the seat of the United Nations.

To close this chapter, let me return to the question of how to study 'normal lives' ethnographically. My interlocutors did not exactly hope for 'normal lives'. Rather, they desperately longed to hope for them. For this reason I decided to formulate the core object of analysis in this book instead as people's yearnings (for 'normal lives'). 'Yearning' denotes a persistent longing. It is continuous and prolonged, and its object is known to be out of reach: it can be both lost in the past and deferred in the future. The ambiguous backward- and forward-orientation of yearning directs our focus to the temporality of practices and to the analytically productive tensions between the 'is', the 'ought' and the 'was'. As such, it can capture disappointment, frustration, impatience and even fury. Yet the term yearning also evokes a wistfulness, a bittersweetness, a melancholy. This prickly combination – a ferociousness verging on tenderness, a sense of entitlement verging on disbelief – along with the tension between familiarity and normativity, and the simultaneous backward- and forward-orientation, make yearnings for 'normal lives', I believe, a promising object of analysis.[7]

Focusing on yearnings for 'normal lives', then, a key aim of this book is to provide insight into prevailing regimes of temporal-political reasoning at a particular historical conjuncture, in a particular location: Dobrinja, Dayton BiH, 2008–10. I am aware that this is a risky endeavour: at the very least it raises questions of periodisation.[8] Moreover, such an attempt to address widely 'shared concerns' is explicitly generalising in ways that are bound to elicit criticism; as writings on the political economy of hope remind us, prevailing temporal reasonings affect people unequally and the possibilities that they open up are never evenly distributed. Yet, trawling through my ethnographic observations, through interviews, media reporting and documents – and through my ongoing everyday engagements in Sarajevo – I cannot help but be struck by strong regularities, common denominators, shared patterns and dynamics, similar experiences and dispositions around yearnings for 'normal lives'. It is in that way that these yearnings initially emerged as the core theme of my study and it is for this reason that I decided to systematically outline them in this book. I believe that the prevailing regime of temporal reasoning, of which we can make out the contours in those yearnings, does constitute a key factor shaping life for most Dobrinjci, most of the time, and therefore does tell us something important about Dayton BiH and, ultimately, about life in the EU's 'immediate outside' in this historical conjuncture.

As already indicated in the introduction, I have an additional reason for taking on the challenge of generalisation. Whether officially 'on research' or not, 'here', in Serbia, Croatia and BiH, is where some of the most significant threads of my life have been unfolding since 1996 and 'here' is where I have spent more time than anywhere else. Since 2007, 'here' has been Sarajevo, where I am writing these lines and where I hope to await their publication. I do not wish to conjure up a mystic bond with people in BiH but I think the reader ought to know that, as I write this, it is amongst them that I am trying to make a life for myself – probably not a 'normal life', but a life nevertheless. And this is perhaps why writing these lines is so intimately painful, for – I better admit to it – the prickly yearning for things to move, and the inability to see concrete scenarios for such movement on the horizon, is 'replicated' in those ongoing endeavours of mine to make a life here too.

This does not imply that I have 'gone native'. Sometimes, my interpretations of the past and of the present in BiH differed from those of my Dobrinja interlocutors. There were divergences between our political reasonings and hopes for the future too. The shared concern with 'normal lives' I found in Dobrinja was often formulated in conformist terms: many expressed a desire to reestablish a platform from which to launch lives in terms already known. In this book I try to understand this against the background of people's war and postwar predicaments. Yet it is only fair to acknowledge that I did not register such yearnings from a neutral position, a view from nowhere. Many evoked the value of order, direction and convention in ways that I personally found painfully petit bourgeois. In short, unlike many other recent studies in political anthropology, I did not deliberately pick a group of interlocutors on the basis of certain shared aspirations or a common cause. Nor could they be considered a prefigurative vanguard of a politics of my liking. Instead, my argument on 'normal lives' and regimes of temporal reasoning aims to compassionately convey a sense of what, I believe, is a central tragedy in Sarajevo as I write this, one appearing from the future that retroactively structures dealings with numerous inherited misfortunes in this city today: the sheer difficulty of producing hope.

In this sense, my use of the term 'yearning' resonates with hooks' (1990) writing about the black liberation struggle in the U.S., in which she proposes that this notion can function as a much needed bridging mechanism between the longings, the desires and the fantasies of everyday life on the one hand, and the struggle for radical political change on the other. She calls for a 'shared space and feeling of yearning' that would open up the possibility of a common ground where a host of different desires might be articulated into a potential dynamic of change (ibid.: 12–13).[9] And this is why I chose to focus on yearnings for 'normal lives': 'sensing the political' in them is my own modest attempt to seek connecting points for political hope – not just for BiH, but for the world. This dimension remains subdued throughout this book – which is first and foremost intended as an ethnographic account that provides insight and understanding – but readers may as well be aware of it. Despite my reservations about the term, then, this book does deal with hope. In this it inadvertently reflects the tendency of many writings on hope to interweave the hopes of research subjects with those of their authors. Yet what may be specific in my study – or perhaps more precisely: what may be especially clearly visible in it – is that what I share with my interlocutors is not so much hope but an ill-defined, stubborn yet resigned, modest yet grand, ferocious yet tender, *yearning for* hope.

We are ready now to enter Dobrinja. Instead of a grand entry, parachuting into Sarajevo's Ottoman-cum-Austro-Hungarian historical centre and visiting the four houses of worship mentioned in the introduction, I propose we approach life in this city from its most outlying planned prewar settlement: the apartment complex of Dobrinja. More precisely, let us start from the Dobrinja *okretaljka* – a city transport terminus on an asphalted, oil-stained parking lot with a few sheds and a lot of overhead cables – doing what people do there: let's wait. Ethnographically, I start my tale there, at the end of the line, or, for an average Dobrinja day, its beginning.

Notes

1. Kelly uses the term 'the ordinary', noting its corollaries 'the normal' and 'the everyday' (2008: 353).
2. At least in Serbia and in BiH, where many experienced the loss of 'normal life' during the 1990s as a veritable 'fall from grace' (Jansen 2005a, 2009), it was not unusual even for public figures with strong anti-communist, anti Yugoslav attitudes and strong investments in the new structures to refer to previous 'normality' in order to deplore current predicaments. The centrality of previous lives in the formulation of standards for 'normal lives' is confirmed in large-scale interview research (for Serbia, see Spasić 2013: 140–63).
3. Studies in former Eastern Bloc states also indicate that the discourse of 'normality', even when focusing on consumption, includes evocations of the need for political stability and efficient social order (Galbraith 2003: 2).
4. As we saw, this did not prevent some from considering it routine, at least since the war and, in evocations of BiH's exceptionalism as a place where abnormality has become the rule, in the longer term.
5. The title of Crapanzano's article 'Reflections on hope as a category of social and psychological analysis', seems to promise some clarity but the author explicitly refuses any formulation of a coherent argument (2003: 4). His ruminations mostly hover around the question of whether hope is a valid cross-cultural category. No answer is provided.

6. For a broader critique of Deleuzian ethnographies of hope, see Ringel 2012.
7. An additional reason why 'yearning' seems a particularly appropriate term to capture concerns with 'normal lives' in the Dayton Meantime lies in its resonance with the emic term *sevdah*. This term is used widely to denote an affect related mainly to certain forms of Bosnian music and people's engagements with it. Derived from the Persian for 'black bile', and having travelled to BiH through Arabic and Ottoman Turkish, *sevdah* is never precisely defined (indeed, its significance in cultural intimacy rests partly on the belief that this cannot be done). Like melancholia and the Portuguese *saudade* (both also derived from 'black bile'), *sevdah* is considered to be a profoundly ambiguous affect. It looks backwards and forward, it is painful and ecstatic, it incorporates love, loss, longing and unattainability. Its passionate pining is extended over time and its fulfilment always remains deferred. In *sevdah* one does not hope for love, one yearns for it.
8. See some of the comments on Guyer's 2007 article.
9. Rofel, whose book on gender and modernity in China (1999) carries the term 'yearning' in its title, takes it from a television series, but does not develop the term conceptually.

– Chapter 2 –

WAITING FOR A BUS
[or, Towards an Anthropology of Gridding]

in which we trace yearnings for 'normal lives' at the Dobrinja city transport terminus through people's clamourings for insertion into an organised city transport grid, which allow us to sense the political in mundane desires for ordered movement through the concept of 'gridding'

Dobrinja, summer 2008. I am waiting for a bus. Come to think of it, taken altogether, I must have waited for buses an awfully large proportion of my life. And in this, of course, I am not alone. It is a weekday, and many are waiting here with me at the *okretaljka* – the city transport terminus where trolley cables make full circle and where bus and trolleybus drivers pause before starting their return journey. Some people are going to work, in or near the city centre, served by trolleybus 103 and bus 31e, or in Ilidža, which requires changing at Nedžarići, served by bus 31. Others, judging by the folders they carry, will chase some paperwork at one of the municipal, cantonal, federal or state institutions that make up the logistics of government in Dayton BiH. Some carry coffee and sweets, perhaps on their way to visit relatives or friends. Others still, women mainly, carry empty shopping bags, probably on their way to the green market at Otoka, about halfway to town, served by bus 42. Due to the elongated shape of the Sarajevo valley, the beauty and the curse of this city, the ten kilometres drive to the centre may take anything between twenty and forty minutes, and almost all destinations removed from that axis require walking or changing lines. An exception is trolleybus service 107, which may bring this woman and two children to the zoo, or, in a less idyllic scenario, to the Koševo hospital. Other than that there are not many young people – it is probably too early during school holidays – except a few backpackers who stand out not only by speaking Spanish, but also by their clothing and by that beyond tired expression that comes with an overnight coach ride across the mountains. Judging by their growing numbers over the last few summers, Sarajevo has become a fixture on the backpackers' circuit. The ones waiting with us at the *okretaljka* have arrived from neighbouring Serbia: the intercity coach station Istočno Sarajevo [East Sarajevo], which has direct services to many towns in Serbia, is only a few hundred metres away. To reach the city centre, they could either take a taxi or walk over here to catch city transport.

Already at this early morning hour, the *okretaljka* is trembling with heat. The glass shelter provides only a few strips of shade, which have long been occupied by the more forward thinking amongst us. I should have known better – from the balcony of the flat where I live I can see the bus arrive from the centre. The driver's break allows me to gather my things, sprint down the stairs and through the grassy area past the basketball court to the asphalted space that serves its original function of parking lot as well that of city transport terminus. Usually I make it in time. Even with a few metres to spare, sometimes the driver will wait for me. Sometimes he will not. I have not worked out a logic behind such decisions yet.

FIGURE 2.1. Map of Dobrinja and a part of Istočno Sarajevo, with the airport bottom left. The dotted line that runs more or less vertically through the map is the Inter-Entity Boundary Line (IEBL). The *okretaljka* lies just to the west of the IEBL. The Istočno Sarajevo coach station, at the site of the prewar terminus, is located just to its east, at the very edge of the Dobrinja apartment complex (© openstreetmap contributors, www. openstreetmap.com)

Some people seek out the sparse shade provided by the ticket booth and the shed with a sign saying *dispečer linijski* [line dispatcher]. A cabin toilet a few metres away provides another option but an unattractive one, especially in this heat. Better to stay close to the shed where drivers take a break between their runs, making coffee on an electric mini cooker and keeping one eye on a television set. Waiting for buses and trolleybuses, it was on that tiny screen that I gained glimpses of some goals on the European Football Championship in June. It was there, a few days ago, that I first saw what Radovan Karadžić, former president of Republika Srpska, looked like after he had shed his disguise as Dr Dabić, a healer, and switched back from alternative medicine to defending Serbdom at the International Criminal Tribunal for former Yugoslavia in Den Haag. At the ticket booth, several categories of Sarajevans (pensioners, students, persons with disabilities, recipients of war-related allowances, etc.) qualify for travel at reduced prices with monthly *kuponi* [bus passes]. Firms and institutions also provide their employees with *kuponi*, which are subject to a brisk black market trade. Many passengers do not buy tickets at all and take their chances that no *revizor* [ticket inspector] will appear on the way.

The vehicles pausing at the *okretaljka* display their usual visual variety. A ramshackle 107 trolleybus still carries the original passenger messages of the donating German city council, such as *Barzahler bitte vorne einsteigen* [Cash payers please enter in front]. It also retains fading advertisements for the *Solinger Tagesblatt* [Solinger Daily] and appeals for a Solingen charity organisation. Some of the original advertisements have been covered by new ones and passenger signs in Bosnian have been added. Although the doors are open, no one gets in just yet – in this heat people prefer to wait outside. A 31 bus carries a few signs of EUFOR, the acronym for the EU-led military units stationed in BiH. The women with the shopping bags board that market bound bus. A 42 bus arrives, without advertisements but with a sun-bleached sign saying *Japan Official Development Assistance - Japan za Bosnu i Hercegovinu 1998*. Many are now moving towards the place in the middle of the asphalted area where we know it normally stops. But the driver waves them away as he passes, taking the vehicle to the *remiza*, the garage, located about halfway between Dobrinja and the city centre.

Dissatisfaction is mounting now and some people angrily address the *dispečer*, or whoever looks like an employee of KJKP GRAS [*Kantonalno javno komunalno preduzeće Gradski saobraćaj Sarajevo*, Cantonal Public Communal Enterprise City Transport Sarajevo]. Will anyone

FIGURE 2.2. The *okretaljka* in Dobrinja (photo by Vanja Čelebičić, 2010)

FIGURE 2.3. A trolleybus waiting at the *okretaljka* (photo by Vanja Čelebičić, 2010)

consider using the routes for complaints and requests advertised on the *dispečer*'s booth? There are two of them: one provides an email address and a phone number for *korisnici usluga* [service users], whereas the other one, attached to a letterbox, addresses *građani* [citizens]. Warning signs on vehicles address the people they serve as *putnici* [passengers]. Whether as service users, passengers or citizens, people complain amongst themselves or loudly vent their dissatisfaction to no one in particular. '*Pa gdje to ima!?*' [Well where does that exist!?; see introduction], a woman exclaims. Using another polyvalent phrase in Dayton BiH, a man sighs, '*Da je ovo normalna država…!*' [If (only) this was a normal state!]. Judging by the reactions from the crowd waiting for bus 31, their grudge seemed to be summarised effectively by a woman in her late fifties, smallish but straight-backed, her long hair pinned up: 'They're skipping again', she says, 'Of course now they'll tell us there's a problem and they'll send a *komercijala*. That's how they do it!'

Sure enough, this is precisely what happens. A newish 31e bus, painted in the colours of a credit card company but without any advertising inside, arrives: it is universally known as the *komercijala*, even in GRAS announcements. The *komercijala* is much less frequent but faster and on the whole more reliable than other services. While its actual movements are sometimes rather loosely related to the timetable on the *dispečer*'s booth, you can always count on it turning up at some point. Other services are more erratic and, especially in the mornings, the *okretaljka* is therefore often occupied by crowds with *kuponi* waiting to go to work or to school. On the *komercijala* all passengers must buy tickets from the driver. Except on a few late night services, the price is the same as that of individual tickets bought at the booth for other lines. The crowd is thus faced with a dilemma: wait for a vehicle on which they can travel with their *kuponi* or pay for a ticket on the 31e bus. For me there is no issue: I do not qualify for a *kupon* anyway.

Some people do try to board with their *kuponi*. The woman with the pinned-up hair who predicted its arrival argues with the driver but to no avail. Some grudgingly get out their purses, while others decide to wait. We drive off. I always have a place to sit – a privilege of those who live near the *okretaljka*. This advantage is counterbalanced by the fact that many passengers, weary of the draught, object to open windows, which often leaves only those in the central standing area partly open. I am lucky: my favourite seat, immediately behind those windows, and with the added luxury of extra leg space, is free.

When the middle and backdoors open to let passengers disembark two stops further along, two middle-aged women and an elderly man board the *komercijala* – believing, or, more likely, pretending to believe that they do not know their *kuponi* are not valid here. As always when this happens, they are called to order by the driver who gets up from his seat and tells them to buy a ticket. The man grumbles and steps off the bus. One woman waves her *kupon* and loudly states that she refuses to disembark. The other woman stands by silently. From the front of the bus, the driver shouts: '*Ovo ti je k'o taksi, morate platit'* [This is like a taxi, you have to pay]. The first woman remarks disparagingly on GRAS claims to taxi standards and the destination of the money she would have to pay for a ticket. Now agitated, the driver shouts he will not drive off before the women buy a ticket or leave the bus. The silent one buys a ticket, the other one steps off, fuming. She will have to wait for the next standard service but I know that other people are still waiting for that one at the *okretaljka*.

Amongst them is the woman with the pinned-up hair. I know her. Mrs Sejda Šehović – a seamstress, divorced mother of two adult children – sits on the council of one of the four *Mjesne Zajednice* [local communes, MZ] in Dobrinja.[1] The MZ, an institution founded in the 1942–45 Partisan liberation war and developed as part of Yugoslav workers' self-management, is the most localised form of self-govern-ment in BiH. Like many other councillors, Mrs Šehović had been an active participant in the self-management bodies of her now defunct prewar work organisation, a pre and postwar house representative for a set of flats in her building and an activist in the Civil Protection structures in besieged Dobrinja during the 1992–95 war (see chapter 3). In our conversations, she combines positionings that initially seemed incompatible to me, but then turned out to coexist for others too: she is an active SDA member, a practising Muslim who says she never joined the League of Communists for this reason, a vocal BiH patriot and a staunch defender of the previous, Yugoslav socialist po-litical order, which her party helped to implode, as superior in most everything to the current one, in which SDA has been a dominant factor for almost two decades.

At a meeting of Mrs Šehović's MZ council not long before her outburst at the *okretaljka*, as at other ones I attended, city transport had been a priority issue. Following up on citizen complaints, the council had sent an assertively phrased letter to GRAS and to the can-tonal authorities, under whose responsibility it resorts. Firstly, they demanded that the advertised time schedules be respected, making an end to the 'skipping' of many services, with only the *komercijala* a reliable option. Secondly, they wanted a solution for the dangerous situation created by arriving vehicles letting people disembark on the other side of the road before they turned around on the *okretaljka*. On the council's invitation, the cantonal authorities and GRAS had sent inspectors to assess the situation. Regarding the second issue, councillors agreed to submit a demand for a zebra crossing and a warning sign but they doubted they would gain the cooperation this would require from another Dobrinja MZ, because, as they pointed out, the current situation did suit those living on the other side of the road. Months later, the MZ was still waiting for a reply.

When the Bus Does Not Arrive

In his *Critique de la Raison Dialectique*, Sartre (1985) uses the example of people waiting for a bus on the place Saint Germain to illustrate what he calls a *série*. Considering it the fundamental structure of human sociality, he defines a *série* as an inert, contingent gathering of inter-changeable people whose unity is only perceived from outside (1985: 371). These persons, Sartre says, represent a plurality of solitudes: they do not communicate with each other and they form a group only 'insofar as they are standing on the same pavement that protects them from the cars that cross the square, insofar as they are grouped around the same stop' (ibid.: 366). They are there, Sartre adds, because they share a 'present interest': an identical relation to the 7h49 bus that will allow them to engage in particular pursuits. Using this example as the starting point for a theory of group formation, as *séries* may fuse into groups and organisations, Sartre focuses on the logic of political action. Discussing Sartre's example, Badiou (2009) alerts us to the possibility that the bus does not arrive. 'There will be protests and mutterings', he says, 'people will start to talk to each other about the inhumanity of their external conditioning', and we will witness fusing in action as 'the awareness of its intolerable nature ... dissolves the *série* and creates a new reciprocity' (ibid.: 23). Relating this to the questions of movement and entrapment, Hage (2009) suggests we can thus understand the bus queue as a mode of self-government. Yet in contrast to Badiou's revolutionary optimism, he argues that, 'today', the metaphorical non-arrival of the bus would not lead to critique and possible exploration of alternatives. Instead, Hage states:

> [E]nduring the crisis becomes the normal mode of being a good citizen and the more one is capable of enduring a crisis the more of a good citizen one is. ... heroism of the stuck seems to signal a deeper form of governmentality,

a governmentality that is reproduced even in times of crisis. Even when the bus does not come, even when people are feeling stuck in a queue that is not moving, they heroically keep on queuing. And this is self-reproducing: the more one waits and invests in waiting, the more reluctant one is to stop waiting. (2009: 104)

I discuss the experience of being stuck in chapter 5. Here, I want to use Sartre's example, and Badiou's and Hage's elaborations, more literally than they were ever meant to be. I refrain from attempts to model revolutionary politics or comments on 'the crisis of today' (which, as we shall see, did not feature much in Dobrinja reasonings). Instead, I deploy engagements with city transport as a window on yearnings for 'normal lives'. What can we learn about life in Dayton BiH from our vantage point amongst those who wait for a bus at the Dobrinja *okretaljka*? How can we use the prism of yearnings for 'normal lives' to draw out shared concerns from those vignettes that shed a light on the Dayton Meantime? I take GRAS to be a provider of material vehicles for transport and, thereby, of discursive ones for yearnings for 'normal lives'. Below, after a brief detour into urban discourses of culturedness, I proceed to my main topic: the 'gridding' of lives into the ordering framework of city transport.

City Transport and *Nekultura*

In Sarajevo, and perhaps especially in an outlying settlement such as Dobrinja, to speak, as Badiou does, of 'protests and mutterings' would be a grave understatement when describing the intensity with which city transport emerged as a shared concern. Few themes could match it as a topic of social commentary. Everyone, it seemed, had an opinion about it and few of those opinions were favourable. This echoed a wider post-Yugoslav choir of social commentary deploying the quality of city transport as a symptom of societal problems, and particularly of the lack of normality and order (see Simić 2009).[2] When in 2008 a teenage boy was stabbed to death in broad daylight on a Sarajevo tram, debates on how to dam in 'youth delinquency' revolved to a large extent around city transport – and later that year GRAS did introduce security guards on some of its services. Yet many Dobrinjci expressed passionate feelings towards city transport beyond such relatively rare occasions of violent crime: its importance and shortcomings – oh its shortcomings! – were discussed in the chance gatherings at the *okretaljka*, in MZ meetings, but also around kitchen tables, in cafés, in newspapers and on websites. Complaints abounded that its vehicles were old, filthy and badly maintained. Exasperation was expressed with regard to virtually all dimensions of GRAS' work as an inefficient, oversized, clientelist, subsidy-dependent public firm.

Bad services and high prices (often compared to cities elsewhere in Europe, where transport was considered to be better yet cheaper) were often blamed on drivers who, as we saw, were also criticised for not respecting schedules. A favourite target of letters to the editor in Sarajevo dailies – often from Dobrinjci, who were amongst those within the urban agglomeration with the longest travel time to the city centre – was the 'inappropriate, uncultured' behaviour of GRAS drivers.[3] People complained that they caused crowding by opening one wing of the entry doors only, that they ate *pita* [savoury pastry] or *ćevapi* [patties of seasoned grilled minced meat] or smoked in the bus, and that they played distasteful music. *Revizori* were blamed for being aggressive and impolite, for targeting confused tourists on crowded vehicles and for being rude to other passengers wanting to help them.[4] Special criticism was saved for the management of GRAS, often depicted as a nest of corrupt enrichment. Some Sarajevans embedded this in the blanket assessment that GRAS only employed *Sandžaklije* [people from Sandžak, a region in Serbia and Montenegro from which many 'people with Bosniak names' had moved to Sarajevo], who had turned the firm into their exclusive vehicle for *uhljebljenje*. This wonderful term [litt. em-breading] refers to the successful pursuit of material benefit and security. While it is used in different contexts, with regard to GRAS it referred mainly to the capture of stable salaried positions and to being securely 'tucked in'.

Beyond complaints about *Sandžaklije*, it was common to hear general condemnation not of the origins but of the *nekultura* [unculturedness] of GRAS personnel as unworthy of city life. Such litanies reflect a wider post-Yugoslav urban discourse of culturedness, whereby city transport functioned as a vehicle for the articulation of urban self-positioning through denunciation of the uncultured behaviour of others (Jansen 2005a/c, 2008b; on Sarajevo, see e.g., Bartulović 2013; Maček 2009; Sorabji 2006; Stefansson 2007). The coexistence of righteous disobedience in some ways (except on the *komercijala*, many did not buy tickets and defended this with a haughty, 'I am not paying for this!') and moralistic conformism in others, resonates with some of Lemon's findings in the Moscow metro (2000) and with Appadurai's laments of the loss of dignified bus transport in Bombay (2000). In Sarajevo too, this discourse of culturedness contained tensions. While GRAS personnel was particularly vilified, there were also voices arguing that some passengers were little better, elbowing their way to a seat, talking loudly on their mobile phones and smelling badly. In 2000, a Sarajevo weekly commented on GRAS' plans to modernise their equipment with a cynical: 'Nice try. If only someone added something about the "repair" and "modernisation" of passengers, drivers and inspectors' (Mulić-Bušatlija 2000). As one outraged newspaper letter writer concluded, 'Europe is still far away'.[5] Moral outrage at the behaviour of individual GRAS drivers and inspectors was thus often broadened into a sense of doubt about the comparative culturedness of what was frequently referred to as *naši ljudi* [our people]. In all these ways, standards of city transport emerged as a point of geocultural ranking in which Dayton BiH came out far below the *uređene države* [ordered states] of Western Europe that many had got to know as refugees or as *gastarbajteri* [guest workers, from the German 'Gastarbeiter']. People who had not resided abroad were still wont to make such comparisons in which BiH always featured as a place that was unable to catch up.

Such comments display a tension, akin to Herzfeld's description of 'cultural intimacy' (1996), between exasperation with the ways of 'our people' (the 'is') and righteous statements of entitlement to 'normal lives' (the 'ought', embedded in recollections of the 'was'). However, it is important to note that many complaints did not focus on the behaviour of individuals but on the inadequate functioning of city transport as a system, e.g., on what was seen to be the 'irrationality' of the network and of non-integrated ticketing policies. This brings us to the role of city transport as a structuring factor in (sub) urban life. Considering its significance in many people's routines, anthropologists have paid strikingly little attention to city transport.[6] Millions, perhaps billions of people around the globe wait for buses, trolleybuses, trams, tubes and trains on a daily basis. In a (sub) urbanising world, the rhythm of our daily routines is 'calibrated' (Lemon 2000: 18) by the arrivals and departures of city transport vehicles – and those passages are more or less (often less) anchored in some sort of set timetable. The habit in Sarajevo, like in other post-Yugoslav capitals, to turn line numbers into proper names (e.g., *Trojka* in Sarajevo, *Osamdesettrojka* in Beograd, *Šestica* in Zagreb) may be an indicator of the degree to which they have been domesticated into everyday life. With around two thousand employees (Šimko 2006: 113), GRAS was said to be the largest employer in Novi grad municipality, of which Dobrinja was part. But people's relationship with the city transport system was mostly one of passengers and citizens/tax payers. During my research, GRAS figures spoke of over four hundred thousand passenger trips daily, implying an average of roughly one trip per inhabitant of Canton Sarajevo per day.[7] Many Dobrinjci had cars but large numbers relied on public transport for their ordinary movements within the agglomeration. Before the war, Dobrinja had been known as a dormitory settlement: its inhabitants had been predominantly oriented towards other parts of town for employment, administration, health care, recreation, most secondary and all higher education. As we shall see, this changed somewhat with the war, but during my research many still travelled from and to Dobrinja on a daily basis. Dobrinjci thus spent much time inside city transport vehicles or waiting for them; GRAS formed part of the shared infrastructure that calibrated their routines.

Appadurai's lament about disintegrating queuing manners at Bombay bus stops is embedded in a comment on it having once been a 'well-managed' city, 'a civic model for India' (2000: 628). Likewise, I suggest in Dobrinja city transport did not simply serve as a particularly rich metaphor for *nekultura* but also as a 'place-trope' (Lemon 2000: 18) for a broader sense of entitlement to some 'ordered framework' in which 'normal lives' could unfold. To grasp such concerns I now introduce the notion of 'gridding'.

Gridding

In his original example from the place Saint Germain, Sartre draws attention to the importance of schedules and regularity, rendering the 7h49 bus the 'object' that makes the gathering of people at the stop into a *série*. Assuming they live in the neighbourhood, he says that their 'present interest' as individuals engaged in particular pragmatic endeavours already contains indications of 'fuller and deeper structures of their general interest: public transport improvement, price freezes, etc.' (Sartre 1985: 366). These people's presence in that time and place is anchored in a schedule and thus in an expectation of daily circulation of the bus in a network of transport provision, which means 'the city is present' in and through them (ibid.: 365). In Paris, Sartre notes, the medium for this anchoring is the city transport provider RATP, a giant equivalent of Sarajevo's GRAS. Yet where Sartre, Badiou and Hage are interested predominantly in formulating a critique of this embedding of bodily circulation (and, ultimately, of people's lives) into ordering frameworks as a form of governmentality, I approach this question from the opposite direction. It is not simply that I focus on the experiences of the people who are waiting for the bus themselves; my ethnographic research led me to pay particular attention to how they *sought* such embedding. Unlike what Hage suggests, when the bus did not arrive, people at the *okretaljka* in Dobrinja insisted that this should be seen as 'an unusual state of affairs' (2009: 204). And, on the whole, rather than celebrating endurance, they raged against 'the given (dis)order'. Yet their complaints and criticisms did not herald revolutionary 'forms of reciprocity' (Badiou 2009: 23). Instead, they channelled yearnings for more, and more effective, 'calibration'.

The calibration of routines through city transport – the ways in which it orders everyday lives in particular ways – relies on the degree to which it functions itself as an ordered framework. I conceive of such ordering and ordered frameworks as 'grids'. Using the term more as a visual metaphor, Scott, in a sustained critique of 'high modernist' forms of statecraft, has spoken of 'a standard grid' (1998: 2) that registers and monitors the unruly diversity of people, places and things and thus allows their government. This, he argues, involves ever more encompassing processes of simplification (ibid.: 76–83). Scott convincingly shows how this grid is central to the way states 'see', that is, the way state projects seek to make peoples, places and things legible. He then proceeds to trace the devastation caused by high modernist state 'schemes' that aspire to the 'sweeping, rational engineering of all aspects of social life in order to improve the human condition' (ibid.: 88).

For my purposes in this book, I reformulate Scott's conceptualisation of a 'standard grid' into a more multilayered, dynamic and plural understanding of grids. A better, more three-dimensional term would be 'grid-matrix'. Stemming from the Latin root for 'mother', matrix also means 'womb' and refers to a substance within which something is enclosed, takes shape and develops. In anatomy, for example, it refers to the formative tissue from which a tooth or a nail develops and in geology to the matter in which a fossil or crystal is embedded. Amongst its other meanings is that of a binding substance, like cement in concrete. To crystallise my dialogue with the libertarian paradigm in the anthropology of the state, as exemplified by Scott, I stick with the term 'grid', understood as grid-matrix.[8] This also allows me to emphasise crucial practical dynamics through the notion of 'gridding' (rather than the unacceptably clunky neologism 'grid-matrixing'). Grids, then, are ad hoc cumulative results of ongoing gridding. If Scott's grid metaphor conjures up mapmakers or administrators, who wish to make people and things legible, I turn it around to evoke people's routine reliance on trolleybuses, taps, cookers and light switches – and the wire and pipe grids in which this occurs. In this way, I fold my analysis into writings that trace ongoing performative effects as well as disruptions of material infrastructures of connection and circulation in postsocialist states (e.g., Alexander 2007; Collier 2004; Dunn 2003). Within this, I develop a specific emphasis on temporal dimensions, that is, on the way in which gridding calibrates mundane routines on the short and on the long term.

Focusing on gridding as process and practice avoids the structural-functionalist emphasis on stasis and equilibrium and resonates with work on assemblages (Ong and Collier 2005) and actor–networks (Latour 2005). Yet my entry point consists of yearnings for 'normal lives' and it is people who harbour them, not things, so my approach requires a distinction between different kinds of 'actants' and a grasp of hierarchy incompatible with the assumptions of a 'flat social' in actor–network theory (Jansen 2013a). My analysis underscores Greenberg's point that desires for 'normality' in Serbia evoked 'an *external environment* in which one has the agentive capacity to translate a promise or a wish into reality' (2011: 93, my italics). Yet, as we shall see, griddings can be mobilised in an unstable, partial convergence of self-organisation and imposition that, to an extent, questions such 'externality'. The latter term reflects the way in which Dobrinjci usually verbalised the importance of a framework of regularity and predictability to make 'normal lives' possible, placing themselves outside of it, but it obscures the intimate ways in which the routines that were said to make up 'normal lives' were implicated in the very production and maintenance of that framework. It is to capture this tension, and its processual and practical aspects, that I propose the notion of 'gridding'.

Where Scott privileges the imposition of grids, I propose 'gridding' as a complementary analytical tool that allows us to also highlight what we could call 'grid desire'. This is not to imply that the 'normal lives' for which people in Dobrinja yearned would be maximally stable and regimented, but rather that, to a degree, they were projected to be calibrated by a normalised and normalising order. Such incorporation would ideally be on their terms. This order was not imagined as a closed grid but as the cumulative effect of a set of ongoing gridding processes. As our entry from the *okretaljka* indicated, people's practices and words evoked the normative self-evidence of such gridding – often implicitly, sometimes explicitly, and predominantly through exasperated confrontations with the fact that, in practice, it was not self-evident at all. Through 'gridding', then, I will shed light on the frequent evocations of reaching into, and thereby making, an ordering framework in Dobrinja yearnings for 'normal lives'. This framework would be regular: the 'normal lives' that people yearned for required a framework of institutionalised predictability that would provide a basis on which one could mobilise one's 'agentive capacities'. It would be regulated: there would be an order to it that would to an extent be experienced as organised 'from above' and which would persist independently from individual practice. And it would be regulating: the effectiveness of such gridding would depend at least partly on disciplining technologies, themselves fore-grounded as one dimension of the conditions in which 'normal lives' might unfold. Indeed, the disintegration of regular, regulated and regulating gridding was recalled as having been central to the col-lapse of 'normal lives' in the early 1990s. Making the latter possible again, from this perspective, required some degree of integration in a regular, regulated and regulating framework, the substance within which 'normal lives' could develop.

Elaborating on issues of city transport, schooling and the 'govern-ment of a population', this book will approach questions of statecraft as a set of contested processes of gridding. While the libertarian para-digm proposed by Scott usefully confronts top-down state schemes to coerce, discipline and expropriate, it is important to note that gridding may consist of a variety of practices in different fields, on different scales and with different intensities. If we conceive of them as three dimensional, we may picture people as always already moving in some grids. Yet those grids are themselves in process: they consist of griddings that may be growing, integrating and intensify-ing or shrinking, disintegrating and lowering in intensity. Gridding processes, moreover, may unfold in interaction with each other and can be hierarchically nested: smaller-scale gridding may be depend-ent on and/or precipitate larger-scale gridding. The degree to which statecraft is effective may then be traced through the extent to which people experience institutionalised practices as gridded in 'vertical encompassment'. My use of this term is inspired by Ferguson and Gupta's call for 'an ethnography of encompassment' that analyses processes 'through which governmentality (by state and nonstate actors) is both legitimated and undermined by reference to claims of superior spatial reach and vertical height' (2002: 995). This Foucault-ian 'governmentality' framework allows us to trace technologies of government as they unfold in dispersed institutional sites such as ministries, NGOs, schools, private companies, foreign intervention agencies and so on. Yet it is not sufficient to grasp two crucial dimen-sions of lives in the Dayton BiH Meantime in which I am particularly interested. Firstly, as for the 'is' – the empirical description of how statecraft effectively works – governmentality approaches offer few if any tools to address issues of legitimacy, interests and complicity. In chapter 6 I therefore turn to hegemony theory to discuss those questions. Secondly, the governmentality paradigm would struggle to analytically capture the affective centrality of statecraft in Dobrinja yearnings for 'normal lives', where the 'ought' and the 'was' intersect. Gridding, let me reiterate, does not necessarily have to be associated with statecraft at all, but my research in this Sarajevo apartment complex – where plenty of 'non-state' actors provided services that gridded in some way or other – found that grid desire was overwhelmingly expressed in the 'language of stateness'. The notion of 'gridding', I propose, can help us grasp the fraught dynamics not only of claims to vertical encompassment by agents of statecraft but also of people's exasperation at their perceived failure to calibrate lives as they should.

High Noon at the *Okretaljka*

Spring 2010. I am waiting for a bus at the *okretaljka*. Again. It is unusually cold for this time of year. Around the *dispečer*'s booth, GRAS employees on their breaks agitatedly comment on the coaches we see passing on the main road. These belong to the company Centrotrans, which has started running services on two Sarajevo lines, one of which links Dobrinja with Vijećnica, in the centre, served by GRAS' *komercijala*. Centrotrans was founded in 1963 and privatised in the early 1990s. It provides scheduled and chartered intercity transport within BiH and across Europe and now uses some long-distance coaches for the Dobrinja–Vijećnica line. This incongruence leads to humorous comments amongst passengers – *Jarane, k'o da smo krenuli za Beč!* [Mate, this is as if we're on our way to Vienna!] – but many people do take advantage of the 1 KM promotional fare (against 1.60 KM on GRAS). It has been reported that Centrotrans accepts GRAS *kuponi* too. Its vehicles do not turn around at the *okretaljka*; instead we see them pass on their way to the Istočno Sarajevo coach station, a few hundred metres further. They carry large anti-GRAS signs, and GRAS buses and trolleybuses pausing at the *okretaljka* carry posters in response. Some contrast GRAS' status as a public service to Centrotrans' profit-orientation, but many more slogans, accompanied by photos of destroyed vehicles, remind Sarajevans of GRAS' wartime role.

CENTROTRANS SLOGANS

Konkurencija Da, Monopol Ne

[Competition Yes, Monopoly No]

Do kada će te biti građani, do kad će te biti taoci monopola GRAS-a? [sic]

[Until when will you be citizens, until when will you be hostages of GRAS monopoly?]

Građani, pitajte ministra Krmpotića zašto nemate kvalitetan prijevoz

[Citizens, ask minister Krmpotić (cantonal minister responsible for GRAS) why you have no quality transport]

GRAS COUNTER SLOGANS

Mi nismo monopolisti, mi smo javni servis Kantona Sarajevo

[We are not a monopoly, we are a public service of Canton Sarajevo]

Grasovi vozači u ratu voze građane Sarajeva jer ovaj grad ima dušu koju oplemenjuje i obogaćuje kretanje ljudi. Gras je branio dušu našeg grada

[GRAS drivers drove Sarajevo citizens during the war because this city has a soul that is ennobled and enriched by the movement of people. GRAS defended the soul of our city]

I u najtežim trenucima bili smo uz vas

[Even in the most difficult moments we were with you]

Između granata brži od PAM-a i PAT-a

[Between grenades, faster than PAM and PAT (artillery types used in the siege of Sarajevo)]

2. maj 1992. Gras – medju prvima na udaru. Da bi se ubio ovaj grad, trebalo je ubiti Gras … I danas???

[2 May 1992, GRAS – amongst the first under attack. To kill this city, GRAS had to be killed … And today …?]

> *Autobusi Gras-a su stajali na barikadama i štitili građana od snajpera … i bili tanka nit života …*
>
> [GRAS buses were on the barricades and protected citizens from snipers. They were the thin line of life …]
>
> *GRASovi vozači voze pod snajpera i ginu zajedno sa svojim građanima.*
>
> [GRAS drivers drive under sniper fire and die together with their citizens]
>
> *Gras se podigao iz pepela, ne iz profiterstva*
>
> [GRAS emerged from the ashes, not from profiteering]

The *komercijala* arrives. It carries a photocopy of a 1997 document in which then BiH president and SDA leader Alija Izetbegović congratulates GRAS on its wartime work. A woman who enters the bus with me asks, no doubt to provoke the driver, if 1 KM will be enough today. The driver does not take the bait but tells her she is free to go and catch a Centrotrans service. Still, on our way to town we see that Centrotrans' attempt to insert itself onto certain city lines has angered GRAS personnel. On one occasion a GRAS bus blocks Centrotrans vehicles from using designated bus stops. A shouting match between the drivers entails. On the whole, Centrotrans coaches avoid these situations by stopping just before or after the bus stops. A GRAS press statement, read out and reproduced in written and electronic media, explains that the posters on its vehicles serve to:

> [I]nform the public about what GRAS does for the city and for its citizens over the last 125 years – and especially during the years of aggression on BiH and on the capital – about its human mission and its permanent efforts to provide its users with the best transport of the highest quality, without any intentions to damage citizens' interests in any way, or to earn profit at their expense.[9]

A press statement by Centrotrans, in contrast, criticises 'privileged public enterprises', who, 'despite enormous humanitarian donations and subsidies, continue amassing debts through their overemployment, unrealistically high wages'.[10] Some GRAS services, it is argued, including *komercijala* ones, have in fact been declared illegal by various state institutions, yet the cantonal government does not intervene. Instead, GRAS' *nerad* [non-work], it is said, is paid for by the citizens of Sarajevo, whereas Centrotrans is an enormous 'help to the state' through its regular tax payments. And in response to GRAS accusations of war profiteering, Centrotrans also takes pains to emphasise it wartime credentials, referring to the material losses it suffered and to its involvement in refugee transport and repatriations.

This city transport conflict, referred to as a 'war' in some media reporting (e.g., Mustajbegović 2003: 30), was an eruption of a longstanding dispute which saw an earlier culmination point in the winter of 2003–04, when Centrotrans introduced five 'inter-entity' services linking Sarajevo with what was then still called 'Srpsko Sarajevo' (now Istočno Sarajevo). Three of those services, with the promotional fare of 1 KM, passed through Dobrinja. Just before that, inter-entity transport regulation had been moved from the entity governments, which had obstructed such services, to the BiH ministry of Communications and Transport, which had granted Centrotrans a licence. GRAS personnel protested vehemently against what they called an attack on public services, condemning Centrotrans for using dumping prices, and fearing job losses.[11] They also insisted that the city transport network, including its timetables, its stops, its shelters and so on, should be governed as one system, pointing out the duty of public firms to provide nonprofitable services and respect ecological standards through the increased use of trams and trolleybuses. In any case, GRAS argued, bus stops fell under the responsibility of the cantonal and not the BiH state government because these public surfaces were owned by Canton Sarajevo and served city, not inter-entity traffic.[12]

At the time, the GRAS director suggested that Centrotrans 'used the situation of lawlessness in order to skip the cantonal level to address the top of the state' (Mustajbegović 2003: 30) and, after an intervention by the cantonal minister on GRAS' behalf, the BiH ministry withdrew Centrotrans' licence until further notice. [13] Negotiations to reach a compromise about lines and stops failed and Centrotrans turned to the BiH Court, which confirmed the legality of its licence. Announcing four days of completely free services, they started with a service Vijećnica–Dobrinja–Srpsko Sarajevo, thereby effectively extending the *komercijala* service with one stop.[14] Four other lines were introduced a few days later. GRAS buses blocked Centrotrans vehicles until the police intervened and there were protests by taxi drivers in Srpsko Sarajevo, who had long relied on the absence of inter-entity transport in the Sarajevo agglomeration to attract customers.[15] The Office of the High Representative (OHR), the supreme in-country organ of the foreign intervention in BiH, intervened and the BiH ministry withdrew the licence, after which the cantonal minister and Centrotrans representatives agreed an OHR-brokered deal on a public tender for inter-entity transport in the Sarajevo region.[15] Yet a few months later Centrotrans won its case against the withdrawal of its licence by the BiH ministry and once more announced five inter-entity lines for the promotional fare of 1 KM. It also planned a set of monthly passes with special rates for pupils and students. Predictably, GRAS protested and Centrotrans replied with accusations of monopolistic behaviour. A Centrotrans representative hastened to make clear that they too were in favour of an 'integrated city transport system'.

Six years later, in the late spring of 2010, as I am on the *komercijala*, such a system is still not on the horizon and the conflict between Centrotrans and GRAS remains unresolved. The complaints letterbox on the *dispečer's* cabin has recently been replaced with a typed notice. It contains two phone numbers and an email address for *primjedbe, pohvale i sugestije* ~~uposlenika~~ *putnika* [complaints, compliments and suggestions by ~~employees~~ passengers]. The typed word 'employees' is crossed out, and 'passengers' has been added in handwriting. The original error neatly reflects the widespread feeling amongst Dobrinjci that GRAS acts as if it exists for itself, rather than for the people it transports. My balcony view on the *okretaljka* is changing somewhat, as a *dispečer's* centre is being built to replace the cabins, but for Dobrinjci the only effect of the 'war' with Centrotrans so far has been a directive that reduced the number of *komercijala* services. So it has become more difficult to travel to or from the city centre, especially later in the evening. This change is drily announced in a statement attached to the *dispečer's* booth.

Two motifs run prominently through this conflict between Centrotrans and GRAS: war and the state. In Dayton BiH it was almost impossible to politically articulate anything about one without mentioning the other – indeed, this is one of the most important ways in which concerns with state*craft in* BiH tended be overshadowed by issues of the state*hood of* BiH. In the following two sections, after a brief excursion into Dobrinja's prewar history, I explain the particular significance of city transport in wartime experiences and then relate this to questions of the state, gridding and 'normal lives'.

The First Tram

While the Dobrinja city transport lines, like the settlement itself, were the product of late Yugoslav socialism, the infrastructure of Sarajevo public transport was not straightforwardly associated with that period. Local patriots often proudly pointed out that Sarajevo was one of the first cities in Europe to be served by an electric tram in 1895 (although not the first, as some claim). The Austro-Hungarian occupation also oversaw the building of intercity transport infrastructure, such as railways. But it was in the socialist post-Second World War period that Sarajevo's massive expansion occurred (52 per cent of the city's 361,735 inhabitants in 1991 had been born elsewhere), spurring investments in tram, bus and trolleybus infrastructure. City transport was thus a key component of successive gridding schemes.

Dobrinja was the last large-scale apartment project to be built in Yugoslav Sarajevo. On the whole, people who had settled there in the 1970s and 1980s told me they had been satisfied with its modern flats, spacious streets and child-friendly greenery. At the same time, however, many of my interlocutors, especially those who had moved there from more central areas of the city, recalled they had been put off by its remoteness (ca. ten kilometres from the centre). 'It seemed at the end of the world', they said, or 'people told me: uh, you are moving to a village!' In the early 1980s, when only some parts of Dobrinja had been completed, and it remained largely surrounded by agricultural land (and the airport), its incorporation into city transport grids had been relatively weak. Initially there were minibuses and later buses and trolleybuses – the latter introduced to Sarajevo as part of the city's infrastructural and environmental projects on the occasion of the 1984 Olympic Winter Games. City transport lines also linked Dobrinja to the industries in the Sarajevo valley and beyond, where much of the population worked. In addition, many of the larger socially owned firms ran their own buses for workers. As we saw, through the socialist self-management system of long-term, inheritable tenancy rights, those large firms had been responsible for building and allocating Dobrinja's flats. This outlying settlement was thus very much part of Sarajevo gridding schemes and its inhabitants evaluated their lives there at least partly according to how successful they found this gridding.

Since most people over fourteen had used city transport on a daily basis to go to work or to school, the sense of not being connected well enough was the most important negative assessment of prewar life in Dobrinja I encountered. Some pointed out that Dobrinja had never been served by a tram line, despite periodical pre and postwar announcements by politicians to that effect. In any case, whether positively or negatively, the fact that city transport was spontaneously mentioned so frequently reflects the role it plays in the desirability of peri-urban locations. Mrs Nina Kamenica, for example, a fiftyish medical doctor, had moved with her two children and her policeman husband from further outlying Hrasnica into their new Dobrinja flat. City transport formed the axis around which she spun her tales of satisfaction and dissatisfaction:

> What people from the centre, or from the *soliteri* [high-rise blocks nearer the centre], can't understand is that Dobrinja is the nicest part of town to live in. Because people think, if they live on Ferhadija [central shopping street], that that is beauty. But beauty is when you detach yourself from the buzz and I think Dobrinja is one of the better settlements. Why? Because it has a wire [*Zato što ima žicu*]. You know, once the wire only went from the old town to Čengić Vila, but now it goes until Dobrinja. That is the trolleybus and you know it will come, because one will push the other one. When we moved here, there was a minibus that took forty people. It takes forty and the rest waits for the next one, in that way three times as many people gather. We didn't have anywhere to buy bread, we didn't have anything. If it wasn't for the Olympics, we'd have remained a village [*da ne bi Olimpijade, mi ostadosmo selo*].

I thus found that the degree of gridding by integrated city transport – here evoked literally as the trolleybus wire network – was central to people's assessment of life in prewar Dobrinja. Some remembered it as adequate, whereas others complained about it. Newspapers from the 1980s also indicate that the quality, frequency and reach of city transport were major topics of concern. Yet their vital significance became suddenly and painfully clear at the 1992 start of the war. This time the bus (and the trolleybus) really did not arrive. And when it did, it was not as a city transport vehicle. Even before large-scale military violence in Sarajevo started, at the time of the referendum on BiH independence on 29 February and 1 March 1992, trolleybuses were used to mount barricades at strategic points throughout the city in a show of force. In early April, the besieging JNA – soon to become VRS (see Narrative Glossary in introduction) – shelled tram and trolleybus garages, as well as key points in GRAS' electric network (Novo 1992: 103). Frenetic repair works kept some lines going for a while – indeed, in a display of continuing 'normality', the daily *Oslobođenje* announced an increase in ticket prices on the morning of 2 May 1992. This day, marked also by the withdrawal of JNA from the city's central barracks, with several soldiers killed in attacks on the convoy, became decisive in the encroaching encirclement of Sarajevo. All out JNA shelling also saw the destruction of other public services of 'gridding' such as the post office. Some of the further outlying points of the city transport grid, including the prewar trolleybus terminus in Dobrinja, were taken by the besiegers. Initially, some bus services continued to run along the Sarajevo valley, but by late July 1992, shelling and sniper fire had killed four passengers and wounded eight, and soon after city transport came to an almost complete standstill. The city transport grid had collapsed.

During those early war months, Dobrinja was effectively under double siege: it was cut off from the rest of the city. To a large extent the settlement was suddenly and violently ungridded. After military operations by ARBiH in summer 1992, a precarious corridor to the city centre was opened up again, but no transport was available and many remember the dangerous and exhausting two- to three-hour walks. Yet there were continuous efforts to grid Dobrinja back into the city, not least in terms of transport. Towards the end of the war some limited GRAS services were reintroduced, but even when shelling did not make traffic impossible, lack of fuel often did.[17] Meanwhile, city transport vehicles had been put to new use: trams, buses and trolleybuses served as sniper shields and their parts were used for improvised construction. Yet, the extraordinary significance of a city transport network – indeed, the hopes invested in it by besieged Sarajevans – had grown to gigantic proportions (see Mulić-Bušatlija 2000). As the summer 1992 booklet *I oni brane Sarajevo* [They too defend Sarajevo], aimed to keep up civilian morale, stated: 'And as many have noted, we will know the war has come to an end, amongst other things, when the *Trojka* [Tram No. 3] will make its circle from Ilidža to Baščaršija and when, instead of savage grenades, the bell and the rattle of the trams will wake Sarajevans' (Novo 1992: 104).

As it turned out, the first tram ride, on 15 March 1994, did not herald the end of the war, but it was greeted with widespread excitement. People applauded it from the pavements. In the words of GRAS' general director, this first tram was a 'symbol of the resistance, the pride, and the invincible and indestructible spirit of Sarajevo and Sarajevans'.[18] This attribution of key significance to the 'first tram' is reflected in the fact that there is hardly a film, a book or a media report about the Sarajevo siege that does not contain references to city transport. Photos of bullet-riddled vehicles in unconventional positions are standard fare in the visual representation of Sarajevo's war story of destruction and resistance. They featured heavily in efforts to gain local and foreign legitimacy and, as we saw in the conflict between GRAS and Centrotrans, they could be mobilised again much later for new purposes. In everyday narratives, this fitted into a crucial theme in war recollections: the disruption of gridded 'normal lives' and relentless efforts to reestablish them to some degree under siege.

In this context, a graffiti exchange on Sarajevo's main post office in spring 1992 has become legendary. The first one said *Ovo je Srbija*

[This is Serbia]. Socn after, someone added another one: *Budalo, ovo je pošta* [Idiot, this is a post office]. During my research, this exchange was retold to demonstrate how, at least for some, national categorisation had not been allowed to overtake the pragmatics of 'normal lives'. As so often, such recollections also contained some bitterness, as Dayton BiH 'trivision' now saw three separate postal systems. The war period, then, was reconstructed as a time when a commitment to banal routine had served to resist the onslaught of 'abnormality'. In chapter 3 we shall consider this in detail. Here, with the example of city transport, I emphasise that past and present yearnings for 'normal lives' thus contained grid desire: they indexed a social configuration in which certain structures of expectations were made regular and ordered in an institutional manner.

Dobrinjci recalled that during the war any news of the possibility of city transport resuming was awaited anxiously (a similar focus is present in wartime newspapers).[19] The fact that trams were often singled out may be due to the fact that it is the most 'gridded' of city transport systems and (perhaps partly therefore) widely considered the most urban one.[20] In spring 1994, when the first trams started circulating in the city, a UN-brokered agreement led to the opening of so-called 'blue roads' across and around the airport, creating links between noncontiguous VRS-held areas and between noncontiguous ARBiH-held areas. While subject to a permit system – with checks on security risks and military duties – this provided an opportunity for Dobrinjci and other Sarajevans to bring in (much cheaper) goods from Hrasnica, on the other side of the airport just outside besieged Sarajevo, in private cars but also in special GRAS services. Centrotrans also offered services, and the fact that even on this very short ride luggage was to be paid per piece, indicates the volume of goods traffic. Before, the famous tunnel under the airport, of which one end was located in Dobrinja, had been the only link. The blue roads, monitored by mixed patrols of VRS, ARBiH and United Nations Protection Force (UNPROFOR) soldiers, were an important bargaining tool and their functioning was frequently interrupted. In July 1994 they were closed, and in February 1995, alongside the long-awaited reintroduction of two *komercijala* miribus services on the Dobrinja–Vijećnica line and tram services on the sections closer to town, they were opened again.[21] In about a month's time, some one hundred and ten thousand passengers travelled from the city to Hrasnica and back, including many in cars with trailers full of goods. GRAS and Centrotrans each organised two services, all working on a commercial basis (making it feasible to buy petrol despite chronic shortages). They left the city centre in the morning, via Dobrinja, to Hrasnica, and returned in the afternoon.[22] The other blue road, linking up VRS-held Ilidža and Lukavica across the airport saw some thirty-eight thousand passengers. In March 1995, after the death of two girls in VRS-held Grbavica, attributed by the UN to ARBiH snipers, VRS called the deal off and intensified its siege activities.[23] In the summer of 1995 the blue roads were opened a third time.

It was only well after the Dayton Agreement in November 1995 and the reintegration of some VRS-held parts of Sarajevo in early 1996 that the city transport grid was restored to a degree of 'normality'. To and from Dobrinja, first more buses started running and, in November 1996, trolleybus services were reinstated. If, according to the graffiti, the post office was indeed a post office, the trolleybus was also a trolleybus, the bus a bus and the tram a tram: a vehicle allowing persons to travel from A to B *as part of an integrated public transport grid*.[24] Many recalled the exhilaration they felt when this grid reappeared. Precisely in that way the first tram was indeed the symbol of pride and defiance as described by GRAS' director. In Sartre's words, the city was present in and through it (1985: 365). In principle, cars or private minibuses could provide the means for people to move, as they do in many other cities around the world, yet I believe that in Sarajevo they would not be invested with the same significance as the 'first tram'. The hope invested in a tram or a trolleybus activated a web of associated expectations of public infrastructural provision: roads, traffic lights, electricity supply etc. The reappearance of an institutionalised transport system – embodied by its trams, buses and trolleybuses, but also by its shelters, network maps and subsidised ticketing system – was experienced as a sign of the reemergence of gridding. And with it, it promised a fulfilment, however minor, of 'yearnings for normal lives' and at once, of course, the seeds for further exasperation at its continuing incompleteness.

Still Waiting for a Bus…

A decade and a half after the reappearance of the first tram, city transport remained a key topic in Dobrinja yearnings for 'normal lives'. Bitter complaints about the *nekultura* of GRAS personnel were accompanied by statements of entitlement to a much better organised city transport system. I have shown how, waiting at the *okretaljka*, people sought incorporation (on their terms!) into a well-functioning grid. We also saw that the same people might prefer to remain non-gridded

– illegible – when it came to paying tickets. Still, their dissatisfaction contained more grid desire than grid evasion: they were exasperated with the fact that they still could not count on self-evident gridding, so many years after the war. The use of city transport thus inserted Dobrinjci into publicly organised networks, and people's waiting for buses and trolleybuses (and trams, when closer to the city centre) was shot through with a yearning for the orderly movement – bodily and existential – that they associated with 'normal lives'. With 'life kept on hold' (Navaro-Yashin 2003: 121), blaming GRAS for not being able to adequately provide for their circulation in the city, I suggest, simultaneously served as a channel to express their sense that, collectively, they were not 'moving well enough' (Hage 2009: 99). And that, as we shall see in chapter 5, was seen as key predicament of life in the Dayton Meantime.

In socialist Yugoslavia, the expansion of public transport had formed part of a modernising developmentalist project – including industrialisation, urbanisation and the spread of communication infrastructure – and it reflected many of the tensions that underlay this project. Concomitantly, more than a decade after the war, Sarajevo city transport provided an interesting prism on contradictions of Dayton BiH. The *komercijala* was a GRAS service, but it ran outside of the subsidised ticketing system. While Mrs Šehović and many others accused the company directors of favouring this service in order to line their own pockets, its 'premium' character was not unambivalent: 31e buses were cleaner and newer than most others, and they ran relatively more punctually, but they often picked up passengers at unmarked locations just before or after certain standard stops. In terms of advertising, the *komercijala* did not look 'more commercialised'. Many official bus stops functioned as sites for formal and informal business in kiosks, on folding tables, cardboard boxes or blankets. Also, city transport, like much else, was characterised by unsystematic juxtapositions of public service, private enterprise and humanitarian intervention. GRAS notices and press statements addressed people interchangeably as 'citizens', as 'service users' and as 'passengers'. Moreover, through abundant signs that it was dependent on foreign humanitarian donations, public city transport also contained stark reminders of what many deplored as the absence of a 'functioning state'.[25] As the man waiting for bus 31 on the *okretaljka* exclaimed, 'if only this was a normal state!'

With the 'war' between Centrotrans and GRAS, dissatisfaction intensified and media reporting became near frenetic. I did not hear many people explicitly argue either for or against the breaking up of GRAS' monopoly by a private firm such as Centrotrans, but there seemed to be a far-reaching consensus that GRAS was a hopeless case. If people pointed out the non-work of GRAS cadres and their tendency to milk the firm in a process of ever expanding *uhljebljenje*, this lent it even more eminently to social commentary on the nature of public services, on citizenship duties and entitlements – and, ultimately, on the state. Rather than assessing whether most Dobrinjci were opposed to the privatisation of city transport or not, I note that city transport was engaged with as a public service that one was entitled to, as one of the mundane, practical channels through which citizens sought to encounter something approximating the state. Much of this emerged as a desire for proper state*craft in* BiH and concerned the transformation of socially owned firms set up under Yugoslav socialist self-management and their role in a configuration moving towards some form of capitalism. Yet issues of the state*hood of* BiH were present in engagements with city transport too. As we saw, GRAS and Centrotrans both claimed legitimacy through invocations of wartime sacrifice for BiH statehood. Moreover, the conflict between them was partly shaped by the territorial division of BiH into Entities and the labyrinthine institutions set up to govern the country. The postwar *okretaljka* was located on the site of what had been the penultimate stop of the prewar network. No public transport linked it up with the former terminus – a few hundred metres further – which now housed the coach station of Istočno Sarajevo, across the Inter-Entity Boundary Line, in Republika Srpska. The two companies could therefore mobilise the distinction –even regarding travel within the Sarajevo agglomeration – between cantonal transport and inter-entity transport, governed by different ministries. In chapter 4 we shall return to the questions of inter-institutional 'verticality' that the evocation of the 'top of the state' entailed.

We find ourselves here right on the intersection of postwar and postsocialist transformations. GRAS was a public institution, but the slow reestablishment of city transport after the war – within the boundaries of the new subpolity of Canton Sarajevo – did not straightforwardly involve the restoration of a 'normality' in which services were publicly planned and provided; neither did it imply the straightforward introduction, through 'transition', of a new normality of privatised city transport. Instead there was a contradictory, partial recalibration of mundane practice through changes in city transport, in which GRAS, its competitor Centrotrans and passengers could and did all reach for the 'language of stateness'. In this context, city transport, or rather the exasperation at its incompleteness and inadequacy, was a significant factor in producing what we shall explore, following Mitchell (1999), as the 'state effect' in chapter 4. But first, in the next chapter, we turn to recollections of wartime gridding for 'normal lives'.

Notes

1. Except when citing media reports, this book uses pseudonyms for all research partici-pants. The pseudonyms I devised are equivalent to their originals in terms of relative national (in)distinguishability. Many, but not all, names in BiH can be categorised as reflecting Muslim, Orthodox or Catholic heritage, with the difference between the latter two less systematic. A key identitarian presupposition is that such ethnoreli-gious heritage equals a sense of subjective belonging to a nation, leading people to be categorised as *being* nationals (Bosniak, Serb, Croat, respectively) and ignoring ques-tions of the relative intensity of any sense of belonging (Jansen 2005b). In this book I sometimes speak of 'people with Bosniak (or Serbian, or Croatian) names' where the argument requires that readers know what fellow-Bosnians might know, or might think they knew, if they so wished. Furthermore, rather than conjuring up intimacy by using first names for all interlocutors, I use surnames except when referring to people I know beyond the confines of my research engagements. In the case of married women, my pseudonyms reflect the surnames (usually their husbands') they normally used.
2. In Serbia, the theme of public transport has long been central to the merciless sarcas-tic columns of Teofil Pančić (2006). In *DJ Majstor*, he depicts intercity bus drivers as emblematic figures of a not-so-postsocialist era. In *Osamdesettrojka*, he describes the stoicism required by the extended waiting times for Beograd bus 83, declaring the 'incandescent, neglected centre of the Darkest Balkans' (ibid.: 289). And I am sure I was not the only one who wished there was truth in the initial (later disproved) reports that Dr Karadžić-Dabić was arrested precisely on that line – the 83 that reput-edly never ran on time, if it ran at all. In any case, it was on bus 83 that two members of a clerofascist movement beat up Pančić in 2010, while his co-passengers looked on without offering any help. In *Oh kalkuta*, Pančić discusses the partial deregulation of Beograd city transport, allowing private entrepreneurs to make quick profits by selectively covering certain lines. These private firms specialised, Pančić argues, in humiliation, and while 'in public city transport they humiliate you too, at least they don't play *narodnjaci* [commercial folk songs] on top' (ibid.: 271).
3. For example, 'Bahatost GRASovih vozača' [The brutish arrogance of GRAS drivers], *Oslobođenje*, 14 April 2008. 26.
4. Perhaps I have been extraordinarily lucky, but I have always been treated correctly by *revizori* (and, yes, I have paid a few fines). I have also attended occasions on which passengers without tickets shouted abuse at *revizori* and drivers, which I will censor here, limiting myself to mentioning that it concerns their presumed regional origin (Sandžak) and unspeakable activities with regard to their female family members.
5. Reader's letter [no title], *Cslobođenje*, 28 April 2008, 21.
6. But see for example, Lemon 2000; Rizzo 2002.
7. See www.gras.ba. Just before the war, GRAS realised some eight hundred and fifty thousand passenger trips per day (www.ddh.nl/org/poo/bsh/introduk/gras.htm). By

mid 2007, the population of the City of Sarajevo was estimated to be around three hundred thousand and that of Canton Sarajevo around four hundred and twenty thousand, about a fifth less than in 1991 (*Statistički bilten…* 2008).

8. In Scott's case this entails an explicit anarchist positioning. To broaden the argument, I follow European conventions and use the term 'libertarian' to denote a concern with autonomy and freedom from grids. This is not exclusively associated with either the left or right side of the political spectrum.
9. www.gras.ba
10. www.centrotrans.com
11. 'Danas kreću autobusi na međuentitetskim linijama' [From today buses on inter-entity lines], *Nezavisne Novine*, 16 February 2004, 6.
12. 'Od ponedjeljka još cetiri linije Centrotransa' [From Monday four more Centrotrans lines], *Nezavisne Novine*, 20 February 2004, 10.
13. 'Ministarstvo saobraćaja BiH blokiralo međuentitetske linije' [BiH Ministry of Transport blocks inter-entity lines], *Nezavisne Novine*, 02 December 2003, 11; 'Zaustavljeni autobusi između dva entiteta' [Buses between two entities halted], *Nezavisne Novine*, 22 December 2003, 11.
14. 'Danas kreću autobusi na međuentitetskim linijama' [From today buses on inter-entity lines], *Nezavisne Novine*, 16 February 2004, 6.
15. 'Vozači GRAS-a blokirali autobuse Centrotransa' [GRAS drivers block Centrotrans buses], *Nezavisne Novine*, 17 February 2004, 2; 'Od ponedjeljka još cetiri linije Centrotransa' [From Monday four more Centrotrans lines], *Nezavisne Novine*, 20 February 2004, 10.
16. 'OHR se uključio u rješavanje problema javnog prevoza' [OHR joins search for solution of public transport problems], *Nezavisne Novine*, 21 February 2004, 6; 'Novi prevoznik biraće se javnim pozivom' [New transport provider will be chosen by public tender], *Nezavisne Novine*, 25 February 2004, 9.
17. 'Dobrinja je specifična' [Dobrinja is specific], *Dobrinja Danas: Bilten Mjesne Zajednice* 50, 27 March 1995, 1.
18. www.ddh.nl/org/poo/bsh/introduk/gras.htm
19. 'Krenuli tramvaji i autobusi' [Trams and buses start running], *Oslobođenje*, 19 February 1995, 10.
20. In Antwerpen (Belgium), where I was born, people who pride themselves on being really 'of the city', known as *Sinjoren*, make this brutally clear. When railgrids were expanded to commuter villages, elderly *Sinjoren* distinguished between *den tram*, serving only the central parts of the agglomeration, and *den boerentram* [the peasant tram], referring to the trams (and sometimes even buses) that served outlying villages like the one where I grew up.
21. 'Autobusi (i dalje) čekaju naftu' [Buses (still) wait for petrol], *Oslobođenje*, 6 February 1995, 11.
22. 'Autobusima do Hrasnice' [By bus to Hrasnica], *Oslobođenje*, 08 February 1995, 10.
23. 'Bajka se rijetko ponavlja' [A fairy tale rarely repeats itself], *Oslobođenje*, 14 March 1995, 2.
24. And, likewise, it was important to insist that a school was a school (chapter 3).
25. In that context, it is telling that almost fifteen years after the end of the war, the Director of GRAS specifically announced that the second-hand purchase of seventeen trolleybuses from a city council in Switzerland would be their first transaction that used commercial credit and did not involve any foreign donations ['bez posrednika'] (e.g., 'Gužve u špicama biće prošlost' [Crowds at peak times will be confined to the past], *Oslobođenje*, 3 April 2010, 18).

– Chapter 3 –

WARTIME GRIDDING FOR 'NORMAL LIVES'
[or, Towards an Anthropology of Hope for the State]

in which, through a discussion of wartime schooling in Dobrinja, we embed yearnings for 'normal lives', their temporal structure and their evocations of the state in a critical dialogue with replications of hope in the libertarian paradigm that dominates the anthropology of the state

Spring 2008, early in the morning. I am woken by playful children walking under my bedroom window to the primary school next door. Except during holiday periods, they function as my weekday human alarm clock. In fact, like most schools in BiH, this school employs a shift system, so I can tell four times of day on that basis. There are other regimented markers of the daily passage of time: the arrival and departure of less than a dozen daily airplanes at the nearby Sarajevo airport; the chiming of the bells of the nearby Serbian Orthodox church in Istočno Sarajevo (the construction of which started just before war, to be completed afterwards), visible from the same bedroom window; and, depending on the wind, the five calls to prayer from the somewhat more distant, recently built mosque, hidden behind apartment blocks. As we saw, the comings and goings of buses and trolleybuses at the *okretaljka* are rather too loosely related to the schedule pinned up on the ticket booth for them to work as an effective time marker. For me, it is the movement of schoolchildren that is the most noticeable regularity. This is the case for many Dobrinjci: if they have school-age children of their own, it shapes their daily routines, and if they do not, the prominence of one secondary and three primary schools in Dobrinja's otherwise relatively uniform landscape of apartment blocks still makes the traffic of pupils very visible.[1] I need to get up. Today I am attending a School Day celebration.

FIGURE 3.1. The mosque in Dobrinja and the Serbian Orthodox church at the far edge of Dobrinja, just inside Istočno Sarajevo (photo by Vanja Čelebičić, 2014)

The central atrium of the modern, spacious and well-equipped primary school building is packed with pupils, teachers, some parents, a few media people and official guests, such as the mayor and the police chief of Novi grad and the cantonal minister of education. We are treated to a celebratory programme consisting of songs, folklore and ballroom dances, a recital of a poem and a piece of dramatised dialogue. I have been doing research in this school for a while now – attending meetings of the pupils' council, led by pedagogue/psychologist Mrs Fahra Maglajić, sitting in on meetings of the parents' council, interviewing staff and trawling through its in-house publications. I have learned that the fundamental motif that underlies this school's story about itself is one of wartime survival, of heroic commitment to 'normality' and civilisation, and, crucially, of self-organisation. If a polity label is used to refer to this, it is that of the state of BiH. The speech at this event given by Mrs Senada Redžić, the director, provides an example. Mrs Redžić explains how, 'with the values we are facing in our society today', they consciously selected a positive theme for this School Day: 'I am proud of …' 'What can we be proud of?' the director asks, 'Perhaps of something we achieved in one of our subjects, in sports or in an art project. But also of small, everyday things we did: help a friend to find her way in

FIGURE 3.2. One of Dobrinja's primary schools, reconstructed after the war (photo by Vanja Čelebičić, 2014)

new surroundings, carry shopping for our neighbour, or show that we can be trusted with a secret.' In that way, Mrs Redžić continues, the school has much to be proud of too: it introduced a pupil-centred education system in 'impossible circumstances', it has always been a multinational, it secured funding for rebuilding and equipment, and it stood firm when 'our country' faced extreme challenges.

2008. A few weeks later. I attend the School Day of the Dobrinja Gimnazija, the settlement's only secondary school, where I have also been carrying out research for a number of months. Unlike the three primary schools, the Gimnazija does not have its own building but is accommodated in improvised ground floor spaces of apartment blocks. Originally intended for storage or commercial use, these spaces have been converted into classrooms, largely with humanitarian donations of equipment. I attended classes in the cramped classrooms, with almost no natural light and with noise spilling through wafer-thin walls. I surveyed documents in their windowless library and director Mirsada Pucar generously allowed me to sit at the table in her office to consult the Gimnazija's Diary. During breaks, I joined the teachers in their equally windowless teacher's room, where a dozen people could just about squeeze around a table to have a cup of coffee and a cigarette. Since there is no large enough room in any of the spaces occupied by the Gimnazija, the School Day is held in the rarely used premises of the Cultural Centre of Dobrinja.

FIGURE 3.3. The entry to the main premises of Gimnazija Dobrinja, in former storage and commercial spaces on the ground floor of an apartment building. These were in use until late 2010 (photo by Vanja Čelebičić, 2010)

It is a scorching hot day and, with many people standing, even breathing is hard inside. A screen is being set up next to a piano. Pupils' artwork adorns the walls. Snacks and drinks are spread out on a table. The audience is similar to the one at the primary school, including teachers, pupils, some parents, some media people, the mayor of Novi grad and a woman representing the BiH presidency. Most of the pupils, especially the girls, are dressed up, but within bounds that (so I find out some days later) will be drastically transcended on their graduation day. While we wait for people to find a place, the music teacher loosens his fingers on the piano and the pupils in the choir chime in when they recognise last year's winning entry to the Eurovision contest from Serbia. They know all the lyrics of the ballad and sing it with more confidence than the Latin school hymn that officially opens the ceremony, which also includes poetry recitals (partly in French), two more songs by the choir and a short film about the Gimnazija. Certificates and flowers are awarded to the 'pupils of the generation' and one pupil reads out a letter in the name of the cantonal minister for education. Congratulations are passed on in the name of Željko Komšić, the current presiding member of the three-headed BiH presidency, who swept the board in the elections in Dobrinja. Certificates of gratitude are handed to the head of the school's board, the cantonal minister of education, the mayor of Novi grad, the school's inventors' club, and so on.

The ceremony is chaired by a pupil who starts off with a reference to the 'impossible circumstances' in which the school was born, speaking for generational continuity when she emphasises that, even then (she was about one year old), 'we believed we would live and survive'. The Gimnazija's director, Mrs Pucar, makes a virtue of the location for this event; pointing out the improvised surroundings, she expresses determination and hope 'that we will have a better place next year'. She too makes reference to the Gimnazija's birth in exceptionally adverse conditions and insists that, when it moves into better premises, the school will retain its name: *Dobrinjska Gimnazija*. The mayor of Novi grad municipality, himself a Dobrinjac, expresses support for this and a month later he will reinforce it in a media interview.[2] He too underlines the school's 'special credibility' due to its wartime genesis. The director's and the mayor's rallying calls are met with cheers. This does not surprise me: over the last few months I have grown accustomed to the strong sense of achievement and ownership amongst the school's staff and pupils. Yet it is in contrast with a conversation I had last night over beers with my friends Iskra and Lejla about the recently commenced construction of new, purpose-built Gimnazija premises nearby. These two women attended secondary school in other parts of the city before the war. Lejla later completed her secondary education in besieged Dobrinja. 'Pfff, a Gimnazija … why would they need that?' she said, meeting with Iskra's approval, 'Dobrinja is not a place for a Gimnazija. Everyone will be locked up here, they won't leave the settlement at all. Everyone liked going to school in town [*pa svima je bio merak ići u školu u grad*]!' This may have been the case in their time, but, as the reception of the director's comment on the Gimnazija School Day indicates, the current mood amongst teachers and pupils is bullish; they finally want to move into appropriate premises and give Dobrinja a secondary school that actually looks like one.

The 1992–95 war in BiH is not mentioned directly in any of the speeches at those two School Days but it is evoked in the numerous references to survival, endurance and self-organisation. Chapter 2 explained how the value attached to city transport gridding was amplified when its network was devastated in spring 1992. For many, the war was made an experiential reality partly by the fact that they could not get to work anymore because the 'bus didn't arrive'. In this chapter, I focus on this early war period in Dobrinja, delving deeper into the dynamics of, and desires for, gridding, the centrality of temporal calibration in Dobrinja yearnings for 'normal lives' and their evocations of the state. Tracing the sudden disruption of routines that presume the plugging of lives into grids – mainly those of schooling – and feverish attempts to reestablish them, I enter into critical dialogue with anthropological studies of the state.

School is Out Early

During the early days of the 1990s violence, many schools in BiH announced a premature end to the school year. For Dobrinja teachers, pupils and many parents, war thus started in part as an interruption of routines organised around the daily rhythms and longer-term trajectories of schoolwork. Three primary schools had been built as part of the construction of this apartment complex during the 1980s. In May 1992, not only were they closed early but they were also destroyed by shells fired by Serbian nationalist forces as they laid siege to the city. Three months earlier, during the referendum on BiH independence, these buildings had served as polling points guarded by SDA-affiliated militias. The latter had put up barricades, controlled by armed men, to counter those set up by SDS militias who wished to prevent independence and had called for a boycott (see Narrative Glossary in introduction). I was told that militias associated with both parties had previously been using schools, and especially their sports infrastructure, for training exercises.[3]

By the time of the destruction of the schools and the closure of the siege, most Serbs had left Dobrinja in a convergence of SDS evacuations, intimidation by militias associated with SDS and SDA, and their own belief that they would be better off 'with their own'. Especially just before and after the proclamation and international recognition of the independent Republic of Bosnia and Herzegovina (RBiH) in April 1992 (as per referendum outcome), many Serbs moved to territories controlled by the besieging forces, the now Serbian-dominated JNA, local militias and paramilitaries from Serbia. Others sought safety abroad. Many other Dobrinjci also left: especially women and children evacuated, often intending to return soon – at the latest by the start of the new school year. Meanwhile, Dobrinja started receiving Bosniaks expelled from eastern BiH by Serbian nationalist forces, now congealing into the Army of Republika Srpska (VRS). The latter quickly took some outlying parts of Dobrinja, imprisoning hundreds of civilians, but then their progress was blocked by hastily

organised and logistically much inferior local units, including improvised 'guards' of individual apartment blocks and SDA-led militias
– sometimes operating in uneasy alliance. They were joined by RBiH
military and special police and later these formations merged into
the Army of BiH (ARBiH). After the discovery of arms and of the
signalling of targets to besiegers, remaining Serbs in Dobrinja came
under increasing scrutiny as suspected fifth columnists. Some were
imprisoned and mistreated – often by criminals-turned-commanders
who operated semiautonomously from local ARBiH structures, but
with support from SDA figures in the RBiH government (Andreas
2008). These posed a threat to other Dobrinjci too. Many remaining
Serbs fled through the lines. Prisoner exchanges followed and a temporary corridor allowed many women and children to move to the
city centre. Some returned to Dobrinja some months later, when a
precarious connection to the centre was established.

In the 1992–95 war, Dobrinja was a relatively separate, heavily
damaged settlement on the siege line with a drastically changed
population due to inward, outward and internal movement (for
example, proportionally more adults, more men, more people with
'Bosniak names'). Military defence was accompanied by the work
of *Civilna zaštita* (CZ, Civil Protection), subordinated to the former.[4]
CZ activities started with a population census and then included,
for example: allocating accommodation to displaced persons;
constructing anti-sniper shields, trenches and tunnels; repairing
utilities (gas, electricity, sewage …), buildings (roofs, stairs …) and
equipment (stoves, generators, bicycles …); sewing and washing
soldier uniforms; digging water wells; running a fire brigade; maintaining hygiene (rubbish collection, pest control, water disinfection
…); distributing humanitarian aid; coordinating burials between
buildings; running public kitchens, hairdressers', a print shop and
a music studio; creating a hospital; organising blood donations
and breast screenings; staging cultural events; distributing seeds
and advice on growing plants on balconies; and so on. Premises
for these activities were improvised in shop spaces, offices, flats or
common areas. Equipment from former workplaces was put to new
uses: a tailoring workshop, for example, was equipped with sewing
machines saved from the premises of a burning folklore club, and
a man who used to make sports badges and banners started producing flags and emblems for ARBiH. With central heating down,
much energy went into making improvised stoves, with chimneys
peeking through mostly blackened, boarded up or bricked up flat
windows.[5]

The Making of 'Staircase Schools'

In addition to infrastructurally supporting the armed defence of Dobrinja, then, CZ coordinated efforts to mobilise the skills, knowledge and labour of Dobrinjci to guarantee survival and to reestablish functionality. It was in the extreme conditions of the early war period that the seeds for an emergency schooling system were planted.[6] Mrs Azra Zumbul, a Dobrinja teacher with over thirty years of experience, told me:

> On 15 May 1992 our school was shelled … They had already taken Dobrinja IV and [my family] had to move to Dobrinja II [a more central part]. On our own initiative, some of us started to gather children from the building in the staircase. I kept them busy with some lesson or activity. We wanted to protect the children, to keep them inside, but also to give them something to do, something valuable. To show them what was important, even then.

After the destruction of her workplace, Mrs Zumbul thus organised educational activities in staircases, the safest parts of the apartment blocks – hence the name that became common later: *haustorske škole* [staircase schools]. Colleagues cut off from their schools elsewhere in the city joined in. Recalling those days, teachers often stressed their desire to establish a degree of meaningful routine. In the words of Mrs Pucar, the director of Dobrinja Gimnazija:

> During the war, different people reacted differently. Some fled, some withdrew into the basements, and some came out. We started all kinds of things then: schooling in the staircases, plans for this Gimnazija, all kinds of cultural manifestations … If you'd have asked me before the war, I'd never have been involved in anything like folklore, but during the war … we did. It seemed smarter to be busy with that than to think about which shell was going to kill you.

Still in May 1992, the CZ secretary for schooling gained approval from municipal authorities to form a 'Schooling Centre'. Dobrinja's military commander allocated them a venue in a former games parlour. All teachers then present in the apartment complex were called to participate. Spontaneous initiatives were thus coordinated into a system. Classes were still organised in staircases and basements, referred to as *punktovi*, i.e., 'points', nodes in a network. To minimise pupils' exposure to shelling, teachers moved between *punktovi* through trenches and along sniper shields, which provided the safest possible movement between buildings even in the central parts of Dobrinja. Mrs Zumbul and Mrs Pucar continued their activities, now under the umbrella of the Schooling Centre, and many others joined. Mobilisation for CZ work could include coercion, for example for trench digging, but in their recollections many Dobrinja teachers emphasised their willing participation. Mothers of small children, for example, were exempted, but some, like Mrs Maglajić, now pedagogue/psychologist at a Dobrinja primary school, volunteered anyway. Most able-bodied men of working age were by now mobilised into Dobrinja's armed defence, so, in an already female-dominated profession, wartime schooling involved a large majority of women teachers (although some men did combine soldiering with teaching). Over the next three years, thousands of pupils participated in a system designed to provide education in extraordinary circumstances of siege. In their recollections, they emphasised the extreme conditions of wartime schooling in Dobrinja. Lejla, who had so enjoyed going to school in the city centre before, now started attending the Dobrinja school:

> Schooling in the staircases was chaotic, but somehow, incredibly, it worked … Improvised, everything changed all the time, there was heating or not, how much shelling. We reused paper and wrote in tiny letters. We almost only had general subjects throughout the war – it was by the old curriculum, but they threw in some BiH writers. Classrooms were improvised, some teachers were real teachers from other schools, stuck here, some simply people who could and would teach something. I wrote my final history project about ancient Greece. I can't believe now that I could actually concentrate on that. But it was so boring that people focused on doing things that probably made no sense in those circumstances, but they devoted much attention and time to them. And so did I with my schoolwork.

The reference to boredom was very common in the recollections of those who had been children during the war. Several young men recalled how initial excitement quickly turned into frustration with the lack of anything to do (cf. Kelly 2008: 353; Allen 2008: 473). Asked to describe an ordinary day during the war in Dobrinja, Mr Tarik Uzunović explained:

> What has stayed with me most from the war is the cold. So … well, perhaps these details are not interesting, but details stayed with me. Dandruff, for example. Details. Like, you get up, you have no duties at all, so you get up when you get up. Maybe, if there is some trouble, you get up earlier to get water, or you go in the middle of the night. And then, you know, you have two/three things you can do, and that's it. So you can try to figure something out to get water, you can try to find some solution, some idea to find some wood, and that's it. Wait for humanitarian aid. In the meantime you could … read comics, some books, hang out with friends. In the beginning we played

games, but, well, we got bored with all of it after a few months. While it was still interesting, it was great, you know, without electricity, without this … So a day, on the whole, that was it. You get up, you have no duties, you have two/three things to do and as for the rest: figure out how, simply, how you will spend that day.

Many adults did have various regimented duties, in the army, in CZ, or as carers for family members and others. Yet whether one was standing guard, waiting to participate in a military operation, queuing up for water at one of the collective wells, or spending long winter nights in dark flats, the need to 'spend time' was ubiquitous. Safety concerns were crucial: movement in Dobrinja was strictly limited due to its location on the siege line and for much of the time people were condemned to stay inside, surrounded by equipment that was unusable in the absence of electricity, gas or running water. The boredom that featured in the recollections of wartime Dobrinja was thus conditioned by the suspension of 'normal lives', which included a crucial temporal dimension. As Maček (2009: 64) has pointed out in her wartime ethnography, conditions in besieged Sarajevo were marked not by the total absence of basic utilities but by their unpredictable supply (notably, people blamed this not only on besieging forces but also on the city's SDA authorities). Daily routines were thus rendered impossible. The burden of collecting water was especially significant, as it involved queuing, competition with others, and the exposure of bodies weakened by poor nutrition to cold and potential shelling. One of the largest massacres in Dobrinja occurred when a water queue in the ruins of a primary school was shelled. More than a decade later, Ms Jasmina Musić, a web developer in her mid thirties who had been a teenager during the war, said:

Really … survival [*preživljavanje*], and that's the worst. I also found it the hardest to deal with, you know, those tinned foods, carrying water, waiting, endless queues, ten hours in the queue so you would fill up two gallons of water. What was always harder than that, what I found the hardest, that feeling of powerlessness, that someone has reduced you to a level that is not dignified for an animal, let alone for a human being. That was what I found … that was the hardest thing to take for me, harder than, say, practical things.

Yet, clearly, it was precisely 'practical things' that constituted humiliation. Well into the postwar period, Sarajevans anxiously waited for water or electricity, which 'made people feel that they were able to live more normally' (Maček 2009: 65). Chapter 2 noted a similar pattern of expectation and gratification with regard to the first tram. The suspension of ordered predictability associated with 'normal lives' was thus crucial to the war experience. With regard to schooling too, the calibration of everyday life had been thrown into disarray. In the words of then pupil Mr Uzunović:

> Catastrophic … They constantly moved us between locations every few months. School was two/three times a week in the afternoon. I often completely forgot to go. Because after two/three years without any obligations, you totally lose the feeling what it means to have an obligation, to arrive somewhere on time, to go there, to be there, to do something. So, on the whole, there were some basements where we were, like, protected, and then they quickly rattle off five/six subjects. You, like, listen, manage to take some notes, and then another time is arranged … Like the majority of kids, I finished with three notebooks and my level of knowledge in the end was zero.

Leaving aside their differing senses of achievement – with Lejla more positive than Mr Uzunović, who was three years younger – former pupils present a vivid picture of extreme conditions due to shelling and infrastructural problems. Mrs Refika Fejzić, then already an experienced teacher, now lived with one of her two sons and his family. Her husband had been killed in the war and she had later retired early to take care of one son who was heavily wounded and disabled for life. She said:

> I worked in the war school. Here in our building, in the basements, we organised primary and secondary schooling. We organised everything ourselves. All those who found themselves in Dobrinja and who were in the teaching profession, we all became active. So I went from *punkt* to *punkt*, and in one summer we completed an entire school year. Because we had no heating … So we had shortened classes. … Conditions were catastrophic. We ran a truncated curriculum, adapted for war. This meant holes in the children's knowledge, but we had to. It was difficult for them to get used to, but there you go. They all took a little longer.

'The Class Takes Place': Rhythms and Trajectories of 'Normal Lives'

Education is often an instrument for nationalist indoctrination, seeking to impose particular imaginations of the state (e.g., Wilson 2001). There were plenty such efforts by the SDA-dominated RBiH government too. Moreover, SDS and its allies defined the entire situation exclusively in nationalist-identitarian terms: under Serbian flags, they justified the VRS siege as a defensive operation against the city's 'aggressively Muslim' population (see, e.g., Donia 2006: 324). People targeted *as* Muslims could perhaps be expected to develop a narrative of resistance in those terms. Yet the recollections above, as well as the School Day celebration, do not use this register. This is not to say that we find no sense of belonging in national-religious terms at all,[7] but that this does not markedly feature in self-positionings. Strikingly, the thousands of wartime entries of the School Diary of the Dobrinja Gimnazija, kept by its director, contain almost no reference to Bosniakness, Islam, or nationality generally.[8] Gimnazija personnel and pupils included people with 'non-Bosniak names' and the first pupil to be killed by shelling was one of them. In more recent documents from the Dobrinja primary schools and the Gimnazija, national classifications are also absent. When one of the foreign intervention agencies requested such data in 2003, this met with protest from pupils and school staff. In the Diary, references to the war are systematically written in the key of 'BiH', 'our country', 'our state' or 'our people'. It does, of course, display a close association with ARBiH, the army that defended Dobrinja against besieging forces and the ultimate authority in the settlement. Yet the main preoccupation in the Diary is phrased as a determination to maintain civilisation while targeted by savagery and working in 'impossible circumstances'. 'Quiet in Dobrinja', says the entry for 31 March 1994, 'there's gas, there's electricity. Briefly water too. Are we approaching civilisation?' Evocations of the values of professionalism, knowledge and self-development are also prominent. On 29 November 1993 the entry reads:

> All of Bosnia is waiting. Today the Geneva Convention starts its work on BiH. Regular classes are held, although working conditions are impossible. There's no water, no electricity, no gas, and still one lives well and works a lot. That is out of defiance [*iz inata*]. Such are the people from these parts: defiant and proud. Such will they remain and nothing can change them, not even this war.

A Gimnazija anniversary publication describes the first organised class, in January 1993, as follows: 'The class takes place and this is experienced as a miracle and also as a patriotic deed … Work and learning versus darkness and hatred, i.e., the civilisational duty of all those who decided to resist evil and destruction' (Šurković 2003: 5). This class was a patriotic history lesson on BiH statehood, but what is considered most patriotic about it was the very act of running it. Dobrinja wartime sources and recollections highlight a determination that life had to go on – insofar as possible, 'normal life', in which post offices were post offices, buses were buses, schools were schools and classes were classes. Clearly, the notion of 'normal life' derives its significance here from the fact that life was anything but normal. It is against this background that the phrase 'the class takes place' gains its intended power as a descriptive statement. The message is: 'Despite everything, the class does take place'.

During the war, this representation was integrated in foreign-oriented appeals by public figures in Sarajevo. On a number of occasions, Dobrinja schools and its hospital were visited by foreign journalists, humanitarian activists and politicians. Accessibility for global media corporations and people's hopes that this would help to alleviate their predicament by enticing a foreign military intervention were important dynamics in the siege of Sarajevo (Andreas 2008). In this context, SDA deployed a doubly ambiguous narrative: of Bosniak nationalism *and* BiH multiculturalism, and of heroic armed struggle *and* 'barehanded' civilian resilience-as-resistance. In their narratives of war, almost all my interlocutors who spent that period in Dobrinja sidestepped the Muslim/Bosniak angle of this story completely and many actively rejected it. Like director Redžić in her speech at the School Day above, they often referred to the fact that, even after the exodus of many Serbs at the outset of the war, Dobrinja had continued to house people with Serbian, Croatian, as well as 'mixed' and other backgrounds. Yet they did not make this the main theme in their recollections. In fact, the imposition of such national differentiation, often scathingly referred to as *brojanje krvnih zrnaca* [counting blood cells], was itself a cause of indignation for many. The single most important theme in their war narratives was a stubborn insistence that, despite the violence, Dobrinjci had maintained standards of 'normality'; they evoked the fabled determination of Sarajevans to maintain their civilian and civilised dignity during over three and a half years of murderous siege. The war period, then, was reconstructed as a period in which, to a degree at least, abnormality had been resisted by a commitment to routines, and wartime sources suggest that this was also how it was experienced at the time.

This is rather different from the 'routinisation' that has been described in contexts of even more protracted war (e.g., Lubkemann 2008). Instead, as Maček explains, a sharp tension ran through what she calls the 'negotiations of normality' in besieged Sarajevo: on the one hand, people adapted their expectations to new conditions but, on the other hand, they continued to consider those conditions shamefully 'abnormal' (2009: 66–70). Some School Diary entries report special events, such as an exhibition on the tenth anniversary of the Sarajevo Olympic Winter Games, but most concern what would, in 'normal' circumstances, be nonspectacular routine. The dense 1993–94 entries detail classes (dates and times, places, interruptions, number of pupils); the weather; the (un)availability of utilities; food prices;

humanitarian aid; city transport; struggles for space, equipment and heating (energy and safety problems remained after the installation of some central heating in February 1994). Mentioning the relative intensity of shelling, many Diary entries end with exhortations like 'We'll hold out! Despite everything, we are going on!'

Recalling wartime experiences many years later, some Dobrinjci spoke of 'surreality', detailing situations that would be unthinkable in 'normal life' – funny, scary, often both at the same time. Alongside stories of fear and boredom, I heard many about crazy parties and wild abandon. Yet most autobiographical war anecdotes concerned things like cooking dishes without required ingredients, cleaning without running water and fashion within the bounds of clothing donations. Especially in interviews, people's stories on the whole mirrored that of the School Diary: they too emphasised the defence of civilised humanity under uncivilised, inhuman siege through stubborn continuation of everyday practical routines. Seen within broader Balkanist representations of their predicament – e.g., Western media portrayals of Bosnians as savage and prone to violence – it is easy to understand how that effort itself came to be considered a civilisational cause.

The attempted continuation of mundane practices in wartime conditions was widely remembered as Sarajevo's prime form of dignified resistance. Yet it is crucial to understand that people recalled this commitment to everyday 'normality' not primarily as one of brave, atomised individuals. It did not occur in a vacuum, nor in total chaos; it included a deeply social dimension. Many Dobrinjci contrasted current economic inequalities and 'messed-up values' with the wartime sharing of food, water or firewood and the relative lack of economic differentiation in the bomb shelters, when 'nobody had anything'. When they had collectively hit bottom, they recalled, socialising and mutual help, key to the self-image of people in BiH, had been deeper and more sincere. In a few cases, people mentioned there had been discrimination (for example, of Serbs, and of displaced people coming into the settlement, even of those from the outlying parts Dobrinja now taken by VRS or evacuated by ARBiH). Others reported selfishness and said that the war had allowed the worst in people to emerge.[9] Yet this was rare and usually embedded in a broader affirmation that it had also allowed the best in people to appear, and that solidarity had certainly been stronger than after the war.

This, I suggest, should not be reduced to a generic celebration of human warmth in extreme adversity. Far beyond an affirmation of solidarity as a human trait, many Dobrinjci emphasised the work that went into channelling this into an organised system. They proudly recalled wartime self-organisation. Alongside military defence, they referred, for example, to the allocation of flats to refugees, humanitarian aid distribution, the linking up of apartment blocks through a network of sniper shields, tunnels and trenches, the setting up of a hospital and, of course, of a primary and secondary schooling system. Highlighting the infrastructural and safety problems of the staircase schools, people signalled an experience of temporal unmooring – a lack of regularity and predictability – as a key dimension of the 'abnormality' of siege circumstances. They referred to the incessant revisions of timetables and locations, themselves due to the unpredictability of shelling and energy supply. As Mr Damir Kešo, now an electrical engineer, indicated, this was implicitly or explicitly measured against the regimentation of schooling in 'normal life':

> I started the fifth year [of primary school] before the war, so I did not manage to finish it, and during the war I did the rest of my fifth, then sixth, seventh and eighth year. And then on to secondary. A school day, well, we had some timetable as in normal schools, shifts, but they were corrected according to the safety situation … So our school day started with … running under sniper fire, shelling, to our basement. In the basement we tried to have some kind of normal schooling activity, until some shelling, some danger erupted, and then we had to interrupt class.

In their critical reading of E.P. Thompson's classic text on time-discipline (1967), Glennie and Thrift state that he conflates three different processes: regularity ('the degree to which people's time–space paths involve repetitive routine'), standardisation ('the degree to which people's time–space paths are disciplined to be the same as one another's') and coordination ('the degree to which people's time–space paths are disciplined to smoothly connect with one another') (Glennie and Thrift 1996: 285). While these processes may overlap, the authors argue, it is in fact a specificity of high Fordism that we find a high degree of all three. Unlike what Thompson implies, they contend, these processes do not necessarily have to be part of a single disciplinary force, but 'various permutations of these three elements are possible' (ibid.: 286). I argue that the siege of Dobrinja, an apartment complex that was itself the product of 'high Fordist' Yugoslav self-managed socialism, made its inhabitants extremely aware of the importance and interweaving of those three processes in their everyday lives up to then. Suddenly they became conscious of the 'temporal structure' that had – largely unnoticed – governed their mundane practices. It is in this light, I suggest, that we must understand the extraordinary emphasis on the value of 'normal lives' and the collective efforts to restore conditions that would allow them to unfold.

These continuously frustrated efforts had short- and long-term dimensions. On the short term, Dobrinja wartime schooling aimed to reinstitute what I call school 'rhythms': the way in which schoolwork calibrates routines through the standardised schedule of school days, of school weeks and weekends, and of school holidays. Here, feasibility was determined mainly by the intensity of shelling and the availability of energy. Yet there were longer-term factors as well. In September 1994, for example, some pupils rejoined their original secondary schools elsewhere in Sarajevo, only to return a month later when transport was halted again (Šurković 2003: 25). This alerts us to the importance of what I call 'trajectories', the longer-term framework in which school rhythms exist, and their cumulative effect. In his study of the 1968 events in academia in France, Bourdieu calls this the 'temporal structure of the field, as shown in careers, curricula vitae and accumulated honours' (1990: 183). The trajectory associated in Dobrinja with schooling in 'normal life' was also constructed around progression, with every school year building on the former, eventually leading to a diploma and, ideally, employment. Perhaps, then, it was a concern over irreversibly lost time in such trajectories – making adults out of children – that rendered education so important in Dobrinja attempts to reestablish 'normal' temporality.

Dobrinja had never had a secondary school, so teachers designed a system to provide pupils whose school year had been broken off with home study and consultation with appropriate instructors resident in the settlement. Initially, future reintegration into educational trajectories was facilitated through 'modified linear-programmed teaching units' (a kind of Bologna model *avant-la-lettre*), and pupil records were maintained for transferral to their 'home' schools. Ms Musić's recollections confirm the importance of temporal continuity:

> [In the beginning of the war,] I met a former teacher. At the time they had not yet organised those, what are they called, those *haustorske škole* ... They made it possible for us to sit exams for subjects with exceptional status. So that we wouldn't have to, we wouldn't lose, we wouldn't wait, because it wasn't known what would happen with the school system at all.

In January 1993, the Schooling Centre founded a Gimnazija in a network of *punktovi*. By the summer, 126 secondary school teachers who lived in Dobrinja, from twenty-eight different Sarajevo schools, responded to a call to teach during the next school year (Šurković 2003: 22). Some 330 pupils from different schools started classes, rising to 800 in autumn 1994. Contractual regulations for teachers were established, involving some disputes. There were no salaries during the first eight months, but teachers sometimes received payment in kind or food vouchers. However, these vouchers were worth little and availability of goods was minimal, so I suggest that, for teachers too, the temporal dimension was crucial (see Maček 2009: 64–66). The fact that most Dobrinja teachers emphasised their altruistic commitment, I believe, cannot simply be dismissed as strategic self-portrayals, but work in the Schooling Centre, or indeed in any other capacity (Sorabji 2006: 8), was certainly also driven by more pragmatic motivations. On the short term, contractual arrangements helped shape daily practice around rhythms of schoolwork: they provided some degree of temporal structure. On the longer term, too, temporality was important: working in the war schools could preempt problems related to noncontinuous employment (which did indeed amass after the war). They also provided recognition of teaching as professional work – an important factor given the valuation of education and work in 'normal life' (see Baker 2011).

Central to the staircase schooling system in besieged Dobrinja were thus attempts to calibrate the flow of life back to 'normal'. The Schooling Centre tried to establish a degree of predictability, from the daily rhythms of schooling to the movement of pupils along a trajectory towards further study or employment, and that of teachers towards pension entitlements. It aimed to keep young people safe and to provide them with a formal education associated with 'normal lives', including its rhythms and timekeeping. Furthermore, it contained a future-orientation on the longer term: pupil work was recorded in ways that reflected the 'normal' procedures as much as possible, aimed at allowing smooth progress into further education. Yearnings for 'normal lives', and the efforts to make them feasible, thus evoked a social configuration in which expectations were structured through their institutional embedding. The concept of 'gridding', I argue, allows us to capture this analytically.

Anthropology and Hope For/Against the State

In chapter 2 I introduced the term 'gridding' in dialogue with Scott's critique of rational state-organised attempts to impose 'a standard grid' in order to govern (1998: 2). I now disentangle his approach and an associated paradigm in anthropological studies of modern ordering processes, to then return to Dobrinja.

For Scott, state grids always appear as imposed on people, seeking to replace bottom-up, authentic, local self-development with a top-down, inauthentic, larger-than-local system aimed at discipline and expropriation. He argues that such grid impositions necessarily fail due to their disrespect for *mētis*, people's local, experiential wisdom, embodied in collective terms by '(civil) society', posited as separate from and opposed to the state. Scott's analysis is often criticised for being too static, too dualist, and for lacking nuance in terms of the internal dynamics of the two 'sides'.[10] Here I zoom in on another aspect of his work: his reduction of statecraft to *imposed* gridding. If, in Scott's approach, grids are always represented as forced upon people as enclosures, thwarting preexisting freedom, when addressing people's engagement with such grids, he focuses squarely on how they evade or, sometimes, counteract them. Radicalising his earlier work on resistance (1985; 1990), he places the key to human agency in marginal subversion of overwhelming, systematic domination. Despite disclaimers, his work is decidedly anti-modernist. In *The Art of Not Being Governed* (2009), Scott's millennia-spanning narrative aims to reinstate hill people in southeast Asia, expert grid evaders, to their righteous place as subjects of history. Rather than treating those outside of state enclosure as backward barbarians who are not-yet-state subjects, he argues, we should take seriously the perspective of 'barbarians by choice' (until recently, he says, the global majority), who opt to evade the state's grasp, maintaining political autonomy and, at most, entering a mutual parasitical relationship with it.

If Scott's *The Art of Not Being Governed* is a self-confessed epitaph for a disappeared world – with its polemical verve offset by a knowing resignation that it is written after hope – Graeber does not see state enclosure as ever-increasing. Tracing grid evasion in rural Madagascar, he emphasises self-organisation, seeing the establishment of 'provisional zones of autonomy' as hopeful signs 'that alternatives are still conceivable, that human possibilities are never fixed' (2007: 172). In Madagascar, Graeber argues, autonomy emerged from a convergence of people's desire to self-organise, based on their awareness of the arbitrary, coercive nature of the state, and of the government's (dis)interest and (in)capacity to impose grids on them. For our purpose here, I note that Graeber writes that his informants include schools in this view, seeing them as, 'designed to produce the competences required to maintain an infrastructure of violence, … premised on social relations completely unlike those current in other aspects of daily life, ones that could only be maintained by a constant threat of physical harm' (ibid.: 176–77). Graeber identifies an ambivalent attitude towards schools as places where one could learn skills that were valuable but which were also tools of repression. In his analysis, people's limited and tactical engagements with state grids, then, ultimately serve as reminders of its opposite: things considered 'Malagasy', centring on ungridded self-government through consensual, egalitarian democracy (ibid.: 176). In fact, Graeber argues, the state effectively existed only as a hollow 'ghost-state' constituted through a consensual 'scam' (ibid.: 169). Like Scott, but more optimistically, Graeber explicitly places his work at the cutting edge of social inquiry, hopefully speculating that there might be many, 'similar communities in other parts of the world – communities that have withdrawn from or drifted away from the effective control of the national governments and become to all intents and purposes self-governing, but whose members are still performing the external form and tokens of obeisance in order to disguise that fact' (ibid.: 177).

In divergent ways, Scott and Graeber are particularly explicit, consistent and eloquent examples of a paradigm in the anthropology of the state that conceives of it specifically as anthropology *against* the state, in at least two ways: empirically, it privileges its subjects' evasion of statecraft, and politically, it locates its own hope in those subjects' hope for evasion. Both authors seek to 'replicate' (Miyazaki 2004) the hope of their subjects for autonomy, thus formulating hope for an anthropology that counters the impoverishment of political imaginations by state-centred thinking. Both position their self-declared 'anarchist' analyses as subversive of dominant knowledge production and they do indeed provide valuable antidotes against the suppression of grid evasion in official state narratives. Yet, at least since Clastres (1974), such suppression is hardly dominant in anthropological treatments of statecraft. In the study of self-proclaimed modern ordering schemes, such as states, anarchist writings represent particularly consistent crystallisations of a paradigm – a format of questions asked and of ways to seek answers – that has permeated much anthropology for decades (Spencer 2007; *Critique of Anthropology* 2012). This libertarian paradigm posits the state predominantly as an imposed externality, approached along two separate analytical paths. The first path, often inspired by Gramsci or Foucault, unmasks top-down modern statecraft's claims to enlightened progress. The second one documents people's resilience in opposition to, or oblivious to, statecraft thus conceived.

Far from being the preserve of anarchist anthropology, the libertarian paradigm combines favourite ingredients of our discipline more broadly: for example, a celebration of difference, an emphasis on modernity's discontents, a privileging of small-scale phenomena and sympathy for (often culturally conceived) underdogs who generally favour 'authentic' resilience over 'modern' change. We find varying degrees of activist intent and differential emphases on culture, but with regard to the operation of modern grids, a convergence exists around a conception of anthropology as being particularly apt for the study of local, authentic resilience. As anthropologists we thus become experts on how people resist, ignore, or, at most, cleverly accommodate to top-down ordering schemes. The popularity of this libertarian paradigm is, I believe, not merely an analytical reflection of our interlocutors' libertarianism: it is at least also (and perhaps mainly) a function of the hope it allows for anthropologists. Through replication of the hope of our subjects, it promises a lasting political purpose for anthropology. Tracing how, against all odds, plucky little people throw spanners in large-scale grids and retain difference against standardisation, we can reinvigorate our hope for humanity by uncovering political hope where we could have mistakenly feared there was none. Furthermore, this paradigm seems to rely on a broader assumption on human nature too: combining anthropology's romantic anti-modern roots with a Camusian affirmation of *L'Homme Revolté* (1985), it suggests that, ultimately, people prove their humanity through authentic grid evasion.[11] Especially if authenticity is conceived of as cultural, this allows identification with resistant underdogs by sympathetic anthropologists.[12] In that way, the libertarian paradigm also facilitates the replication of people's hope against the state in the search for our discipline's continued relevance.

Studies in the libertarian paradigm, whether by self-identified anarchists or by others, have proven very valuable. They document the contingency of state making and the often catastrophic realities behind triumphalist, teleological state narratives. They provide effective analytical tools to critically deconstruct reason(ing)s of state, to theorise people's evasion and thus to facilitate the possible development of alternatives. Yet the paradigm's popularity and its contributions come at a price. Its limits become especially visible in cases where libertarian hopes are not prominent amongst our research subjects, as in my 2008–10 research in Dobrinja. To reach back to the subtitle of Scott's (1998) book, over and above any resentment of how 'certain schemes to improve the human condition have failed', I was struck by how much 'certain schemes to improve the suburban condition were being *hailed*'. If anything, it was the lack of more such schemes that was resented.

Clearly, that such hope for the state exists should not surprise anyone. My objective is not simply to show that some people's hopes (and fears) do not sit easily with libertarianism. Instead, I probe the limits of the libertarian paradigm in analytical terms and propose complementary conceptual tools. Having become experts in grid evasion, I ask, how can we enrich anthropological understandings of grid desire? If we have an elaborate and effective toolbox for study-ing hope against the state, can we also develop concepts to grasp hope for the state? Short of dismissing it as false consciousness, successful disciplining, or feigned compliance, here anthropology offers a much poorer array of conceptual tools. A critical unmasking of oppression, disciplining and manipulation through state grids usually occurs alongside a celebratory analysis of people's resist-ance to them. This reinforces the assumed boundary between 'state' and 'society', or, allowing for the political charge in the libertarian paradigm, between the horrors of modern statecraft and the beauty of resilience-in-authenticity. In contrast, this book learns from writ-ings that aim to overcome this dichotomous model (e.g., Das and Poole 2004; Fuller and Bénéï 2001; Hansen and Stepputat 2001) but also seeks to extend them in a particular direction. This is because on two specific accounts such writings often leave me dissatisfied. Firstly, despite statements of intent, empirically, many such studies still (separately) focus on top-down disciplining schemes and peo-ple's evasion attempts, paying little attention to their non-evasion. Secondly, when hopes for the state are acknowledged, they are incorporated all too easily into the author's hope against the state: since the analyst unmasks the state as an ideological construct, peo-ple's investments in it are swiftly reduced to internalisations of the insidious circularity of statecraft (e.g., Aretxaga 2003). State grids are thus still mainly conceived of as imposed externalities, and an-thropologists still focus mostly on how people – at least could and should – evade them. To a large degree, the libertarian paradigm remains untouched.

In asking how we can anthropologically replicate hope for the state, I thus seek to contribute to an emerging body of anthropological work that theorises people's investment in statecraft in a nondichotomous, integrated way, reluctant to locate people and their hopes always already outside of state grids (e.g., Corbridge et al. 2005; Dunn 2008; Li 2007; Navaro-Yashin 2002; Nuijten 2003; Obeid 2010; Reeves 2011; Spencer 2007; Ssorin-Chaikov 2003).[13] I aim to extend such work by adding 'gridding' to our conceptual toolbox. Let us now explore this in relation to besieged Dobrinja.

Self-organised Upward and Outward Gridding

In Dobrinja, I found that a sense prevailed that one lived after gridding, and that gridding was necessary to allow the unfolding of 'normal lives'. In 1992, this planned apartment complex was unmoored from its city centre and its gridding infrastructure was devastated. Yet this was far from a gridless situation. The proclamation of an independent RBiH attempted to detach it from what was left of Yugoslav gridding, upgrading grids of a federal unit to state ones. The army that many Dobrinjci had until recently considered to be a coercive guarantee – positively and negatively – of their gridding, had turned its artillery on those who favoured an RBiH grid, effectively siding with those in favour of a grid of a Serbian Republic of BiH. This restructuring thus affected people differentially as they were now made legible through pro-BiH / anti-BiH gridding, partially articulated with nationality. In wartime Dobrinja, an array of new, initially relatively autonomous gridding processes were set in motion to cope with violence and destitution. The most effective capacity to impose these lay with the armed formations of the ARBiH and the CZ structures.[14]

Key figures in CZ Dobrinja prided themselves on gridding organised civilian life as effectively and with as much orderliness as possible under siege. Similar processes, including the organisation of schooling, occurred elsewhere in BiH, but Dobrinja was frequently mentioned as a prime example. Military commanders emphasised how the defence of Dobrinja by poorly armed units, and indeed the survival of its population, had only been possible due to tight civilian organisation.[15] They sometimes approvingly called wartime Dobrinja a 'little state' (e.g., Bećirović 2003), and one spoke of the need for an iron hand to establish 'Churchillian organisation like the one in Second World War London'.[16] Recalling a famous case of self-organisation in Paris, a journalist described it as a 'Komuna':

> There are ever more rejections of invitations to come 'into town' and ever more requests of those who are now here [in the city centre] to return there. There, clearly, war did not win, but people did. From the trauma caused by days and nights of loneliness and hiding from the killers right next to every flat, resistance was born, poured into a movement, into organisation, and, as we see now, into a kind of Commune, unprecedented in this region. That part of town lives its life, for which many 'normal people' in the rest of the city envy it, although they don't like to admit it openly. There, simply said, it's well known who drinks and who pays [*tamo se dobro zna ko pije i ko plaća*]. There, it's known how many people there are, in what kind of flats they are

accommodated, who can or can't share those flats, who can carry a gun, who can clean and wash, cook and distribute aid, write, sing or act. Dobrinja today knows about all its elderly who are immobile and need their allocations to be delivered at the door. Dobrinja knows about all its children who lost their parents, whom this little city will try, insofar as it can, to compensate for this loss ... It's different in many other parts of Sarajevo, especially in places where, from the start, there has been an insistence on those new people who have been honoured even before the first bullet was fired. That story about initiators of the struggle [*prvoborci*] well before the struggle began, is well-known. Luckily, look, ordinary people in Dobrinja didn't recognise them then, and don't do so now. So there is hope.[17]

Of course, claims to successful state making by those who considered themselves its leaders require scepticism. Some testimonies I gathered indicate that the siege and violent claims to sovereignty by self-appointed strongmen on whose armed defence survival depended, posed an unequally distributed threat of a reduction to 'bare life' (Agamben 1998). Some also resented certain dimensions of top-down gridding by CZ and ARBiH – its military-style discipline, its official ban on alcohol, its curfew, its security checks and the public role awarded to Islam by certain military commanders. Yet no one denied the need for gridding per se. It was not just that, threatened by besieging violence and potentially at the mercy of would-be sovereigns, people sought security in gridding – for example, limits on mobility were crucial to survival in this apartment complex on the siege line. In addition, a commitment to gridding emerged also precisely through yearnings to live beyond 'bare life'. If lives had been partly 'bared' by the collapse of the sovereignty–discipline–government triad (Foucault 1991), gridding played a central role in efforts to 'clothe' them again, and to approximate 'normal lives'. My analysis thus folds itself into Lubkemann's argument that, rather than portraying all people living in a war-affected place as 'stripped-down humanity' (2008: 7) and focusing exclusively on how people cope with violence, our approach should be more encompassing, showing how they seek to pursue broader life projects in extreme and unforeseen conditions. In besieged Dobrinja, in the absence of what was considered a 'normal' state, large numbers of people became involved in an intricate gridding exercise that mimicked stateness as much as it could. And in these efforts – involving armed defence, census taking, trench digging, food distribution, schooling, etc. – the combined concern for physical survival and a 'beyond-bare life' starkly exposes the interdependence of claims to territorial sovereignty, disciplinary technologies and the improvement of the condition of the population (Foucault 1991).

It is notable that, while my research was not focused on the war, Dobrinjci often put wartime experiences centre stage in discussions of their settlement. They evoked victimisation, but, over and above that, many proudly told me that wartime Dobrinja really had been 'better organised' and that *they had organised it themselves*.[18] Many other Sarajevans too confirmed that wartime Dobrinja – particularly initially – had been marred less by looting, racketeering and misuse of humanitarian aid than the rest of the city. This self-organisation was considered a major achievement in such a recent apartment complex: rather than pulling together as a longstanding, 'organically' grown community in defence of a common home, many Dobrinjci recalled how they had needed to build solidarity with neighbours they hardly knew. Zlaja, then in his mid forties, worked as head technician in CZ repair workshops throughout the war. He said: 'In the beginning, no one knew anyone. Everything had to be organised ... and we organised everything'. Survival required cooperation, which required coordination. Anti-sniper shields, a hospital, flat allocation, humanitarian aid distribution – they all involved gridding. So did work on a gas-pipe network towards the end of the war, when the city still did not have maintenance teams in Dobrinja.[19] In fact, people often related 'good organisation' precisely to the settlement's relative physical isolation from central RBiH authorities. Over time, however, Dobrinja's reputation faded due to increasing attempts by SDA figures to impose their priorities, including a more Bosniak nationalist vision, in all ARBiH-held territory.[20]

A libertarian interpretation can handle this narrative. Some dimensions of the wartime organisation of Dobrinja by the military (ARBiH) and civil authorities (CZ) could be seen as miniature versions of the schemes lambasted by Scott (1998). While hardly in a position to cherish 'high modernist' aspirations, they could be represented as starting, through mimicry, to 'see like a state' in order to ultimately become part of one. A libertarian analysis could celebrate self-governing, small-scale gridding in Dobrinja and mourn its decline due to its vertical encompassment into RBiH state grids. It could point to a historical tendency of states to appropriate ordering initiatives that emerge outside or in resistance to it. This process is awarded a central place in Foucault's history of the rise of disciplinary power as part of the changes that ushered in modern industrial social formations (1994). Using examples from eighteenth-century England, Foucault writes about petit bourgeois citizens gathered in minority religious communities, 'who assigned themselves, without any delegation from a higher authority, the task of maintaining order and of creating new instruments for ensuring order, for their own purposes' (ibid.: 60). Initially, he says, they organised such measures, for example against lower-class drunkenness, in order to evade state power. Yet, over time, Foucault shows, such self-defence mechanisms were hijacked by more privileged groups: bishops and prominent members of the bourgeoisie and the aristocracy established reform societies, and the very rich founded paramilitary squads and private police societies. Increasingly, these 'mechanisms of control' came to rely on state sanctioning. In other words, what originated as resistance was transformed into support for state appropriation of disciplinary tools.

When applied to besieged Dobrinja, such a libertarian reading of anti-state self-organisation (bottom-up gridding) being incorporated and thereby neutralised by the establishment of state control (top-down gridding) would miss several important points. Firstly, there was no blank slate: as we saw, Dobrinja's construction in the SFRY was part of centrally organised top-down gridding in the first place, and even after the collapse of preexisting grids we can hardly speak of a Hobbesian state of nature at the outset of war. Once they are accustomed to lives that are gridded in modern ordering frameworks, people may actively seek the reestablishment of such gridding when it disintegrates. With regard to schooling, studies by Corbridge et al. in India (2005: 50) and by Rockwell (1994) in Mexico have shown how state attempts to deploy formal education as a disciplinary technology do not imply they are merely top-down impositions. Instead, they demonstrate how schooling was produced in dialogue and dispute between a hegemonising project of a 'modernising' state and the labour, aspirations and professional commitments of people they were supposed to modernise. My Dobrinja research underscores this and further emphasises that these aspirations and commitments may be cherished by people who cannot be defined in any way as state agents.[21]

Secondly, and this is the point I want to emphasise here, wartime top-down and bottom-up griddings were not simply counterposed to each other, although they sometimes were in some ways. As shown in historical studies of urban utilities, such as the absorption of local, private initiatives in a more encompassing public sewage system in New York (Goldman 1997), conflicting interests and priorities do not necessarily prevent a degree of compatibility and convergence. To understand how this interaction of top-down and bottom-up processes worked, I analyse wartime schooling as a contingent, partial convergence of self-organised and imposed gridding. Both attempted to incite certain activities, models of behaviour and temporal rhythms and trajectories of practice. Convergences always remained unstable and contested: for example, teachers felt classes should be held despite of CZ warnings; conflicts over space emerged between the Schooling Centre and CZ officials; some resented increasing SDA interference, and particularly Islamisation agendas. Yet the bottom-up dimension of schooling initiatives always included a gridding dimension beyond itself – reaching 'upward' and 'outward' into the vertical encompassment of the RBiH state.

The Schooling Centre could only operate with approval from Dobrinja's military commanders, who incorporated it in their own embryonic state-making projects. But its efforts to grid its activities upward and outward went beyond that. Even when gathering children on their own initiative as the siege closed around them, teachers kept school diaries, listing the space, age group, number of children present and class theme according to an administrative format (Musić 1998: 11). Later the School Diary too was maintained according to a surviving socialist law. The Schooling Centre, co-ordinating teaching activities, immediately sought approval from municipal and state institutions. After its opening in 1993, the Gimnazija applied for and received a 'Decision' from the RBiH Ministry for Education, Science and Sports authorising it to function as a public schooling institution according to curricular requirements (Šurković 2003: 15).

While keen to safeguard their autonomy in some ways, schooling initiatives thus included attempts to have local gridding vertically encompassed into gridding understood to be higher and broader. In addition to curricula and administrative procedures, we saw how such upward and outward gridding concerned accreditation of marks and diplomas and contractual arrangements for personnel, aiming for continuity in the educational trajectories of pupils and in the employment trajectories of teachers. The 'linear-modular module' set up to provide continuity for secondary school pupils was then further developed in collaboration with the Department of Pedagogy at the University of Sarajevo and the Pedagogical Institute. From spring 1994, the Gimnazija was included in the latter's inspection rota, and, with its approval, the 'Dobrinja model' was later applied elsewhere in RBiH (Šurković 2003).

This last point not only highlights the mutual constitution of self-organised and imposed gridding – largely concerning what I call statecraft – but also alerts us to a more symbolic dimension of Dobrinja's upward and outward gridding. Aretxaga has argued that we should see the state 'as the subject of excess that bypasses any rational functionality. What articulates this excess is fantasy' (2003: 402). In Dobrinja, I found a strong pride in self-organisation but also in practices that explicitly sought to call the state into being. For many, this included a patriotic commitment to RBiH statehood, yet even this 'fantasy' dimension consisted to an extent of desires to establish rhythms and trajectories. The state was then called forth as the hoped-for structural effect of multilayered gridding processes in vertical encompassment. For example, the arrival of an RBiH flag and coat of arms for the Gimnazija in April 1994 deserves mention in an in-house anniversary publication (Šurković 2003: 29). In another example, many teachers proudly recalled that the Gimnazija secretary walked the risky ten kilometres to the city centre, across the barricades, to get an official stamp for the school. 'Work is victorious! Good luck!', says the Diary entry (10 July 1993). We should not reduce this to tactical pretence only – to a 'scam'. The hope invested in this stamp included hope for ratification of the Gimnazija as a 'real' school, by standards of 'normal life', for recognition of its teaching activities in their contents (curricula), methods (models of teaching), products (certificates and diplomas) and labour (teacher employment). And those hopes, in turn, were embedded in hope for one's own survival and, largely seen in conjunction, RBiH statehood.

If we think of states as a structural effect, schooling in wartime Dobrinja can be considered an example of nesting gridding projects that contribute to state making. Teachers aimed to reestablish rhythms and trajectories of 'normal' schoolwork; they sought to grid these gridding activities upward and outward into institutional statecraft; and the largest-scale grid of vertical encompassment considered here – that of the state of RBiH – was itself attempting to reduce its precariousness through seeking upward and outward gridding in a global grid of states. On every scale, this involves a desire for upward and outward gridding into a more vertically encompassing grid. And the temporal dimension is central: it is practices that are gridded here, small or big future-oriented projects that require some predictability shaped by gridding – from getting drinking water in an apartment complex in order to survive, to completing one's studies in order to potentially enter an employment trajectory. This is what 'normal lives' in Dobrinja were deemed to require: a far cry from a wish for ungridded freedom, we find pride in bottom-up self-organisation that seeks gridding.

Limits of Libertarian Critique

This chapter insists that anthropologists should attempt to account for both hope for and hope against the state, overcoming the tendency to flatten out grid desire in a dichotomous model that registers gridding predominantly in terms of imposition and evasion. This latter paradigm, privileging the subversive in 'the margins', leaves little place for practices that actively comply with, confirm the relevance of, and call into being various degrees of gridding. Locating their hopes (and the hopes of the people they write about) in the authenticity of autonomous, self-consciously non-gridded people, libertarian analyses are poorly positioned to account for other hopes that these or other people may cherish. In addition to evading them, people may deeply and continuously invest in engagements with existing (as well as possible) gridding, including planned, top-down statecraft. If people move in and out of states/grids, as both Scott and Graeber argue, they provide no conceptual tools to understand why people would move into gridding, except when coerced. Indeed, Scott points out that many state subjects in southeast Asia were captives, so that, when they fled back to the hills, 'perhaps, for some of them, the journey away from the state was something like a homecoming' (2009: 165). Perhaps it was, but, looking at the issue from the other end of the story, I consider here the experiences of people who had long been positioned within state grids and who self-consciously positioned themselves as being righteous participants in a world structured by them.

The 'ought' and the 'was' – in opposition to the 'is' – were thus again entangled in the yearnings for 'normal lives' I encountered. Remembered lives in Dobrinja had long integrated cookers and light switches, as well as the less obviously material infrastructural – but no less gridded, and no less expected – work of schooling. I found that the normative self-evidence of such gridding was emphasised through confrontations with the fact that during wartime it was not self-evident at all. Most Dobrinjci recalled the outbreak of war as a shock of sudden ungridding. They were forced to collect water from outside wells, to grow vegetables on balconies, to bury their own dead between parking lots and to carry out household chores without electrical equipment. Some experiential knowledge – *mētis* – of elderly household members, who had once led less gridded lives, helped people cope with siege conditions. This, of course, would be a ready-made topic for anthropological analysis, so attuned to small-scale resilience understood as cultural. A replication of the hope embodied in this resilience could spark both political hope for un-gridded autonomy and hope for anthropology as the specialist study of it. Yet, while Dobrinjci sometimes recalled this with amusement, I never heard it represented as an emancipatory return to authentic autonomy. More commonly it was deplored as humiliating.

As well as evoking humiliation, fear, cold and poverty, many contrasted life under siege with postwar conditions through posi-tive references to wartime solidarity and to what they as Dobrinjci – thrown back on themselves – had collectively been capable of. And this itself was frequently phrased in terms of gridding. Mrs Sabiha Barjaktarević, a key CZ activist, said: 'First we did a population census. I went from flat to flat, seven hundred of them, writing down every man, woman and child. Then we set up the schooling system and a folklore group and a women's choir. *Za vrijeme rata, bili smo super* [During the war, we were great]'. Not everyone was as com-mitted to wartime gridding as Mrs Barjaktarević, who was also an SDA member at the time. People are never equally able to mobilise nodes in particular griddings. Indeed, they may not want to. Clearly, besieged Dobrinjci did not hope to become automatons in a perfectly predictable environment. Ideally incorporation into gridding would be on their terms and yearned-for 'normal lives' were projected to be calibrated by the right degree of predictability. Grid evasion existed in tension with grid desire. One could view Mrs Barjaktarević, and teachers for that matter, as state agents with much to gain from grid-ding, but it has to be understood that Mrs Barjaktarević's own chil-dren went to the staircase schools, just like those of Mrs Zumbul and Mrs Maglajić. Likewise, the workers who constructed sniper shields, and their loved ones, themselves hoped to be protected by them. The repair technicians themselves, and their loved ones, were dependent on the infrastructure they patched up with improvised means. The hygiene inspectors, and their loved ones, drank water from the wells and the nurses, and their loved ones, needed medicine and care.

Li's (2007) introduction of the notion of the 'will to improve' in her study of development projects in Indonesia can provide inspiration here. Yet, I argue that understanding Dobrinja's wartime gridding requires us to go one step further. While critical of Scott, Li's focus is nevertheless on the 'will to improve' exacted by the 'centre', i.e., in the work of government institutions, transnational aid organisations and other entities to impact on a subordinate population. Instead, I draw attention to an array of practices through which people themselves may pursue a 'will to improve' – at the very least, to counteract the 'baring' of lives – and to the ways in which this involves gridding. In recollections of wartime Dobrinja, the will to survive was recounted as the will to lead 'normal lives', which was itself understood as containing a 'will to improve'. As research in Palestine shows, in such situations we cannot simply separate personal aspirations from political activism and loyalty (Jean-Klein 2000; Kelly 2008). Dobrinjci recalled their determination to maintain some vestiges of 'normal lives' not simply as heroic acts of spontaneous improvisation, nor only as autonomous self-organisation, but also as bottom-up gridding for improvement. And this gridding included, as we have seen, a strong temporal dimension, combining regularity, standardisation and coordination. In besieged Dobrinja, spontaneous and CZ-coordinated activities set in motion replacement gridding bounded and made possible by military discipline. The 'population' that was thus produced – people who had remained in Dobrinja and newly arrived displaced persons – engaged with this in different ways. All submitted to a degree, since some gridding was coerced and survival was dependent on it, but here too some tried to evade discipline and mobilisation. Anthropology's libertarian tradition provides conceptual tools to investigate such resistance. However, Dobrinjci directed my focus instead to hope for gridding, to the suppressed yearnings, loud clamourings and tireless struggles of people to be incorporated into griddings of improvement, and their investment in becoming, not to put too fine a point to it, part of legible populations. The fact that at other points and in other ways these same people also wish to remain illegible and ungridded does not discount this desire as irrelevant, nor does the fact that they seek incorporation on their own terms.

In the postwar period, when barricades and snipers that had rendered its connection to the city centre tenuous had disappeared, School Diary entries increasingly depicted Dobrinja as a neglected periphery. Despite strong local objections, the hospital was closed and the Gimnazija was threatened with the same fate. If Iskra and Lejla, who had been teenagers in prewar Dobrinja, could dismiss the notion of having a secondary school in Dobrinja, this was because they had always been oriented strongly towards the city centre. Much of this had changed. What had largely been a dormitory settlement in the 1980s, had now become a more self-sufficient apartment complex, with shops, services, a sports venue, and so on. For a decade and a half after the war, teaching staff, pupils and their parents put up a fight not only to maintain the Gimnazija, but also to accommodate it in purpose-built premises. With the battle for its continued existence won, a donation from the government of the People's Republic of China made possible the start of building works. While these premises would also house another secondary school, as Director Pucar's speech on School's Day indicated, they were adamant that they wished to maintain their identity as a school. Throughout my research, the Gimnazija was still housed in the improvised venues created in wartime conditions, but, after a long and meandering road of negotiations with different authorities, it finally moved to purpose-built accommodation, shared with another Gimnazija, at the end of 2010.

This could be deplored as imposed vertical encompassment into disciplining statecraft, a sad end to autonomous self-organisation. In contrast, however, teachers themselves now integrated their self-organised activism under siege into their narratives as the first episode of a contested, stop–start campaign to grid their work upwardly and outwardly, on their terms, into a state education system. Yet the relevant institutions were no longer those of RBiH, which expired with the 1995 Dayton Peace Agreement, but those of Canton Sarajevo and the Federation of BiH (see chapter 4). During my research in 2008–10, many Dobrinjci bemoaned insufficient state gridding as one key reason why they were still unable to lead 'normal lives'. Hope for the state had meanwhile become yearning. It is against this background that they proudly – and with some melancholy – recalled their own

FIGURE 3.4. Building works for the new Gimnazija premises in Dobrinja (photo by Vanja Čelebičić, 2010)

wartime efforts to restore rhythms and trajectories of 'normal life', not simply as resilient acts of spontaneous improvisation, nor only as autonomy, but also as self-organised upward and outward gridding for improvement, including vertical encompassment into RBiH state griddings.

Notes

1. During my research Dobrinja's three primary schools were attended by over two thousand five hundred pupils and several hundred were educated at its only secondary school.

2. 'Gimnazija Dobrinja ima poseban kredibilitet' [Gimnazija Dobrinja has special credibility], *Oslobođenje*, 2 June 2008, 24.

3. This is confirmed by leading figures in those units (Bećirović 2003: 45). See also 'Ubice u školskim klupama' [Murderers on school benches], *Dobrinja: Ratne novine 1. Dobrinjske Brigade*, 31 August 1992, 15–16; 'Doba ilegale' [The era of clandestine resistance], *Dobrinja Ratne novine 1. Dobrinjske Brigade*, 19 September 1992, 11.

4. Much of this wartime organisation was modelled on the Yugoslav socialist doctrine of *Opštenarodna odbrana i društvena samozaštita* [All-People's Defence and Societal Self-Protection, ONO i DSZ], inspired by the Second World War Partisan guerrilla movement (Bećirović 2003; Hamzić 2004). As elsewhere in Sarajevo, some of the leading figures involved in the initial organising were ONO i DSZ specialists as well as former JNA officers.

5. 'Dobrinjski spektar' [Dobrinja's spectre], *Dobrinja Ratne novine 1. Dobrinjske Brigade*, 23 November 1992, 4; 'Najveći kompliment: pohvala borca' [The greatest compliment: praise from a fighter], *Dobrinja Ratne novine 1. Dobrinjske Brigade*, 23 November 1992, 17–18.

6. For a very detailed reconstruction of wartime schooling in Dobrinja, see Berman 2007.

7. During my research, around two-thirds of all pupils at this primary school attended (optional) classes of the subject 'religious instruction'. Almost all of them took Islam and a few took Catholicism. Dobrinjci who wish their children to take Serbian Orthodox classes tended to send them to school in Istočno Sarajevo. No alternative was offered for pupils who do not attend any religious classes.

8. The *Ljetopis Gimnazije Dobrinja* is a multivolume school logbook. An administrative requirement, its detailed wartime sections offer great insight into life in besieged Dobrinja. At times it clearly also addresses a future audience, positioning itself as testimony and the Gimnazija as a self-conscious historical agent.

9. In the words of Mrs Meliha Hodžić, an active participant in Dobrinja wartime self-organisation and a merciless critic not only of the state she lived in but also of her fellow citizens: 'And everyone ... that's interesting, everyone swears by Allah that ... everyone interestingly talks about *merhamet* [litt. compassion] being the basis [*osnovnica*] of our people. No. It's not true. They lie. People were very selfish in the war'.

10. See for example, *American Anthropologist* 2005. Scott has graciously accepted certain criticisms (2005) and nuanced his argument somewhat in a coauthored article (Scott, Tehranian and Mathias 2002). The charge that he is seeking to 'locate pristine spaces outside of power, pure sites of resistance' (Li 2005: 385), he flatly denies (2005: 400).

Yet, even if he may not be looking for such actual pristine spaces, his argument, I contend, does rely on the possibility of them. More generally, occasional disclaimers tend to be swept away by the torrent of his dualist story, which, precisely because he makes his case so clearly and consistently, I posit here mainly as an inspirational counterpoint for my analysis.

11. This, I suggest, may explain the appeal of de Certeau's writings (1990) amongst anthropologists.
12. This may be related to a specific generational conjuncture in academia marked by disillusion with modernist grand narratives and by an institutional framework in which most senior anthropologists in North America and Western Europe operate from positions where they can remain largely unaware of the role of statecraft in the creation of conditions of possibility for their work and lives. This question calls for research on contemporary dynamics in the academic field and its political–economic (trans)formations.
13. Beyond this work, many writings focus on affective investment in the nationalist wholeness projected by state ideologies (largely matters of state*hood*), but here I draw attention to more practical–processual dimensions of grid making (largely in the realm of state*craft*).
14. Similar patterns of expectations and enforcement have been identified for wartime life across the siege line, in Istočno Sarajevo (Armakolas 2007: 86–88).
15. 'Prva Dobrinjska brigada – primjer drugima' [First Dobrinja Brigade – an example for others], *Dobrinja Ratne novine 1. Dobrinjske Brigade*, 19 September 1992, 3; 'Dobrinja se odbranila srcem' [Dobrinja was defended with our hearts], *Dobrinja Ratne novine 1. Dobrinjske Brigade*, 19 February 1992, 14.
16. 'Dobrinja neće postati etnički čista' [Dobrinja will not become ethnically pure], *Oslobođenje*, 30 December 1994, 8.
17. 'Ponovo Dobrinja' [Dobrinja, again], *Dobrinja Ratne novine 1. Dobrinjske Brigade*, 23 November 1992, 2. This text was written by Zlatko Dizdarević, Sarajevo journalist and critic of SDA. In SFRY, the official category *prvoborci* [litt. first fighters] comprised pioneers of Second World War Partisan resistance. After 1992 it was used for prewar organisers of armed units to defend RBiH. In both cases, *prvoborci* qualified for allowances, and debates raged about who legitimately belonged to this category.
18. In some ways, the disintegration of prewar grids was also experienced as beneficial and some handsomely profited from the unprecedented opportunities it provided. Yet most emphasised the opposite side of the coin.
19. 'Plin na račun' [Gas on bills], *Dobrinja Danas: Bilten Mjesne Zajednice* 51, 16 April 1995, 1.
20. 'Dobrinjska komuna: civilizacijska pouka iz nedavne bh. historije' [The Dobrinja Commune: a civilisational message from recent Bosnian history], *Oslobođenje*, 29 April 2001, 6.
21. Responding to his critics, Scott too has emphasised that, in the footsteps of Polanyi, we can trace a development from peasant struggles against the state to protect their hard-fought 'local social-insurance arrangements' to their acceptance of 'a national system of poor relief and, eventually, the welfare state' (Scott 2005: 397). He even suggests that we understand a large part of social struggle between 1830 and 1950 as, 'the attempt to create, in place of the wreckage of local moral-economies, an analogous "moral-economy state" to provide national social insurance along comparable lines – no longer seen as a matter of local reciprocity but as right of citizenship' (ibid.). Yet Scott's later work, especially *The Art of Not Being Governed*, again offers a libertarian reading, with an exclusive emphasis on grid evasion and, at best, cunning accommodation.

PART II

DIAGNOSING DAYTONITIS

– Chapter 4 –

FIRST SYMPTOM: 'THERE IS NO SYSTEM'
[or, Towards an Anthropology of an Elusive State Effect]

$\mathcal{C}\!\!\!\sim$

in which discussions on housing maintenance in local commune meetings introduce us to the first constitutional symptom of Daytonitis as detected in Dobrinja – the 'lack of a system' – which we disentangle by way of structural diagnoses of dispersion, excessive absence and presence, and moral diagnoses of 'messed-up values'

Winter 2008. A poster on a Dobrinja street announces a lecture organised by a consumers' association on the theme 'Communal Problems and Ways to Solve Them'. Three subthemes are specified – the 'possibility of debts being written off', 'the quality of central heating' and 'other questions and problems of consumption'. All attendees will receive a free copy of a 'Manual for Citizens-Consumers'. The venue for the event is the seat of one of Dobrinja's four *Mjesne Zajednice*, located on the ground floor of a 1980s apartment block. All MZs in Dobrinja maintain an office run by a secretary, employed by the municipality of Novi grad, where citizens can attend to minor administrative affairs and submit requests or grievances for consideration to their MZ council. MZ councils consist of five to seven councillors who receive a small fee for their work, which is considered a voluntary engagement. They are elected for two-year mandates on open citizen's meetings, which in Dobrinja attract up to fifty persons. While MZ work is in theory unrelated to political parties, these meetings are purposively organised along party alignments and most councillors are party members. Indeed, serving on an MZ council is a common 'first step' into politics. During my stay, council meetings – said by the secretaries to be monthly – are held every two/three months. While they are attributed great significance in the rhetoric of foreign-enforced democratisation (as in the previous one of Yugoslav socialist self-management), MZs have no budgets of their own and limited mandates. In some rural areas they play a more active role in local government but in Dobrinja many residents do not even know where their offices are.

The meeting on 'Communal Problems and Ways to Solve Them' takes place in a large room with curtained windows, five tables with white tablecloths and a television soundlessly playing in a corner. In preelectoral periods, this venue is used by political parties. It also functions as a polling station. Otherwise, it serves as a meeting place for Dobrinja clubs and associations. Its most frequent users are members of the Pensioners' Club, who play cards and dominoes, chat and smoke. Indeed, in Dobrinja, many people who rarely or never enter into contact with their MZ think of it primarily as a place; and they think firstly not so much of the MZ secretariat, but of the adjoining room where pensioners gather. At a recent MZ council meeting I attended, there was a discussion about a circular from the municipality. It stipulated reduced working hours for pensioners' clubs and reiterated a ban on smoking, alcohol and gambling. At the time, the council agreed to monitor this and the secretary put up a notice to reinforce the policy. This notice disappeared almost straight away and some pensioners lodged a protest, demanding consultation with MZ councillors. At the next council meeting, president Mr Dino Hadžić agreed that they would publicise the rules, but no more than that, for

FIGURE 4.1. One of Dobrinja's local commune (MZ) secretariats, on the ground floor of an apartment block (photo by Vanja Čelebičić, 2014)

they had not been party to the allocation of this space to the Pension-ers' Club. All councillors dismissed the ban on smoking as unfeasible.

Today, as I arrive for the meeting organised by the Consumers' As-sociation, some pensioners finish their card game while we wait for the lecture to start. Ten people have turned up, including myself: five women and five men between thirty and sixty-five. Many smoke, and due to the cold we all keep our coats on. Mischievously, a middle-aged man says, 'Let's see what our rights are!' Another bristles, 'Our right is to shut up and listen'. And then we listen. The speaker, who arrives late, introduces himself as Professor Roljo, president of the Consumers' Association. His presentation never mentions 'rights' but focuses exclusively on complaints procedures for retail purchases. With examples of meat and electronic equipment, Professor Roljo tells us to retain receipts and contrasts the ability of his association to solve problems quickly and for free with the expensive, slow services of lawyers. He takes pains to emphasise the 'non-political' character of his association as 'a service'. However, interchangeably stating that it works 'for customers' and 'for citizens', he also evokes prox-imity to decision makers, referring to meetings with ministers and other cantonal functionaries.[1] He stresses, 'We are a legal entity, we have a stamp!' [*Mi smo pravno lice, imamo pečat!*]. Indeed, this stamp appeared on the announcement poster. When the lecturer stumbles over his words, attempting to specify who 'we' are – 'an association', 'a service', a 'legal entity' – a man suggests they are 'from the non-governmental sector'. Professor Roljo does not pick up this phrase, but, from then on, he increasingly speaks of 'citizens' rather than of 'customers'.

After ten minutes or so, a woman of about sixty, with short dyed hair and glasses, interrupts him. Ignoring retail complaints proce-dures, she launches into a story about the poor maintenance of her building's staircase. Meat and electronic equipment are not men-tioned from this moment onwards. In other words, while the speaker may have addressed only the third of the three subthemes specified on the poster ('other questions and problems of consumption'), it is clear that people have come to the MZ premises to deal with issues that they do not consider to be within the sphere of retail. 'Communal Problems and Ways to Solve Them', to them, implies a focus on the other two subthemes announced: 'the quality of central heating' and the 'possibility of debts being written off' ('debts', here, unanimously understood as unpaid bills for gas, water, building maintenance, etc.). The woman says: 'People pay 20 KM per month and nothing is done with it. In my building they only put in some new tiles and they sometimes change light bulbs. But my flat is draughty, I have air coming in from under the windows, I have to put blankets on the window sills'. The room comes alive now. Many nod, but a slightly younger woman with a headscarf says: 'They are only responsible for anything up to your door, nothing further than that'. She thus distinguishes between the tiles and the light bulbs in the common staircase and the windows of the woman's flat. Then a stocky, grey-haired woman says maintenance payments are too high. 'My entire pension', she says, 'is spent on utility bills. Can the authorities [*vlasti*] do anything about that?' The woman who spoke first loudly declares: 'They can but they won't. The only thing they know how to do is raise prices'. Several people nod in agreement.

As this point two men intervene. They detail a longstanding dispute about the state of their building, referring to *upravitelji* [litt. managers], the official term for the private firms responsible for maintenance of common spaces in apartment blocks. From now on all present use this term. The older of the two men, sporting a large moustache, accuses the *upravitelji* of neglect and corruption, employing a commonly used metonymic image of one man: 'A year ago a poor sod, and now a rich man! Two years ago he didn't even have a *Fića* [a small, cheap Yugoslav-produced car] and look what he's driving now!' The younger one, fashionably dressed, confirms this and says: 'The people [*narod*] pay 20 KM a month, almost nothing is done and in the end the balance is still zero ... Where did that money go?' At this point, Professor Roljo suggests that 'perhaps there should be some kind of inspection'. He also mentions a possible meeting with *upravitelji*. The young man keeps on referring to *narod*, but the lecturer replies in the register of 'citizens': 'We know that citizens are not satisfied with the *upravitelji* anywhere', he says, 'We have spoken to cantonal ministers about it, but next time we are going straight to the prime minister'. One man says: 'What will they do? They'll get some piece of paper and read what people want them to read'. The woman with the dyed hair exclaims: 'Once they have been elected, they don't care anymore. All they know how to do is to raise prices'.

The discussion now turns to heating and the 'extortionate price' of gas, the most common fuel in Dobrinja. A large woman of about forty-five says: 'They can raise the prices as much as they want. I won't pay. Take me to court, to prison, whatever, I won't pay'. The young man argues, 'All this should be privatised!' but then Professor Roljo and two men who have remained silent until now argue that this is not within their field of operations, so that point fizzles out. Those two men are MZ councillors and they now seek to recruit the

Consumers' Association for their case. One of them, Mr Hadžić, the president of the MZ council, starts:

> We as MZ can't do anything, we're between citizens and the municipality, we can't do anything about this, but with you we can. We have all the paperwork, we have data on these things, we know there have been pilot projects to have people pay actual consumption, not more. But the meters were taken away again because they [the suppliers] realised it didn't pay off.

The other MZ councillor points to the problem of people being billed for years during which they did not live in the flat. This is a reference mainly to temporary wartime and postwar occupation of flats by others, whose unpaid bills were passed on. Mr Hadžić then says:

> We don't need lone wolves [*slobodni strijelci*]. We must work together on those things, we have MZs for that. We should collaborate, we from the MZ, citizens, and you from the Consumers' Association. But this is also a problem, and we have to, people complain, and they're right, but when we say, okay let's try and do something about it together, then they won't.

People nod. Someone murmurs: 'Nobody is willing, nobody is willing'. Mr Hadžić argues that problems with maintenance also emerge because of non-payment: 'If 50 per cent of people don't pay, how can it work?' At this point, the moustached man launches into a long story of his decade-long court proceedings about heating bills. The MZ councillors note his contact details. There is also an agreement that it would be good to have a meeting with the MZ, the Consumers' Association, 'as many citizens as possible' and all the *upravitelji*. This is the last I hear of it. Yet it was certainly not the last I heard about building maintenance and utilities.

Like in the realm of city transport, the dynamics on this meeting on 'Communal Problems and Ways to Solve Them', targeting, as its poster said, 'citizens-consumers', indicate unsystematic juxtapositions of public service, private enterprise and humanitarian aid. Continuing my exploration of the relationship between gridding and yearnings for 'normal lives', I now focus on emic Dobrinja political pathologies – 'studies of suffering' that were at once 'accounts of experience'. I use episodes of engagement with building maintenance and utilities in Dobrinja to address what emerged from people's reasonings as the master grid – the state. Such reasonings tended to concentrate on symptoms, which, I have argued, together with the emic diagnoses that congeal around them, emerge as useful focal points to describe the affliction I call Daytonitis. This chapter, then, traces a first constitutional symptom – a generic affliction: the 'lack of a system'. Chapter 5 deals with a second one.

Who Drinks and Who Pays?

While at the meeting on 'Communal Problems and Ways to Solve Them' he called for concerted action within the appropriate institutions and deplored irresponsible non-payers, on many other occasions MZ president Mr Hadžić expressed his exasperation at the lack of an appropriately working 'system'. At one of the council meetings, where he had acted gruffly towards me, I was surprised, for he was otherwise a jovial man. Afterwards, he put his arm around my shoulders, invited me for coffee and apologised, putting it down to frustration with the ongoing problems he was facing. Not specifying whether these concerned the MZ or other troubles – he was unemployed and aspiring to an electable place to become a municipality councillor – a concise explanation was deemed to suffice: 'You have to understand', he said, 'there is no functioning state here'.

I propose to explore this in line with Mitchell's notion of the 'state effect'. Inspired by Foucault, Mitchell has argued that we should conceive of the state as a 'structural effect. That is to say, we should examine it not as an actual structure, but as the powerful, apparently metaphysical effect of practices that makes such structures appear to exist' (Mitchell 1999: 89). As we saw, Ferguson and Gupta (2002) elaborate on this proposal, arguing that the spatialisation of states hinges upon two central principles: 'verticality' and 'encompassment'. From this perspective, the state exists as a structural effect to the extent to which metaphors of verticality and encompassment are materialised in institutional practices and in infrastructure (Harvey 2005; Trouillot 2001).[2] 'Vertical encompassment', then, is coproduced through a myriad of practices and people's investments in them (Navaro-Yashin 2002; Nuijten 2003; Obeid 2010; Radcliffe 2001; Reeves 2011). Through the example of the 'staircase schools', chapter 3 described wartime collective, self-organised efforts for upward and outward gridding, ultimately entailing an investment in RBiH state making. A decade and a half after the end of the war, many of my interlocutors, now citizens of Dayton BiH, recalled such efforts with a combined sense of achievement and regret at their fizzling out. Their diagnosis of Daytonitis pointed to the lack of gridding, and indeed to the 'lack of a system', as a key symptom.

My analysis differs from most other studies of the production of a state effect in two ways. Firstly, while often reluctant to locate any intentional action in state institutions, most authors focus on top-down attempts to materialise the state as a structural effect. They zoom in, for example, on disciplining technologies (inspired by Foucault, e.g., 1991), on the pursuit of legibility (inspired by Scott 1998) or on modes of interpellation (inspired by Althusser 1971). In contrast, I approach the topic from the perspective of everyday concerns of those who would be its subjects and *their* pursuit of discipline, legibility and interpellation. I ask how such 'grid desire' calls forth the state as a structural effect. Secondly, where the state effect is often studied in terms of its successful reproduction through, and impact on, everyday practice, my Dobrinja research confronted me with a situation where the state was not judged to succeed in conjuring up vertical encompassment to the degree that my interlocutors desired.

The elusiveness of a state effect in Dayton BiH pervaded people's reasonings. An explicit example was provided by Mrs Renata Rihter, an experienced professional in social work, overseeing, amongst others, its Dobrinja branch.

> The main problem here is unemployment and a non-ordered system [*neuređeni sistem*]. It has never been tougher to be a social worker. We're, like, torn [*razapeti*] between the state and people. And whatever doesn't function, give it to the social worker to solve … You know, here no system functions, everything is upside-down.

> **Q: Have things improved compared to just after the war?**

> Well, that depends, for some people yes, and for some no. Some who had nothing are now rich, and vice versa. As I say, now the biggest problem are people who *are* able to work! Before we could help people to find employment, to solve their housing needs. Now, we can't do anything like that and this will last as long as the main problems aren't solved. The state needs to be systemically brought in order. First we have to bring down those thieves up there, then open jobs [*radna mjesta*]. In order to do our work effectively, we need a population census, we need to determine a poverty line, the number of pensioners.

In a separate conversation, her colleague, Mrs Valida Jahić, of the Dobrinja Centre for Social Work, argued along similar lines:

> Of course nothing can be solved in the current situation as long as ours up there [*oni naši gore*] don't know how to communicate. We must bring the state in order, it has to be a lawful and economic state [*pravna i ekonomska država*]. But it is not well ordered [*uređena*]. That is the problem, as long as that is not done … .

Mr Elvir Kahriman, a young schoolteacher who had come to Sarajevo from a small town as a student and served in the army while working in the Dobrinja staircase schools, said: 'In Europe, in the west, things there aren't great either, but it has a system. You see, we don't. We don't have a system, for anything. And we need it for everything. We have good people but we have no system'.

Unsurprisingly, the detection of the 'lack of a system' as a constitutional symptom was particularly explicitly and coherently articulated by people with a professional stake in disciplinary state institutions, whether pastoral or administrative. But MZ councillors, social workers and teachers only verbalised more clearly what many others evoked in vaguer terms. I uncovered a widely shared diagnosis around the symptom of a lack of an ordering framework (see also Kurtović 2012: 128–39). Exasperation was often expressed in the saying *ovdje se ne zna ko pije i ko plaća* [here, it's not known who drinks and who pays]. The missing dimension was referred to as *sistem* [system] and very frequently in terms of statecraft: *uređena država* [ordered, orderly state], *funkcionalna država* [functional, functioning state], *pravna država* [state with rule of law], or simply *država* [state]. Amongst those who remembered the prewar period, such statements of the 'ought' often compared the 'is' with the 'was' of remembered former 'normal lives'. People exclaimed that current problems would have been unthinkable *kad je bilo države* [when there was a state] or even *kad smo bili država* [when we were a state]. Then, they argued, like Mrs Rihter, even if things had not been perfect, there had been a system.

I was thus confronted with a barrage of language of stateness in cafés, at the barber's and in trolleybuses. The work of Bourdieu provides useful tools to analyse this. Conceiving of statecraft as a process of 'concentration', Bourdieu stresses 'doxic submission': 'the state has imposed the very cognitive structure through which it is perceived', involving both reasoned and 'immediate, prereflexive, corporeal submission' to its schemata of 'vision and division' (1999: 69–70). Exploring the figure of the state in Serbia in the 2000s in Bourdieusian terms, Spasić and Birešev (2012) note that it spontaneously emerged as a key theme in their focus group discussions even though facilitators never introduced it as a topic. Asked about values and classifications, participants continually positioned themselves with regard to the state in deeply paradoxical ways. On the one hand, they projected a very negative picture of the 'actually existing state', which served as a master explanation for all that was wrong in Serbia, including undesirable values amongst their co-citizens. On the other hand, they evoked what the authors call 'the State with a big S' – the state as it ought to be – as the source of any possible remedy (see also Spasić 2013: 132–40).

On many counts, my Dobrinja research yielded similar results: the state was ever present as a theme and many of the same paradoxes ran through its evocation. In this chapter, I analyse how, in Dobrinja, such paradoxes emerged as part of diagnoses of the affliction of Day-tonitis, that is, in articulation with Dayton BiH's specific geopolitical position in a world structured around the '"fantasy" of state-centric-ity' (Navaro-Yashin 2003: 114). First I relate this back to my analytical distinction between statecraft in BiH and the statehood of BiH.

All Roads Lead to Dayton

In Mrs Jahić's comment that nothing could improve as long as 'ours up there don't know how to communicate', like in many mundane statements of exasperation with the 'lack of a system', the specific Dayton political anatomy of the postwar BiH polity is a key referent. In the Dayton BiH Meantime, all roads tended to lead to Dayton, and they were very short roads indeed: from maintenance bills or social work, they often arrived at what I call the statehood of BiH in very few steps. Parliamentary debates about reforms of what everyone agreed was a dysfunctional BiH state resulted in a succession of stalemates (Bougarel 2005). All major political parties in BiH presented themselves to their target electorate as holding out for grand solutions that would tilt statehood in their favour. This explains, for example, how, in 2011, BiH was one of only a handful of the world's states to not fulfil Mrs Rihter's (and Eurostat's) demand for a population and household census. Major Sarajevo-based parties called for some centralisation of BiH, whereas those based in Banja Luka (Republika Srpska) and Croatian-dominated western Mostar argued for further decentralisation along national lines. The symmetry in these clashes of maximalist posturing was therefore not perfect: every failure to reach a compromise on reforms of BiH statehood was a confirmation of what the latter parties wished to prove, namely that BiH could not work anyway. Unsurprisingly, every major party in BiH blamed its opponents for unreasonably obstructing any agreement.

This is an important dimension of the background against which we must understand Dobrinjci's tendency to identify the 'lack of a system' as a constitutional symptom of Daytonitis. On the whole, their wartime commitment to BiH statehood was still in place. Yet when the statehood of BiH emerged as a concern, it was often as an implication rather than as a starting point. This was due to the fact that evocations of the 'lack of a system' – a concern with statecraft in BiH – were not immune from the tendency that all roads lead to Dayton. Let us look at this pattern a little closer. Asked what she would do if she had the power to make things better, architect Mrs Nermina Kudo, married mother of two, said:

> First I would abolish Republika Srpska and I would make a normal state. And all those who don't love this state, let them go where they love it. Let Dodik [then prime minister of Republika Srpska, later president] go, let him go where they love him. You don't respect the state, well how will you live in that state? How will you then expect that that state gives you something?

Only on very few occasions did my interlocutors call for abolishing Republika Srpska. Sure, I believe that, if the question was raised in this manner, many other Dobrinjci would also prefer a unitary BiH over the Dayton reward of the violence that kept them under siege for almost four years precisely in order to establish a 'Serbian Republic' on their doorstep. Moreover, Dodik himself regularly called for, and announced, an independent Republika Srpska, and thus the abolishment of BiH. He confidently counted on majority support for this within this entity – and he might well be right, since many of those who were likely to be against it had been killed or expelled from that territory in a 1992–95 military campaign designed precisely to create this Serbian polity. Yet when Mrs Kudo criticised the anti-BiH position of the political elite of Republika Srpska, she did so in the name of the need for a 'normal state'. In Serbian and Croatian nationalist discourses in and outside of BiH, such reasonings were often rejected on the assumption that Sarajevan Bosniaks – which to them means virtually all Sarajevans – were cunning hypocrites playing for the foreign gallery. 'Civic' evocations of BiH statehood were then dismissed as disguised nationalism in which 'the Bosniaks', the largest 'constituent people', sought to capture the state and turn it into an Islamic-Bosniak polity. Even if most Bosniak-nationalist discourse did include a pro-BiH stance, my research disproves this idea that, if we scratch hard enough, we find Bosniak nationalism under the surface of all pro-BiH discourse. Granted, one could argue that my Dobrinja interlocutors did not phrase their concerns in terms of Bosniakness because the national order of things permeated the Dayton BiH to such an extent it did not need to be mentioned. Explicit declarations of civic loyalty to

BiH or concerns with the functionality of statecraft in the country phrased as oblivious to nationality questions could then be seen as a doxic endorsement of incorporative Bosniak-cum-Bosnian nationalism. In Dayton BiH, as elsewhere, most people acknowledged the nationalism of others more readily than their own (e.g , Kolind 2008: 128), and such interpretations can therefore not be simply dismissed. Yet nor can they simply be accepted, even if we approach my Dobrinja findings in the light of questions of the statehood of BiH: when my interlocutors did provide reflexive, explicit commentary on nationality issues, they almost always criticised their centrality in the Dayton setup.

Take Mr Sead Fazlagić, married with two adult sons, and professionally active in SDP, then in opposition in cantonal and federal parliaments. He said:

> The biggest obstacle is this non-orderedness of the state we have [*ta naša neuredenost države*], which is called, you don't know what you are and who you are. Everyone is screaming something: 'You're a state! You're not a state!' But in fact, time passes, it passes very quickly. We don't see things happen that could normally have happened, because they happened in the region. If you see they happened there, why can't they happen here [*kod nas*]? ... The other day I read that next year the Republic of Croatia plans the completion of the motorway to Ploče ... So you wonder, how did that happen so easily and quickly there [*kod njih*]. And we, around thirty kilometres [of motorway] and another three hundred to come we're nowhere [*pa nigdje nas*]! So what is this, people who used to live in the same country, speak the same language, whether called Croatian, or Serbian, or Bosnian, but we understand each other. There it's possible, and here it isn't. What is that? Do people there love their state more? Partly I am 100 per cent sure that that's the case, that there people love their state more'.

Mr Fazlagić also praised the national diversity of BiH's population as a plus and he constantly dismissed all three cleronationalist establishments as 'extremists'. Even amongst Dobrinjci who were religiously observant and/or SDA members, I found it rare to come across any explicit Bosniak nationalist positionings. Indeed, quite a few criticised those outright. In this regard, longstanding Dobrinjci might differ from many Bosnians, including in areas of the Federation inhabited by many people with 'Bosniak names'. For example, many spheres of life in towns in Central Bosnia (Kurtović 2012: 50–65) or in Mostar (e.g., Hromadžić 2012; Palmberger 2013) were ruled through institutionalised bargains between parties claiming to represent Bosniaks and Croats. In Sarajevo, far-reaching national homogenisation of the population – whether by ascription or self-identification – had reduced the frequency of everyday encounters with politicised national difference. This might have increased the tendency of yearnings for 'normal lives' in Dobrinja to focus on statecraft in BiH rather than on the statehood of BiH. Yet, as explained in the introduction, in contrast to the dominant approach in knowledge production about BiH, it is not my aim to pin down Dobrinja yearnings for a 'normal state' in terms of identification and BiH statehood. I believe that questions framed in this manner limit the reach of our understandings. Since all roads tend to lead to Dayton, it would certainly be possible to follow through many dimensions of yearnings for 'normal lives' along such roads. However, I purposively focus on the 'first degree' of the concerns with the state that I encountered. I foreground such reasonings about statecraft in BiH which, as explained, do not necessarily correlate with any particular take on disputes on the legitimacy of BiH's national–territorial anatomy. Anyone in BiH, regardless of their views on identitarian questions and the statehood of BiH, could be worried about the 'lack of a system', about unemployment, about corruption, and generally about what the state was doing and, especially, failing to do. Indeed, open questions in opinion polls show time and again that most people in BiH were indeed primarily worried about these things. Ethnographic and other qualitative studies in Republika Srpska (Brković 2012a) and in neighbouring Serbia (Greenberg 2010, 2011; Simić 2009; Spasić 2013) have highlighted very similar concerns.

In Dobrinja in 2008-10, this concern with statecraft was often articulated with an inclusive pro-BiH stance that was critical of all three cleronationalist structures. This was reflected in voting patterns.[3] Yet to the extent that the lives of Dobrinjci, like those of other people around the globe, shaped up around many practical routines, aspirations and yearnings that were largely oblivious to identitarian questions, I suggest that there is little value in trying to label these reasonings regarding 'normal lives' and statecraft as either nationalist or antinationalist. When Mr Fazlagić and Mrs Kudo spoke of 'those who did not love their state', their main concern was with the effective functioning of the state. This was true even for persons who did feel strongly about identitarian questions. To illustrate this, let us look at the account of a man who said that wartime losses had made national identification, including his own sense of belonging to the Bosniak nation, very important to him. Mr Emin Mujić, a 47-year-old electrician, lived in the *mahala*, a part of Dobrinja that consisted of private houses. He shared one of them with his wife, his son and his parents. Already before the war, SDA had organised armed units in the small mosque near his house. Now, Mr Mujić said, he felt deeply disillusioned by the futility of the war in which he had fought. He expressed support for BPS [Bosanskohercegovačka patriotska stranka, BiH Patriotic Party], which he, characteristically, referred to as 'Sefer's party', after its leader Sefer Halilović. Promoting a strongly unitarist pro-BiH line, this party was generally perceived as Bosniak nationalist too: 'Well, simply, Sefer inspires some trust in me. Since I am a former soldier [*borac*], that man was also active from the first day, he was commander of the Army. Compared to all those other politicians … I have most trust in Sefer, as a man and as a commander'. Yet, when asked what he would do if he had the power to intervene in BiH, Mr Mujić argued he would first 'try to abolish corruption, bribery, thievery', after which 'all the rest would end by itself'. Later, he called for a solution that would be attuned to 'Balkan people':

> Well, we are simply, people, Balkan people who need a boot, a strong hand, so, somebody must be found to lead this country, at least in the economic sense. Then I think that it would be better, but, like this, every street, every city, every one of those *županije*, listen, *županija*, which *županija*? *Kanton!*[4] All these, like, governments, politicians, they all look after their own interest … . I don't know, I only hope and I pray to God that the right person comes to, to rule this country. Not in the literal sense to rule, I mean, to lead the politics of this country, only that … I'd like it most of all if it would be a person of Serbian nationality, I'd vote for him tomorrow. Or Croatian, I'd vote for that too. So I wouldn't take into account that national structure, but I'd only look at that person's ability. Before the war I didn't pay attention to that either, who is Muslim, who is Croat, who is this or that. If he's a good politician, there you go, do it.

Like in the case of Mrs Kudo and Mr Fazlagić, I suggest that reducing Mr Mujić's insistence that his preference for a particular leader would not be nationally inflected to a Bosniak nationalist ruse would be an illegitimate imposition of Dayton 'trivision'.[5] Instead, I take seriously the fact that my interlocutors' yearnings for 'normal lives' systematically raised concerns about the state through prioritisation of what they saw as the urgent need for 'normal' statecraft.

How, then, did the Dayton political anatomy of BiH shape people's diagnoses of 'the lack of a system', from building maintenance to population census? I now disentangle two dimensions in emic diagnoses of Daytonitis congealing around this first constitutional symptom. One focuses on problematic values, and the other one, which I shall deal with first, on dispersion and on the excessive absence and presence of the state.

An Excessively Absent and Excessively Present State

In her critique of Scott's work, Li (2005) proposes a Foucaultian conception of statecraft in terms of an 'assemblage'. Such an assemblage, she says, is never fixed but may be stabilised into a discursive formation when elements become systematised and 'their discrepant origins submerged'; when there is transferability; when it is crystallised into institutions; and 'when it comes to inform individual behavior and to act as a grid for perception and evaluation' (ibid.: 386). While the figure of the state clearly did hold appeal for my interlocutors and did inform – as a set of Bourdieusian schemata – individual behaviour, in Dobrinja we can speak only of very limited stabilisation on the first three counts. Instead, dispersion and confusion were rife.

After a meeting in the premises of one of the Dobrinja MZs of a support group for recovering alcoholics, which had first served to bemoan the lack of proper treatment in the public health system and then to organise ways to raise money to attend a yearly regional meeting in Croatia, Mr Lazar Marjanović, its coordinator, told me:

> Before, you could go wherever you wanted. You could sleep in the forest, on the beach. Now, I can't even get any further than Croatia. Before, as they say, that horrible Yugoslavia, that was a state! That state showed concern [*ta država je vodila računa*]: health care, flats, employment.[6] There was treatment [for alcoholics], the state took care of that. But these ones now, they only think of themselves. They don't do anything. We have ten states, cantons, entities, and not one of them shows any concern [a *nijedna ne vodi računa*].

Instead of being 'embraced' by a state (Torpey 1998) that showed concern, Mr Marjanović thus raised a common worry that people had been abandoned, or, as the phrase goes, *prepušteni sami sebi* [left to their own devices]. We must therefore ask not only about 'sightings of the state' (Corbridge et al. 2005: 9), that is, about how the state 'comes into view' (ibid.: 7), but also about failed attempts, that is, about (mutual) 'non-sightings'. There is nothing particularly Dayton about this; ethnographers have encountered such complaints about the state 'not showing any concern (anymore)' across postsocialist Europe (e.g., Bridger and Pine 1997) and elsewhere. Nuijten (2003), for example, shows how a group of Mexican peasants wishing to gain control over land assigned to their *ejido* in a land reform programme but usurped by private owners, continually appealed to the state – represented by the same institutions that had failed to fulfil their hopes for over fifty years. She suggests we conceive of the state as a 'hope-generating machine', whereby disparate state practices are given coherence by the hopes people invest in them.

Mr Marjanović's diagnosis was very similar to the one by social worker Mrs Rihter, but from the perspective of a 'client'. Yet, like the meeting on 'Communal Problems and Ways to Solve Them', and like Mr Mujić's complaint above, he also alerted me to the fact that the space where he felt the state should be was in fact extremely crowded – in his words, there were no less than 'ten states'. The problem, then, was not simply that the state was uninterested and uncaring. Sure, a common saying goes: *Tito je krao al' je dao; ovi kradu al' ne dadu* [Tito stole, but he gave too; these ones steal but don't give], yet if my interlocutors unanimously detected the 'lack of a system' as a constitutional symptom of Daytonitis, all these diagnoses show that, in contrast to Nuijten's findings in Mexico, and Spasić and Birešev's in Serbia, Dobrinjci's dissatisfaction with the 'actually existing' Dayton BiH state was augmented by its structural dispersion. When people did actually wish to mobilise state mechanisms to solve certain problems, it was unclear where in its labyrinthine structure particular 'gridding' capacities were located. This dispersion itself emerged, again and again, as a symptom of Daytonitis. The mantle of the state was claimed by a myriad of institutions, leaving people without a clear address for their appeals.

Alongside city transport, building maintenance and infrastructural repair were frequent agenda items on MZ council meetings. In casual conversations between neighbours they often arose as points of dissatisfaction too. As we saw in the discussion that interrupted Professor Roljo's 'lecture' above, many did not differentiate between such issues and utility bills. The continued use of Yugoslav self-management terminology facilitated this: many people still referred to the monthly maintenance rates as *komunalije* [communals], although residents of a particular 'entrance' now chose between different for-profit *upravitelji* for the maintenance of their shared spaces. Like before, they elected a representative: usually a pensioner who accepted to do it because no one else would. Even in organs of local government themselves there was no clarity on where one should turn for solutions. At one MZ council meeting in Dobrinja, Mrs Elvedina Mehmedić, a middle-aged lady, brought up the issue of two young people, whom she referred to as children, living in a devastated flat:

> I've talked about this before, I know you've heard it before, but I won't stop until something is done. On the top floor of my building there are two children. They're left without both parents ... The situation in their flat is dreadful, catastrophic. Terrible leaks, it's not fit for life [*nije za život*]. This is scandalous.

They're immediately under the roof. This is war damage, something has to be done about it. When I think about those children, I shudder. How is it possible that in eight years that roof has not been fixed? It's war damage, the state must repair it, and these kids live there, no parents, they're really polite, but they're in a terrible … I speak as a mother here, you know that my husband was killed in the war, that I have two children and that I'm raising them alone. But my children have me to protect them! And they have no one!

Speaking ever louder and addressing the (female) MZ secretary, Mrs Mehmedić repeated her story in several versions. Finally, Mr Edo Kovač, the MZ president, intervened and said 'Okay, we had some emotion now …' Mrs Mehmedić cut in: 'yes, emotions! I'm a mother. Where did all those enormous amounts of money for reconstruction go? They did repair *some* people's roofs! But not their roof, not for eight years. It's not true that there is no money, but someone ate it'. President Kovač drily replied: 'This is the job of the canton, they have a commission for this. There is only so much money and the commission makes assessments. And if they didn't get anything, that means it didn't pass at the commission. We can't do anything about that'.

At the same meeting, Mr Mladen Stanić, a carefully dressed middle-aged man, raised a planning issue regarding the space in front of his shop. This had been an ongoing story for years and he and Mr Kovač had tried to find solutions in all kinds of ways. A particular problem was that two similarly named offices existed in the municipal and in the cantonal administration – dominated, at that time, by two different political parties. These offices alternately ignored and disputed each other's legitimacy. The case remained unsolved on this MZ meeting too and Mr Stanić left frustrated.

Likewise, at a council meeting of another MZ, a letter had arrived from Canton Sarajevo stating the responsibilities of the MZ with regard to fire protection. President Mr Hadžić pointed out they used to have high-quality equipment before the war. It had all been destroyed. Some time ago, they had received fifty-eight fire extinguishers as a humanitarian donation, which was insufficient according to cantonal regulations. A councillor angrily said they should reject responsibility 'as long as the state, that is, as long as someone doesn't sort this out'. One councillor interrupted, 'Who?' Another one hesitatingly suggested, 'Well, the canton'. But no one was quite certain. In any case, it was agreed that the MZ would not accept responsibility before equipment was secured and Mr Hadžić dictated a letter addressed to the cantonal authorities to that effect. I heard no more of it.

If MZ councillors themselves were often unsure about the appropriate addressee for complaints and requests, other citizens found this even more difficult. In my observations in the MZ secretariats, it was common for people to be told by the secretary that they had come to the wrong address, sometimes, but not always, with instructions of where to go next. This, of course, is a classic pattern in bureaucratic institutions across the globe (Auyero 2012) – and one that structures rather a lot of my own physical or virtual wanderings around my university in Britain. Yet my research alerted me to its specific shape in Dayton BiH. In everyday interactions in Dobrinja, but also in those within the bodies of local administration, far-reaching confusion reigned about where and who the state currently was. The discussions on MZ councils show that the elusiveness of a state effect was certainly not due to a lack of institutions. In fact, in Dayton BiH, institutional state making was positively effervescent. Dobrinja was no longer an administrative unit, as it had been during the war. It consisted of four MZs, all part of the municipality of Novi grad, itself part of the (governmentally insignificant) City of Sarajevo, which was part of Canton Sarajevo, one of the ten cantons of the Federation. Recall that the 'Federation' does not refer to the BiH-wide institutions, but to one of the two 'entities' making up BiH, together with the small district of Brčko. Estimated to count under four million inhabitants, during my research the country had five presidents, fourteen executive governments with over one hundred and forty ministers, and fourteen legislative assemblies with hundreds of delegates. The two entities each had their own president, their own parliament and their own executive, consisting of over a dozen ministers each. The ten cantons in the Federation all had their own legislative assemblies and executives consisting of up to a dozen ministers. Four of those cantons had less than one hundred thousand inhabitants, of which two had less than fifty thousand. In the BiH institutions, usually referred to as 'state institutions' by those who favoured BiH statehood, and as 'common institutions' [*zajedničke institucije*] by those who rejected it, there was a legislative assembly, a Council of Ministers, and a Presidency with three members – one for each of the 'constituent peoples'. To this we must add the institutions of Brčko district. Judicial institutions were also dispersed across entities, the district and, within the Federation, across cantons. This list does not include municipal organs, local communes (MZs) or in-country and external institutions of foreign supervision.

During the 'war' between GRAS and Centrotrans detailed in chapter 2, the GRAS accusation that Centrotrans bypassed the canton to address 'the top of the state' when it turned to the BiH ministry shows that an expectation of vertical encompassment was still at

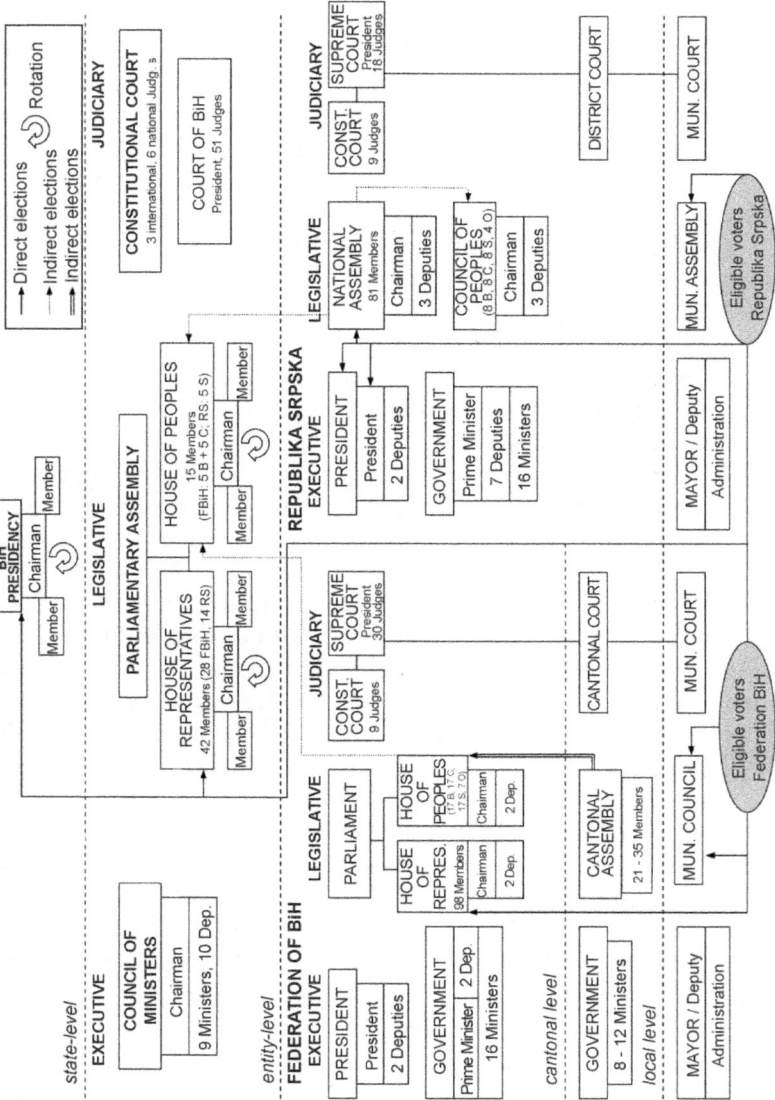

FIGURE 4.2. Organigram of Dayton BiH government institutions (reproduced with kind permission from Gavrić, Banović and Barreiro 2013: 116–17). Note that this diagram only includes one visual representation of the cantonal organs (there are in fact ten cantons) and two of the municipal ones (of which there are 137). Local communes (MZs) are not included. The District of Brčko, with its separate structures of government, is also left out, as are the organs of foreign supervision. Even so, in the original publication the authors saw themselves forced to spread the diagram over two pages.

work in this labyrinth. Unspecified evocations of verticality were also prominent in verbal references to 'up there' and in upward gestures when speaking of the state. Some people, for example, called for a clean up of BiH that would start 'from the top' because 'a fish smells from the head' [*riba smrdi od glave*]. Yet in Dayton BiH, 'the top' or 'the head' was not unambiguously related to any particular site of administration, let alone to the central institutions of the BiH state. Therefore, when emic diagnoses and social scientific writings (including some of my own) refer to those sites as municipal, cantonal, entity and state 'levels', this is in fact problematic. Given the distribution of budgets and agentive capacities across them, such an assumption of pyramidical vertical encompassment fails to reflect the reality of Dayton BiH. It conveys neither the relative capacity to enforce policies in different institutions, nor the way in which my interlocutors encountered the state in their everyday lives. And this is why I have waited until this point to offer an organigram of government institutions in BiH.

Dobrinjci thus encountered statecraft through a variety of juxtaposed and competing institutionalised practices. They found it difficult – as I did – to locate these practices in specific institutions, but they engaged with them in daily routines. The buses or trolleybuses they rode – mostly humanitarian donations – were, like the bus stops and the ticketing system, managed by GRAS, a cantonal institution. Inter-entity transport was governed by one of the ministries that formed the BiH Council of Ministers. The education of most Dobrinja children was governed by Canton Sarajevo and the Federation, but some went to school in Republika Srpska. All schools in Dobrinja were (re)built with foreign aid, and education was subject to monitoring by supra-state agencies. Water and gas supply was run by cantonal institutions; electricity and telephone by firms owned 90 per cent by the Federation. In Dobrinja, most utility infrastructure had been constructed before the war from taxes and salary contributions. Sarajevogas, for example, was founded in 1975 as part of a major ecological policy overhaul in a heavily polluted Sarajevo, and increased its numbers of households/users sixfold during war, largely through humanitarian funding. Nowadays, the categorisation of citizens for welfare benefits, preferential access to housing or credit was governed by municipal, cantonal and federal authorities. With some small exceptions, policing was dispersed too, as was health care. IDs were standardised but issued by cantonal institutions in the Federation and by organs of Republika Srpska. Only very few dimensions of government were uniform BiH-wide. Domestically, real muscle

FIGURE 4.3. One of Dobrinja's boilers for collective heating (photo by Vanja Čelebičić, 2014)

lay in strongly centralised Republika Srpska institutions, and, within the Federation, mostly in cantonal ones. As we saw, it was predominantly in the latter institutions and in municipal ones that Dobrinjci sought solutions for their everyday problems.

As if the Dayton BiH organigram was not complicated enough, two additional paradoxes contributed to the elusiveness of a BiH state effect: first, the foreign intervention in Dayton BiH and, second, reconfigurations of state provision. Let us briefly address them in turn.

Firstly, people in Dayton BiH experienced globalising tendencies in relation to state formation particularly acutely. The U.S. government-brokered Dayton Agreement cemented challenges to BiH statehood by asymmetric projects of state formation from below, yet it also enforced the production of a state effect as a key condition for BiH's recognition in the global state system (Meyer 1999).[7] As we have seen in discussions of city transport and building maintenance, in a partial 'redeployment' of statecraft (Trouillot 2001: 132), claims to vertical encompassment were inflected by many institutions such as NGOs, the UN, the IMF and the in-country foreign supervision organs. Particularly important was OHR (Office of the High Representative), the formal Sarajevo-based embodiment of the so-called 'international community'. Governed by a Peace Implementation Council, in principle OHR presided over the teeming institutional landscape of Dayton BiH as a final arbiter. To implement the civilian dimension of the Dayton Agreement, it could overrule domestic institutions, for example to force through laws and to sack elected officials. Yet while OHR was officially committed to safeguarding the existence of an internationally recognised BiH – its statehood – it did not facilitate the strengthening of a state effect in the statecraft terms of what my Dobrinja interlocutors considered to be a 'normal state'. The anatomy of the BiH state, so the OHR mantra went, should be reformed in a compromise between domestic politicians. Yet such a compromise was extremely unlikely because political representation was structurally organised around national representation with veto powers in the name of the three 'constituent peoples' and of the entities. During my research, OHR did not use its intervening powers in any publicly visible ways. Moreover, the grounds on which it could do so would be to ensure respect for the Dayton constitution, which, according to most Dobrinjci, was itself key to BiH's dysfunctionality and abnormality. As a result, everyone found fault with the foreign intervention (see Delpla 2010; Gilbert 2012). Particularly in Republika Srpska and in Western Herzegovina, its agencies were condemned for insisting on the production of a BiH state effect. In contrast, those who expressed loyalty to BiH, like in Dobrinja, resented their lack of muscular action to establish that state effect.

A second paradox that contributed to the elusiveness of a state effect in Dayton BiH concerns the reconfiguration of public provision. Some interventions by OHR and by IMF, on whose loans BiH became increasingly dependent over the years, reflected a neoliberal commitment to privatisation, and the reduction of welfare provisions in particular. The 'reforms' through which this was to be achieved often involved the self-severing of 'the left hand of the state' – 'the trace, within the state, of the social struggles of the past' (Bourdieu 1998: 9). This left hand was embodied in the remnants of Yugoslav socialist policies of employment, accommodation, health care, education, transport and so on. Some of those disappeared entirely, others persisted only as hollow shells, yet many others still (e.g., allowances, some accommodation and provision entitlements) had been transmuted through an emphasis on war-related categories (veterans, war widows, etc.). Managed by a bewildering array of state agencies, these important forms of entitlement and allocation involved vast assemblages of clientelism, particularly through political parties. All this renders blanket qualifications of Dayton BiH statecraft as 'neoliberal' problematic: it does not correspond to understandings of neoliberalism either as a straightforward rollback of the state or as a reassembling of welfare and punitive mechanisms. Clearly, BiH today cannot be understood without taking into account its embedding in global neoliberalising developments, but, as I explain in chapter 6, the severance and transformation of the state's 'left hand' as well as the selective privatisation of socially owned resources were dimensions of broader dynamics of dispossession and domination that in fact entailed the proliferation of some state activities for the benefit of a ruling caste (see Kalb 2012). Here I return to the question of a 'system'. Mr Mujić, Mr Marjanović and Mrs Mehmedić did not just resent the fact that politicians 'stole without giving anything back'. Despite a large state apparatus in Dayton BiH (the country's sprawling administration was said to eat up over 60 per cent of the budget), they complained that there was no agency doing the organising and the planning that they felt should be done in a systematic, orderly manner. To them, way too much statecraft was going on but it was of the wrong kind, perpetuating the elusiveness of a state effect.

Institutional dispersion, then, made the state seem simultaneously excessively present and absent, and Dobrinja diagnoses saw incompetent, cynical and thieving politicians as taking advantage of this institutional dispersion. An additional factor of resentment amongst Dobrinjci was directly concerned with the statehood dimension. What little effective state effect they discerned certainly did not correspond to the RBiH state that, as we saw in chapter 3, had been projected as the arch of vertical encompassment of their wartime upward and outward griddings. This feeling that the political anatomy of Dayton BiH rendered war sacrifices futile was widespread in Sarajevo (see Sorabji 2006: 8). It was replicated in a sense of being 'left to one's own devices' on a larger scale: many felt abandoned not only by domestic politicians but by 'the world'. As MZ president Mr Hadžić kept on pointing out to me, this referred predominantly to 'my' western governments, who had failed to prevent their wartime suffering at the hands of Serbian nationalist forces and who now guaranteed the Dayton consolidation of the war's results while also keeping BiH confined to the EU's 'immediate outside'.

Here we see once again how a recalled 'was' (Yugoslav BiH) informed readings of an unsatisfactory 'is' (Dayton BiH) in desires for an 'ought', i.e., a 'normal state'. Cast against the expansive hegemony project of the SFRY developmentalist welfare state, people in Dobrinja resented the selective hegemony project to which they were now subjected on different scales (Smith 2011). They were dissatisfied with the limited and transformed reach of BiH left-hand statecraft, with its frail and disputed statehood, and with its adverse and unequal incorporation in EU and global economic and political constellations. To recall a phrase from chapter 1, this is the particular experiential configuration in which one could simultaneously feel that 'nobody fucks us five per cent' [*niko nas ne jebe pet posto*] and that 'everyone fucks us' [*svi nas jebu*].

'Our People', 'Messed-up Values' and Immaturity

Dobrinja diagnoses of Daytonitis that revolved around the detection of a 'lack of a system' and which, in effect, lamented the misfortune of living in a Dayton BiH misgoverned by an array of domestic and foreign institutions, existed in mutual constitution with a value-focused dimension. This is what we turn to now.

At the meeting on 'Communal Problems and Ways to Solve Them', several attendees noted the problem of non-payment. Monthly bills for the maintenance of shared spaces averaged between 10 and 20

KM, but, based on information gathered from house representatives across Dobrinja, I estimate that less than half of all households paid regularly and that many did not pay at all. Mrs Meliha Hodžić, a seamstress in her mid fifties, married mother of two, had recently resigned as house representative. She felt the payment system left much to be desired because many people had never learned the new arrangements:

> People know that someone needs to repair things. Someone. Who is that someone? Especially if they don't pay, who is that someone? No one. On the whole, our roof is falling apart. The neighbour will soon have to swim. No one takes any notice. And no one will pay. When the sewage gets blocked, the *upravitelj* will unblock it. They won't pay. Because people, that's a mistake by the state, if people had paid for their flats [with money instead of 'certificates'], the building would flourish. But because they got some papers, and they have no clue what those papers are, and by God nor do those in the government, so nobody takes care of anything.

Mrs Fejzić, a widowed retired teacher, detailed a recent conflict in which her house representative had also resigned because some residents refused to pay. So whenever they approached their *upravitelj*, Mrs Fejzić explained, they were told, 'You are in debt'. Half of them paid regularly, she claimed, and the other half never paid. This was seconded by Ms Musić, a web developer in her mid thirties, who said she regularly paid her contributions: 'Those who pay, pay everything. Those who don't, don't pay anything'. Mr Tahirović, an electrotechnician in his mid forties, married father of one child, admitted to being a non-payer. Collectively, the residents of his entrance owed several tens of thousands of marks to the *upravitelj*.

> Rarely, I pay very rarely. … I'm of the opinion that it's a lot, that these are very high rates, in light of what they do, what they maintain. For example, in my building, concretely, the intercom doesn't work, they came down to intervene two times and said 'That's a serious defect, we can't repair it'. That provoked me.

High rates and bad services were the most frequently cited arguments to justify non-payment of maintenance bills. Utility bills did not fare much better. Most people did their best to pay phone and electricity bills monthly – they knew services would promptly be disconnected otherwise, and a reconnection fee would follow – but on others many had accumulated debts. This situation was considered to be in sharp contrast with socialist times. Mr Mile Stevanović, who had served as a house representative ever since he moved into a Dobrinja flat in 1979 said:

Today it's very difficult. Then it wasn't. Then, there was another sense of responsibility, morality. People were, well, they were moral, they didn't reject those comm… , those, well, what shall I call them, those requirements that emerged from common life, common residence and so on. So they accepted it, payments for electricity. . . I read the amount of consumption and we paid that sum. I divided the consumption of the staircase by the number of residents. Then, from every resident, that is, from every holder of tenancy rights, how many [household] members, they pay that much for water, that much for electricity and so on. It was okay [*u redu*, litt. in order], there were no problems. It was better organised than now, better organised [*urednije*, litt. more ordered].

To my probing question as to whether everybody had really always paid, Mr Stevanović answered:

Well it happened, let's say, that someone didn't respect, well, then we went to talk to them, a bit of pressure, a bit of discussion about it, and then … But on the whole I can say it was far [pause] better than now, far better. Because there were few people who didn't respect that, [pause] very few, so it was easy to discuss it with them. However, today many people don't pay anything. They won't pay water, they won't pay electricity. No, electricity they have to pay, because they disconnect, but they don't pay water, heating, and so … .

Mr Stevanović's diagnosis of the non-payment problem thus combined two types of factors: on the one hand, the level of order and the threat of disconnection, and on the other hand a sense of responsibility, morality and respect. On both counts, he found the present situation wanting. This linking up of structural failure with moral failure was extremely common in Dobrinja.

Minutes after sketching out the problems of unemployment and the 'non-ordered system', social worker Mrs Rihter, cited above, expanded by lamenting the 'messed-up values' [*poremećene vrijednosti*] that reigned in society.[8] A core reason for the current state of affairs, she said, was a near universal deterioration in respect, work ethic, care and solidarity. Likewise, after denouncing the current lack of 'order', her colleague Mrs Jahić proceeded to a moral evaluation. In less general terms, she lamented the 'messed-up values' she said she had to face on a daily basis in Dobrinja. She attributed this to rural newcomers, providing a range of examples of 'uncultured behaviour', including littering, poor greeting manners, but also hanging out washing and shaking out breadcrumbs in what were, to her, inappropriate ways. Here, Mrs Jahić echoed a view shared by a broader range of self-proclaimed 'urban' Dobrinja residents, who tended to socialise primarily amongst themselves. Having evoked motorways and love for state in Croatia, Mr Fazlagić, for example, proceeded to refer to demographic changes in BiH as an explanation for the poor resonance of 'democratic values'. Although 'he had nothing against newcomers', he said, it would be unrealistic 'to expect from people who saw a tram for the first time when they came to Sarajevo, that they will think in the way you think'. After his declaration that BiH had 'good people but no system', teacher Mr Kahriman, who had quite possibly seen his first tram when he moved to Sarajevo as a student, commented, 'Our people have lost all values, values here are completely messed up'. His young colleague Aida also mentioned 'messed-up values', expressing some hope that the young people she taught, who had not yet been inculcated with those values, had the capacity to 'change the world'. This need to give a chance to a new generation, relatively unsoiled by war, was highlighted by many of my interlocutors (cf. Greenberg 2010). Yet there were also frequent expressions of despair about current youth, blaming this precisely on the fact that they had never known anything but Dayton BiH (see also Čelebičić 2013). In any case, what prevailed in Dobrinja was a combined diagnosis of Dayton BiH as suffering of structural and moral failure. If specified, this was sometimes illustrated with references to the behaviour of particular categories of co-citizens. Occasionally people included themselves too. Yet most frequently, like Mr Kahriman, people made sweeping statements on moral disintegration as a brake on improvement (Bartulović 2013; Henig 2012).

Again, it is unsurprising that politicians, and especially 'pastoral' state agents such as social workers or teachers, linked 'messed-up values' to the lack of an 'ordered system'. It fits their job description and it is in their interest to see a strong system in terms of values rather than, say, domination. Yet, again, while such professionals provided the most elaborated and eloquent versions of this linking, they were far from the only ones to do so. Some people made the connection only implicitly. Take Saliha, who ran a Dobrinja kiosk. A war-widowed mother of four adult daughters, she regularly told me about the 'messed-up values' that reigned in BiH. Referring to the stabbing of a teenager on a tram, to junkies in staircases and to a bomb thrown at a Dobrinja bus stop, she painted a dark picture of 'society'. Saliha did not criticise any politician or party in particular, nor did she, as so many others, blame 'politics' on the whole. Instead she expressed general moral worry: 'Values are totally messed-up. This society is totally rotten. The worst has come to float on top. There have never been so many rich people in Bosnia and there has never been so much poverty. Before, we were the golden medium, but now … .'

It was through reference to life in Yugoslav BiH, then, that Saliha evoked structural factors too, specifically criticising rising social inequality and, on other occasions, national–religious exclusivism. Other particularly common evocations of 'messed-up values' concerned the relation between honest work and reward, and between parenting and youth violence. Like Saliha, Mrs Hodžić targeted fellow citizens more than politicians. As we saw in chapter 3, this seamstress refuted the dominant story of exemplary solidarity during war, although she proudly documented her wartime engagements in Dobrinja self-organisation. Asked what she would change if she was in a position of influence, Mrs Hodžić launched into a tirade:

> Change? Discipline! The discipline of Germany. And rewards within that discipline. You go, you don't buy a ticket in Germany, or they see, you threw rubbish in the wrong container, you get a fine of 50 Marks. Because your neighbour filmed you on his mobile phone, reported you. He is not a snitch, he loves his state. ... Here, they kick stuff across the street, unculturedness on the street, in the shop, wherever you go. Imagine, at school, teachers don't teach children to use formal address. ... People, we sank, we sank into an abyss, we sank. So what would I do first? DI-SCI-PLINE. Only discipline. ... Before we had discipline. Not like in Germany – I coincidentally say Germany because I know it – but there was discipline. ... But there has to be a state with rule of law [pravna država]. There has to be, because as long as that's not the case, we don't have anything. Nothing. If I, in order to get anything on paper, or whatever, anywhere, I go ten times, I rip up the paper and I complain to my sister. And she says, 'You idiot, put 20 KM in the paper and tell them, this is for coffee, when will that paper be ready? Just under the table and leave'. DI-SCI-PLINE. Discipline. Not via daddy, not via uncles!

Mrs Hodžić followed this up with a lament about greeting etiquette on the street and a story about neighbourliness in the old Sarajevo *mahala* where she grew up – including references to warm relations between people of different nationalities. She continued to flick back and forth between the state and everyday practices and manners. 'First democracy, and then neighbourly relations!', she said, proceeding to detail people's envy of hard workers and their unrealistic expectations.[9] Yet, after that, again, she reverted to the state:

> So we need to bring discipline into the state, but urgently. Like, an inspector comes, across the street from my window, and women run from the pizzeria as if they are lost, they hide in the staircases because they are not registered. Why doesn't the state ask: how can a *ćevabdžinica*, how can it function with one person? Hello! No! But the state itself won't do it. It won't. The inspection arrives, my God, I find it pathetic when they come, when I see them walk. Pathetic. All my neighbours have closed their shops, they haven't got, they're

'closed', they left their business 'in preparation' because someone warned them that the inspection was coming.

Likewise, commenting on non-payment of maintenance and utility bills, former teacher Mrs Fejzić said:

I don't know, because here the rule of law [*pravna država*] is also on a very low level and it's all … nobody has that, well, the power to force residents. For example they won't pay heating bills, but they do heat their flats. And then we wonder why they constantly increase prices for us, and we continually pay, every time more, and they, some, don't pay. … And, really, there are people on the list downstairs who have over a thousand, they owe for water. And we pay, and they only increase the price per cubic metre.

Q: Irresponsible people?

Irresponsible people, shameless.

Q: An irresponsible community?

There's no state with rule of law [*nema pravne države*].

Here the symbiosis of the moral and a structural dimension emerges in its most striking form. It was because there was no 'state of law', Mrs Fejzić suggested, that people were irresponsible. Yet we can also detect a lingering sense that the link works the other way around too: it was also because of 'messed-up values' that no state of law was on the horizon. Symptoms and causes were thus not clearly distinguishable and this predicament was itself key to the affliction of Daytonitis, in which a sense of structural and moral failure mutually reinforced each other. In that way, the situation in which 'it wasn't known who paid and who drank' was perpetuated. To change this, to put it in the terms of the irrepressible Mrs Hodžić: the state should 'discipline people' and people needed to 'bring discipline into the state'.

Like the structural dimension of the diagnosis, the moral one also often included a comparison with Yugoslav lives as a superior alternative. Less frequently, it was pointed out that people's values in that period had not been perfect either, particularly with regard to work habits and initiative taking. I will spare readers Mrs Hodžić's elaborate analysis of the widespread abuse of sick leave in the former system. Rest assured she had strong opinions about it. Instead, I cite Mr Meho Džumhur, active in a pensioner's club, who was married and had two adult children. He had worked his entire life in one of Sarajevo's 'socialist giants', starting as a carpenter and eventually managing an entire section. Mr Džumhur believed there was a 'mentality problem' in BiH, telling me a story I have heard in several different versions:

> For example, when we had the Olympics [in 1984]. Fantastic. The entire city was included. Everything organised perfectly. People were polite, things functioned; spaces were clean and in order. This was the civilisational apex [*vrhunac civilizacijski*] for us. Not one problem. But when the Olympics were over, things returned to the previous situation! I remember clearly, on the way back from Ljubljana [capital of Slovenia] I saw a car with Sarajevo plates. I thought, I'll follow him! And we drove through Slovenia, and then Croatia, two republics, now two states, and then we entered BiH and he opened his window and threw out two plastic bags! When we stopped I asked him, 'Why did you do that!?' And he said, 'Well I know here they won't punish me!'

Again, structural and moral dimensions combined in Mr Džumhur's diagnosis, as they did in the words of Mrs Maglajić, psychologist/pedagogue at a Dobrinja primary school:

> In BiH people don't respect anything or anyone. Some messed-up criteria reign here. Our profession is ungrateful, you know ... they don't value us. But that was the same before. In socialism, educational workers weren't valued either. Still, they had a bigger role, and as such, they had a greater effect ... but that was what that society was like, it was different. In this society today there are no values. Our people experience democracy as 'I say and I do what I want.' For them, that is democracy. They say, 'I will do and say what I want, and I don't care about other people's interest, nor about the common interest'.

As we have seen above, Mr Mujić argued that, 'we are simply, people, Balkan people who need a boot, who need a strong hand'. Initially, he did not relate this to a structural diagnosis, although he later disparagingly referred to the proliferation of polities in Dayton BiH. Yet this did not mean this electrician did not see a responsibility for himself. Just as Aida believed she contributed by being a conscientious teacher, so Mr Mujić emphasised honest work. His dissatisfaction centred on the fact that he felt he could not properly fulfil that responsibility in the current situation, and that politicians were not willing to work. 'My duty is to work [*Moje je da radim*]. I am a worker, qualified for the work I do, so I mean, come to work and complete it honourably, conscientiously [*časno, pošteno*]. And let him [the politician who would ideally run the country] do his job, like I do mine. Then I would hope for something'.

Few people were as direct in their qualification of 'our people' as 'not ready for democracy' as Mr Mujić and Mrs Maglajić, who arrived at a similar position about (the majority of) their co-citizens from rather different starting points. This was often formulated as an assessment of others, thus potentially lifting oneself above the mass of 'our people'. Yet I suggest that many other reasonings about 'messed-up values' I encountered were also permeated with a lingering doubt that it might just be the case that war or newcomers did not tell the full story of a lack of moral compass. In principle, a diagnosis of Daytonitis through 'messed-up values' would imply that values had previously been adequate (not messed up yet). Instead, blanket assessments of 'our people' detected something more akin to a built-in deficiency in people in BiH (and in the Balkans more broadly). Insofar as people reasoned in this manner, we can say that a 'lack of a system' ceased to function as a symptom of Daytonitis per se. Resonating with what Herzfeld (1996) calls 'cultural intimacy', such a suspicion of a faulty mentality, a collective self-image of imperfection and inability to abide by the standards one ardently insisted on, seemed to form an important undercurrent to moral laments. In off the cuff, blanket commentaries on political issues, this was very common, often to be tempered in more thoughtful attempts to reason through one's predicament.

The Not-Yet-State and the Not-Anymore-State

What came as a relatively recent discovery in anthropology – the notion that statecraft is better understood by tracing the production of a state effect than through the self-representations emanating from institutions – would come as little surprise to most inhabitants of Dayton BiH. To close this chapter I work through the structural–moral diagnosis constructed around the first constitutional symptom – the 'lack of a system' – to specify the intensity of concerns with the state in Dobrinja and to ask: which state effect was at stake for them? To answer this question, I must specify the intertwinement of postwar and postsocialist dynamics that constituted the Dayton conjuncture.

In the Dayton Meantime, the fact that public discourses inscribed over a hundred thousand deaths into the making of states or state-like entities in the 1990s war, enhanced the 'magicality' of the state (Taussig 1992). As we saw in previous chapters, evocations of legitimacy by Sarajevo bus drivers, school teachers and pupils were grafted into the making of a BiH state, and many of my Dobrinja interlocutors expressed affective investment in BiH statehood. The 1992–95 war, structured around at least three incompatible sovereignty projects to territorialise specific states, thus continued to inflect political reasonings about Dayton BiH. Here, the key point was one of legitimacy: a decade and a half after the end of the violence, and despite its international recognition, the polity called BiH did not project a convincing state effect in terms of its statehood. However, in the yearnings for 'normal lives' of my Dobrinja interlocutors, the precise extent of the 'embrace of the state' and the national–territorial organisation of its vertical encompassment were less prominent than the very capacity of statecraft to effectively grid. Complaints rarely directly targeted the so-called 'state' or 'shared' BiH institutions but 'the state' in a generic sense. While all roads continued to lead to Dayton, here the key point regarding the elusive state effect was one of functionality. Gridding capacity was dispersed in a bewildering proliferation of institutions that Dobrinjci encountered, or sought to encounter, as citizens. And this must be contextualised in the post-Cold War conjuncture, for yearnings for 'normal lives' tended to cast the 'is' not only against the 'ought', but also against the 'was'.

Experiences on both sides of Cold War divided Europe are relevant here, yet in postsocialist Eastern Europe the 'postpresence' of the state has been found to be particularly important: in the first two decades after 1990 there was a widespread sense that the state had lost its 'capacity to order and regulate people and things' (Dunn 2008: 244). As we saw at the meeting on 'Communal Problems and Ways to Solve Them', as well as in the other observations and interviews referred to above, retrospective valorisations of a sense of public order were then often embedded in functional institutional solutions for identifiable problems (Bodnár 1998: 501). Wartime and postwar developments in BiH, I suggest, had sharpened the loss of such a sense of order to further extremes. Relentlessly criticising current actors in the 'actually existing state', most Dobrinjci never abstained from their yearning for a 'proper' state, a 'State with a big S' (Spasić and Birešev 2012). Ideally, for most of my interlocutors, this would probably be embodied by strong, unitary BiH, but in this book I show that, first and foremost, they ardently yearned for statecraft itself. Mundane engagements with the regulation of provision thus turned out to be more revealing for an analysis of statecraft than participation in elections, or even than encounters with the police, the judicial system and other dimensions of the repressive and revenue taking 'right hand of the state' (Bourdieu 1998: 9). In this postsocialist context, the state was called forth most often as developmentalist provider. And since provision was seen as contingent on having an 'ordered state' in the first place, Dobrinja yearnings for 'normal lives' entailed strong calls for order, legibility and discipline – in short, for 'a system'.[10]

In this postsocialist and postwar constellation, then, a key concern in Dobrinja reasonings through the Dayton predicament was that the state did not sufficiently exist *yet* and did not sufficiently exist *anymore*. This, as I have shown in chapter 3, is where the libertarian critique runs into its limits. The state was not experienced as aspiring or able to make everything and everyone legible, to govern rationally through standardised gridding, let alone to improve the population. A decade and a half after the war, rather than displaying outrage against high modernist tendencies to 'see like a state', Dobrinjci still desired more than the occasional eye contact with it. Can we please see the state, they wondered, and, especially, can the state please see us? They were clamouring for legibility and thus called forth the state as a 'hope-generating machine' through desires for protection and possibility. Here, in a 'postdisciplinary' constellation, we have a longing to be subject to no less than 'disciplinary regimes of power' that 'produce regulated and reliable subjects who can translate desire into action' (Greenberg 2011: 97). Knowing all too well that this was a fantasy, people thus appealed to the 'ideal face of the state' (Obeid 2010) and their resentment reproduced a projection of its hope-generating capacity. Dissatisfied with the kind of low-intensity interpellation that the 'actually existing' state provided, they themselves enacted interpellation, as if willing a state effect into being (see also Kurtović 2012). Their 'language of stateness' – steeped in high modernism, but without optimism – resented what the state did, but, much more so, what it failed to do. In the next chapter, I elaborate on the specific temporal reasonings this entailed in the Dayton Meantime.

Notes

1. After the meeting I found that the activities of the Consumers' Association were funded by a grant from the government of the Federation of BiH, not Canton Sarajevo. The fact that the speaker evoked proximity with functionaries in the latter's institutions is significant, since this is where much decision making and budget allocation take place. See below.
2. Trouillot and Harvey call those 'state effects'. Different uses of this notion cause some confusion in the literature. Scott (2009) employs it to refer to a variety of nonstate phenomena that are indirectly generated by – and in his study, often in resistance to – the state. For Trouillot (2001), the notion serves precisely to destabilise such a view of the state as subject. Here, 'state effects' make the state recognisable as an entity. Likewise, Harvey's (2005) tracing of how the state comes into being through road construction speaks of 'the materiality of state effects'. She explicitly refers to

Mitchell (1999) and her fascinating analysis is compatible with the latter's insights. Yet when referring to roads themselves as 'state effects' (2005: 137), I suggest, Harvey departs from Mitchell's intended meaning. In my reading, Mitchell (1999: 89) calls for the study of processes that produce a cumulative, more or less stable 'state effect' (singular). Here, the state itself is considered a structural effect and this is the manner in which I shall use the term. Clearly, conceived of as an effect, the state can itself have numerous effects, and Trouillot and Harvey usefully lead the way in analysing how the state thus becomes recognisable to subjects, including ethnographers. Yet to avoid confusion I do not refer to the latter effects as 'state effects'.

3. In 2008 municipal elections, SDP emerged as the largest party in twenty-seven of the twenty-nine Dobrinja electoral wards, attracting 31.53 per cent of the vote. SDA came second with 21.25 per cent, followed by the antinationalist Naša Stranka with 9.12 per cent. Pro-BiH-cum-Bosniak Stranka za BiH [SzBiH, Party for BiH] and BPS both collected 8 per cent. The incumbent SDP mayor of Novi grad, a Dobrinjac, gained an absolute majority in all Dobrinja wards bar one, where he still claimed a relative majority with 44 per cent. Turnout in Novi grad in 2008 was under 40 per cent, the second lowest in BiH. In the 2010 general elections (Novi grad turnout: 50 per cent), SDP, with a campaign entitled 'A state for people' [*Država za čovjeka*], collected by far the largest amount of votes in all Dobrinja wards. Note also that three parties with more Bosniak-nationalist profiles (SDA, SzBiH and the new Savez za bolju budućnost [SBB, Alliance for a Better Future] together collected many more votes than SDP. Naša Stranka did poorly.

4. Cantons are called *kantoni* in most of BiH, including in Dobrinja. Given the 'trilingual' logic of Dayton BiH, official documents also refer to them as *županije*, the name used for provinces in neighbouring Croatia. In popular parlance in BiH, this is common in areas with Croatian majorities, but when a Sarajevan uses the term *županija*, it would be understood that she or he is making a point of using the 'Croatian' word. Mr Mujić thus 'caught' himself using a term he would not normally use.

5. In the 2010 vote for the three-headed BiH presidency, all Dobrinja wards returned a majority for the SDP candidate. In nineteen out of twenty-nine wards he gained more than double the amount of votes of the second-placed candidate. The incumbent Željko Komšić thus regained the Croatian seat in the presidency. Here, then, we have large numbers of people with 'Bosniak names' who express commitment to an inclusive unitary BiH and who vote for a person who declared his nationality as Croatian (candidacy for the presidency was only possible as a member of one of the three 'constituent peoples'), and who expresses that same commitment (and who had fought in ARBiH during the war). Clearly, Komšić's candidacy was part of SDP's electoral calculations. Serbian and Croatian nationalist reasonings rejected the authenticity of his mandate. In Dobrinja, positive references to Komšić (qualified, of course: he is, after all, a politician) identified him as the least bad candidate. Why would that be any less authentic than a vote for a co-national as the least bad candidate?

6. *Voditi računa* literally means 'running an account', 'taking into account'. In principle this implies a neutral act of paying attention to factors that are considered relevant. However, it is widely used to denote concern: institutions or persons considered to be negligent can be criticised for not 'taking into account' something or someone, for illegitimately leaving them out of their domain of concern. This affective dimension neatly fits with the reciprocal evocation of 'love for one's state'.

7. One of the few visible strengthenings of an all-BiH state effect came about as a result of EU conditionality – a paradox proper to a 'supervised state' (Cowan 2007). Especially after 2002, large EU funds were invested in the securitisation of BiH state borders. A unified border agency was one of the first central BiH state institutions to function and to display BiH state symbolry. We can assume that this contribution to

the spatialisation of BiH statehood was at least partly motivated by factors outside of BiH, namely EU migration and security policies.

8. *Poremetiti* means to disturb, to mess up, to prevent normal development or reproduction.

9. Here I should note that Mrs Hodžić and her husband had bought their Dobrinja flat in the late 1970s on credit. Unlike her and Mr Mujić, who lived in a private house, all other people in this book had been allocated tenancy rights to their Dobrinja flats through a workplace and bought them out for 'certificates' after the war.

10. Indeed, the notion of a 'lack of a system' included charges of dysfunctionality against the institutions that would in a 'normal state' function as part of a repressive state apparatus (e.g., police and prosecutors' offices). These were seen as beholden to political parties rather than dedicated to establishing discipline.

– Chapter 5 –

SECOND SYMPTOM: 'WE ARE PATTERING IN PLACE'
[or, Towards an Anthropology of Spatiotemporal Entrapment]

$e\!\!\sim$

in which we discern the contours of a regime of temporal reasoning amongst my Dobrinja interlocutors by tracing the second constitutional symptom of Daytonitis: 'pattering in place' in the Dayton Meantime, a constellation that was experienced as not quite postwar and not quite on the projected 'Road into Europe'

Summer 2009. Vlado, a young man who lives with his wife and child in a top-floor flat in my building, is collecting money to install an intercom at our entrance. The old one was stolen, the doorbells do not work and loose wires have been hanging out of the wall for years. Visitors wanting to enter have to shout from below. The glass of the entrance door is broken and there has been no lighting for ages. Occasionally messages are written on the walls of our staircase in felt marker to warn against drug addicts. Our house representative, old Momo, has not been successful in sorting out these issues with our *upravitelj* [the company that is responsible for the maintenance of shared premises in our building; see chapter 4]. On the one occasion I called on him with regard to a repair issue he was very, very drunk. This winter a notice was posted in the staircase. It said:

> Residents are asked to suspend payments for the maintenance of shared parts of the building to the firm EKO ING until further notice, because until now it has never invested anything in this entrance. For a year there is no light in the basement, light bulbs have burned out, drug addicts gather, the doors are bad, there is no intercom, etc … From today, we forbid entry to the representative of the residents, Momo, who doesn't do anything to improve the situation. Shared position of the residents.

Vlado, whose top-floor location means he and his family are affected most by the absence of a doorbell and an intercom, has now decided to 'chase' a solution himself.

Going by what they say, people in Dobrinja spend an awful lot of time 'chasing' [*ganjati*] things. When I meet someone on the street, on the bus or in the corner shop, I ask, 'What's up?' [*Šta ima?*]. And perhaps the single most common reply I get is, 'Nothing, look, I'm chasing X' [*Ništa, evo ganjam X*]. On the most immediate level, the object of one's chase, X, can be anything from medical test results, over a certified copy of a municipal document, to a pension arrangement, a bank loan, a stipend, enrolment at university, reconstruction of a war-damaged flat, a welfare payment or visa for foreign travel. The job of house representatives, as we saw, consists mostly of chasing solutions from *upravitelji*. As Mrs Kata Šnajder, a married mother of two who is retired from her job in a GRAS kiosk, tells me about her husband, representative for a nearby entrance: 'He likes that kind of thing [*laughs*], like making phone calls and that … He's a pensioner, he has more time, so, to get in touch with the *upravitelj* and so on'. Our Momo seems to be less committed, which is why Vlado has taken over the chase for the intercom, circumventing the *upravitelj* too. Due to the intermittent nature of concrete activities and the role of documents and procedures, *ganjati* emerges as particularly relevant in regard to bureaucratic institutions, generally considered needlessly demanding, inefficient, confusing and slow. Yet the term flags patterns seen to structure the pursuit of many other mundane projects in BiH too. Someone can be said to be chasing a job [*ganjati posao*] and a person who is taking a long time to graduate can be referred as chasing school [*ganjati školu*]. And again, when someone is said to be chasing university [*ganjati fakultet*], this evokes less the act of reading, researching and writing, and more the practices of signing up for exams and visits to professors' offices to collect the required signatures in one's student report.[1]

Dobrinjci, of course, invest much of their time and resources in practical activities aimed at reproducing or improving their everyday lives. Like for most human beings elsewhere, many of these projects concern household livelihoods and are dependent on institutions, whose support people try to enlist or whose obstruction they seek to overcome. As its equivalent in English, *ganjati* literally refers to the sustained physical pursuit of (parts of) such projects. It implies that one believes – on balance – that a set of activities might lead to an objective, yet it often leaves open the possibility that they might not. There may be uncertainty about precise procedures and it is usually hard to estimate when the objective might be reached. Valid information about obstacles is thus at a premium. Chasing can be facilitated by a *štela* [connection, litt. setup], a person inside who may remove some obstacles for you, help you overcome them, or at least identify them (Brković 2012a, 2012b). Clearly, not everyone has equal access to such connections and chasing a connection – *ganjati štelu* – features as a form of meta-chasing (see chapter 6). To reduce uncertainty, chasers seek information about obstacles, through a *štela*, through a phone query to the sister of a friend who is married to a former schoolmate of a member of staff in the relevant institution, and through conversations with other chasers. This is part of the chase.

The term *ganjati* could in principle be used in a neutral manner for any pursuit – and I have been told it was used in Yugoslav times too. It does not necessarily imply drama or a great burden; on the contrary, it often evokes routine and even boredom. Yet when embedded in the general diagnosis of Daytonitis, it acquired a particularly negative connotation, evoking exasperation. In the Dayton Meantime, *ganjati*, much as it involved a goal-oriented attitude, was experienced as defying fully rational planning. Its accumulated trajectory might be extended but its practices functioned on short-term horizons. Chances of success were experienced as dictated largely by forces outside oneself, particularly bureaucratic gatekeepers. Chasing was considered time-consuming and often treated as sufficient explanation of why one was not engaging in other activities: 'Nothing, look, I'm chasing X', then, conveyed a sense that one was busy. However, although the verb *ganjati* implies active, sustained engagement, in practice, the set of steps to be undertaken was often shot through with uncertainty. So, in Dayton BiH chasing consisted of switching back and forth between making phone calls, visiting offices and filling in forms, on the one hand, and waiting on the other. What united all this into chasing is shared temporal reasoning over a period of time: a goal-orientation based on a degree of expectation of forward movement. Since the course, the duration and precise outcome of the chase were often unpredictable, chasing took place under the sign of a fragile hope, in need of permanent rekindling, that one was getting closer to the objective. In Dayton BiH, the need to chase *so much* could thus itself be seen as a symptom of broader inadequate movement, including collective movement. In this chapter, I disentangle this sense of spatiotemporal entrapment as a second constitutional symptom in Dobrinja diagnoses of Daytonitis.

A Shared Sense of Not Moving Well Enough

Loosely based on research in Australia, Hage has written that notions of a viable life 'presuppose[s] a form of imaginary mobility, a sense that one is "going somewhere"' (2009: 97). After Bourdieu (2003), he proposes a focus on 'the self as it is moving into a higher capacity to act' (Hage 2002: 152) and on its opposite: a 'sense of entrapment' (Hage 2003: 20), a feeling of not moving 'well enough' (Hage 2009: 99). Dobrinjci often articulated such a sense of inadequate 'existential mobility' through a distinction between 'living' and 'surviving'. In the words of Ms Musić, a web developer in her mid thirties:

> Life is hard [*teško se živi*, litt. 'one lives difficultly'] for most people. We have lost that middle layer, people who have permanent employment. People who are living very difficultly, they are actually surviving [*preživljavaju*]. Whatever you try to do, to achieve for yourself, I don't know, for your child, in whichever segment of life, you run into all kinds of walls, into the impossibility to realise some of your elementary rights.

The term 'surviving' [*preživljavanje*, also: *životarenje*] thus denoted a sense that, in the Dayton Meantime, one was condemned to chase in order to approximate the kind of movement that 'living (normally)' required. Clearly, there were inequalities in how well people were moving – and in how well they felt they were moving. Some were more successful in their chasing than others, and, more importantly, some were less reliant on it than others, and thus less reduced to a struggle to 'survive' and more able to 'live'. Although the great majority of Dobrinjci were not destitute, hungry or homeless, most were dissatisfied with their living standards and wary that they might get worse. Some struggled to meet elementary subsistence needs, and many ingeniously assembled resources in an attempt to provide what they felt to be adequate conditions for their households. A minority said 'they could not complain' about their households' living standards, but they always qualified this. Such relative satisfaction was said to extend exclusively to material matters and to be based on comparison with the circumstances of most others in BiH, who were moving (even) worse. It was also considered precarious, always threatened by a turn for the worse. Recalling Bourdieu's findings of Algerian workers being 'on the peak of a negative career' (1979: 62), 43-year-old electrician Mr Tahirović, married father of one, said:

> I'm of the opinion that things will get worse and worse, that we have now come to a line where we will only go down, not up. And I'm afraid what will happen the coming years, whether it will be as it is now, or whether we will

be out of work, or what will happen ... I don't have any hopes. I don't see anything bright in this country for the next ten years.

Even amongst those who considered themselves to be doing fine, the trope of 'surviving' allowed references to continuous struggles to secure what were considered 'normal lives'. A key difference between 'living (normally)' and mere 'surviving' was thus that the former was marked by a reasonable degree of smooth forward movement, unhindered by 'all kinds of walls'. Furthermore, Dobrinjci explicitly measured the quality of their current lives against the 'was', that is, against a background of remembered prewar upward movement. This was possible even for young people. Reaching back to the prewar trajectory of his parents, Mr Uzunović, a 29-year-old employed professional and civic activist, said:

> My parents were not poor before, and, well, they were going upwards, so I could have had a better quality of life [today], not very much, but perhaps a third better ... Personally speaking, I think that everything, regardless of the fact that I also try to fight for the common good, for some other people, that I will still, personally, continue to swim relatively well. So I don't have big fears, although it is uncertain of course, as always.

Contrasting this with the reviled overlapping categories of politicians, tycoons and *mafijaši*, who were seen to 'move well' at other people's expense, ultimately all my interlocutors shared a sense that they were 'not moving well enough'. And long before I arrived with my anthropological tools of contextualisation, Dobrinjci gridded their household trajectories in collective movement, in a broader economy of possibilities. They did so spontaneously when trying to make sense of their predicaments and even more so when asked about their expectations and plans. Mr Uzunović's careful confidence that he would continue 'to swim relatively well' in the given conditions implies that movement was seen as at least partly determined by external forces. If the collective movement of Dayton BiH provided the waters in which one swam, its currents were considered deeply unfavourable, especially compared to remembered SFRY ones. Some people felt they were moving relatively okay (for now), despite collective BiH movement, whereas most felt they moved badly because of it.[2] BiH itself, it turned out, was 'not moving well enough' and failed to provide the gridding that would allow the movement of 'normal lives' to unfold.

While permanently engaged in chasing this or that, Dobrinjci impressed on me, they were collectively stuck in a Dayton Meantime. This second constitutional symptom of Daytonitis was expressed through a range of spatiotemporal metaphors: 'we are pattering in place' [*tapkamo u/na mjestu*]; 'we are spinning in a circle' [*vrtimo se u krug*]; 'nothing starts moving from the dead point' [*ništa se ne pokreće s mrtve tačke*]. Such exclamations were as common in everyday conversations in Dobrinja as they were in the Sarajevo media. A fraught horizon of expectation, centred around projections of gridded movement, was perhaps most sharply visible in matters concerning emigration and return. On a Sarajevo visit from her new life in Western Europe, Belma, a 35-year-old web designer, mother of one, told me that she wished to return. After a pause she added, 'I *would* return, if only I felt things were improving [*da stvari idu na bolje*, litt. 'going towards better']'. Meanwhile, 38-year-old Mr Semir Bučan was chasing immigration visas for his girlfriend and himself. A machine engineer working as a security guard, he had volunteered in a paramilitary formation even before all-out war, and then spent four years in ARBiH. Yet now, he said:

> I don't see the point of life here, because this is just surviving. So you have no back at all [*nikakva leđa*], some protection from the state to organise a family, children, because there's no chance, here and now, there's no place for a family ... During the war, when we did look a little forward, we saw a future, we saw all the things that could be organised. But, well, the end of the war and the years after really turned around such views of the future in me, so I really don't have any vision of a future, of my future in this country.

Mr Bučan's words indicate that the sense of inadequate movement I encountered in Dobrinja had itself a history. Such confrontations with questions of the possibility to articulate and act upon certain kinds of hope led to my conceptualisation of yearnings (see introduction). Let me therefore briefly recall how my approach is embedded in anthropological literature on temporal reasoning.

The short-term horizon of the chasing to which Dobrinjci felt condemned was widely experienced as what Guyer (2007) calls 'enforced presentism'. Writing about the U.S., Guyer argues that people find themselves increasingly suspended between instantaneous, pragmatic mini projects on the very short term and evocations of a very long term and totally different future with which they have little reasoned engagement. Compared to neoclassical economics and biblical tradition respectively, she says, both monetarism and evangelical fundamentalism incite such 'fantasy futurism and enforced presentism' (ibid.: 410) as dominant modes of temporal reasoning. Examples of enforced presentism and fantasy futurism abound in the anthropological record. Recall, for example, subproletarianised

Kabyle in late colonial Algeria who '[lacked] that minimum hold on the present which is the precondition for a deliberate effort to take hold of the future' (Bourdieu 1979: 69). Yet Guyer draws attention to the fact that particular templates of temporal reasoning may come to function to a large degree as hegemonic in particular historical conjunctures. Congruently, Ferguson's 'ethnography of decline' in Zambia (1999) shows how hopes themselves have histories, and investigates how this shapes the way in which people engage with the future at a given moment. Ferguson thus embeds the sense of 'abjection' he encountered in modernist templates from Zambia's developmentalist era that continued to haunt future orientations. Rejecting unilinear understandings, his study nevertheless rests, like Guyer's, on the insight that such relative hegemonies have real effects.

My study addresses questions raised in this literature from a 'semiperipheral' vantage point in the EU's 'immediate outside'. Reaching back into Dobrinja's short history through informal conversations and interviews, this chapter reconstructs emic histories of yearning for movement to analyse temporal reasonings structured around the value of linear, forward movement. I investigate how such temporal reasonings congealed on the intersection of past futures and projected futures. In what follows, I thus first refract the sense of entrapment I found in Dobrinja between 2008 and 2010 against recollections of engagements with the future in the 1980s SFRY period, during the 1992–95 war and immediately after it. Then I turn to futures projected as part of BiH's 'Road into Europe'.

(Mis)remembering the Movement of 'Normal Lives' in the SFRY

Since evocations of 'normal lives' in Dobrinja shaped up on the intersection of the 'ought' and the 'was', one key discursive resource through which people made sense of their predicament consisted of recollections of 'normal lives' in the SFRY. According to their narratives, what kind of hope had that society encouraged? While younger people were sometimes irritated with the nostalgia of older ones, evaluations of prewar Dobrinja lives were unanimously positive. Major themes were, unsurprisingly, precisely those at the centre of current dissatisfaction: employment ('who wanted to work, worked' [*ko je htio, radio je*]), living standards, discipline, flat allocations, social welfare (free schooling, health care, sports and leisure, etc.) and, crucially, all this embedded in a 'functioning system' – an 'ordered state'. Contrary to western images of life in a socialist one-party state, many mentioned 'freedom', understood as freedom from danger (to safely walk the streets), freedom from worry (about livelihoods, about the future) and freedom to enjoy life (ample time and means for leisure). Additional features of previous 'normal lives' that were regularly mentioned were relative social equality, inter-national harmony, weekend houses, coastal holidays, foreign travel with SFRY passports and everyday lives oblivious to 'politics'.[3] In contrast with current precariousness, Dobrinjci recalled lives in which one could reasonably expect to achieve everything associated with 'normal lives' in a process of smooth, gridded reproduction. 'I hoped it would repeat itself', said Mrs Zehra Bašić, a retired hairdresser of fifty-five, married without children, 'that it would be like that in the future too. Nice, rosy'. Mr Haris Borovac, fifty-one, accountant and married father of two said: 'I thought everything would run along its normal course, that life would further, after Tito's death, in 1980, that it would all function completely normally. But it came to a turnaround, war broke out, and everything went totally upside down'.

Like Mrs Bašić and Mr Borovac, when asked about their expectations in the 1980s, many only said that they had not expected what actually had happened in the 1990s. 'That was a nice time', said Mrs Sena Mašić, retired from work in a *buregdžinica* [savoury pastry shop]. Sixty-four years old, she was the mother of two adult children, one of whom lived abroad. 'One saw all the best things ahead of oneself', Mrs Mašić said, 'One didn't think about war'. Or take retiree Mr Stevanović, a house representative who was later internally displaced in Dobrinja and hit by a VRS shell during the war: 'We looked at the future and … we thought it would, we could not expect that what did happen would happen. At that time, no one could foresee that'. Others provided slightly more detail. Employment was considered central to 'moving well'. Through contrast with the predictable trajectories of forward movement they recalled from their 'normal lives' in the SFRY, many expressed concern about the chances for forward movement of their children, lamenting mass unemployment and widespread corruption in hiring policies, particularly for (desirable) jobs in public institutions. Dissatisfaction with current social inequality was itself often phrased in terms of movement. Mrs Sabiha Varešanović, a widowed, retired sales manager in her sixties, mother of two, commented:

> I am old, I have everything, but I feel sorry for young people … Everything is worse, everything … Before, a director and a cleaner had equal rights, a right to a flat, on the basis of years of service, they had that possibility. Loans

for your house. But now, when will a young person get work, buy a house? How? Never!

Yet, as we saw at the meeting on 'Communal Problems and Ways to Solve Them' in chapter 4, it was also common to implicitly take prewar social inequality for granted and deplore inverted movement. 'He who had nothing before the war', the story then went, 'now has everything. And we who had everything, have nothing now'. In any case, rather than being condemned to chase for surviving, my interlocutors recalled 'normal lives' in which SFRY institutional grids had facilitated movement towards accommodation – 'a certain future'. Remembered 'normal lives', then, did not simply feature as a previous state of affairs, as a static baseline. They themselves were recalled as containing movement. Mrs Varešanović, again:

> I looked at the future … all I imagined, all that I thought would come, all that really was realised, materially and psychologically. It all happened in a positive direction. And you knew your child would get a job when completing [education]. … So, since I had a flat and all I wished for, all that an ordinary person can afford, my wish was that my children would complete school, start working, get married and so on. All those wishes of mine eventually collapsed, when the war came.

Mrs Varešanović's two sons did complete school, got married and had jobs, but both lived in the U.S. since the war, contrary to her expectation of continuation of familiar temporal coherence (Han 2011). Mrs Zlata Delić had worked as a typist in a large firm, but at forty-nine she was entering her fifth year of unemployment, having been technically unemployed – or as the phrase goes 'on waiting' [*na čekanju*] – for long periods before that. A married mother of two, she said she never had any great visions for the future. But she still contrasted prewar lives with today:

> It was normal. I didn't think about political stuff at all. … We had it good. I had it good. How would it not be good!? I got a flat. I had a job. A flat, a car. I had everything … It was much, much, much better than this now. Of course, I was younger too … but no, it was better, better. It wasn't stressful. Now it's stressful. Now it's stressful to go the cornershop. At the time, I don't know, it was steadier [*staloženije*].

People thus said they had hoped for their children to make 'normal lives' themselves (to work, to marry, to get a flat). Yet, if a central pattern in these recollections was an expectation of reproduction, this did not imply cyclical repetition of total sameness but a prolongation of an upward trajectory. A good example of this linear model of continued improvement was provided by Mrs Mejra Zvizdić, a retired draughtswoman of fifty-nine who lived with one of her two sons:

> [I hoped] that I'd earn some pension, that I'd reach my pension. I was never a megalomaniac. I never wanted an aeroplane, because I knew I couldn't have one and I've always been modest in my thinking. The most important thing was to give my children school, education, so that they would become people. … It was important to me, my family, how I would school them, to move in the direction in which we had turned [*da idemo pravcem kojim smo krenuli*].

'We were happy', said 55-year-old seamstress Mrs Hodžić, 'Simply, we had work, we had a flat and we had a future'. She emphasised: 'I had a certain [*sigurnu*] future and I thought, God, I will guide my children. My children will go further. I was happy. I was happy, I believed in the future and in certainty'. Mr Tahirović, twelve years younger, said: 'Well, I didn't, I totally didn't; it didn't occur to me that what happened in the 1990s would happen. First that. I couldn't believe it. Simply, I thought that life would continue as it was. Like, everything was going towards, that it would get better. And then, well, 1992 happened. Then everything turned upside down'.

Those whose own 'normal life' – adult version – had not shaped up yet in those days could evoke similar expectations of reproduction via their parents. Mr Bučan, the security guard who was now chasing a visa to leave BiH, was twenty-two at the outbreak of war: 'I hoped for a normal life, to find work when I would complete school, to work, like my parents, that's normal, to fight for something, for your family, I mean to organise a family, I don't know, that was it in that period, and then those kind of thoughts were cut off by the war'. Younger people thus emphasised the interruption of a projected trajectory: just as they were about to take off, their flight was broken. Aida, a 33-year-old teacher: 'Then I hoped I would succeed in life, that I would be as happy as I was then until the end. That I would complete school … Well, I hoped I would become successful, happy, complete school, and so, get work in town, and, least of all, I expected how it actually turned out'.

Dobrinjci, from pensioners to those around thirty, thus tried to make sense of their current predicament through recollections of movement in previous 'normal lives'. They remembered a past which had had a future – steady, certain, normal, going forward. Most understood this past future as largely apolitical. While some recalled their engagements in party organisations, no one mentioned a radiant communist future. Dobrinjci had of course been exposed to some 'teleological' temporal reasoning of socialism (Hartman 2007) – in speeches and textbooks for example – but this did not feature in their recollections. Instead, they narrated the achieved, desired and expected movement of their prewar household engagements as part of predictable and regular collective movement gridded in SFRY institutions, particularly of employment and provisions associated with it. Trying to make sense of their current 'far worse' predicaments, people thus recalled a past in which developments on the polity scale facilitated a future on the household scale. Such recollections selectively omitted the chasing that had no doubt been part of previous lives. Probed about unemployment and periodic shortages in the 1980s – which no one ever mentioned spontaneously – this was brushed aside as a small discomfort that had perhaps hit other people but not oneself. Moreover, although I knew it (and they knew it), few acknowledged that most people in Dobrinja now had access to more, and more technologically advanced, goods than then. In this economy of existential mobility, my interlocutors' worry about 'surviving' did thus not concern physical survival or material wealth per se, but a brutal end to the movement associated with 'normal lives' without a relaunch on the horizon.

None of this was specific to Dobrinja; I was familiar with this sense of interrupted movement of previous lives from my previous studies in different settings in the post-Yugoslav states since 1996. Yet it did seem especially prevalent and outspoken in my Dobrinja research. Why? I offer two tentative explanations. Firstly, my study focused on people who had moved to this newly constructed apartment complex before the war and who still lived there. In the 1980s, a decade, as any history book will show, marked by deep economic crises in SFRY, almost all of them had accrued residence rights to their first (or a better) flat through their work organisations. They had mostly been Sarajevo households from middling social categories – skilled workers, teachers, technical experts, etc. On aggregate, this population was not especially wealthy but it was particularly well inserted into Yugoslav institutional grids of provision. Socialist self-management had shaped the rhythms and trajectories of their lives more so than those of, say, many Bosnians in villages or in the old Sarajevo *mahale*. Perhaps partly reflecting this, in 2008 and 2010, Dobrinja, as we saw, produced electoral victories for the successor party to the League of Communists. Altogether, the longstanding Dobrinja residents that I focused on thus shared a sociological profile that made it particularly likely that they, even more so than many others, would contrast current stagnation with smooth 1980s movement.

A second, and in my view crucial reason for the particular prevalence of the concern with movement in my Dobrinja research lies in the timing of my study. Almost a decade and a half had elapsed since the guns fell silent, and people felt they were still moving inadequately. Hopes have histories – they may turn into yearnings. Exasperation had accumulated. I now explore this dimension in detail.

The 'O' of 'Over'

How had people related to the future when 'normal thoughts were cut off' and when 'everything turned upside down' in wartime Dobrinja, besieged by Serbian nationalist forces? Mrs Varešenović said, 'You know what, in war you don't hope for anything'. Almost all other recollections contained a similar pattern. They recalled extreme enforced presentism and simply stated, 'I hoped my children would survive' or, as the saying goes, 'to save my living head' [*da sačuvam živu glavu*]. The focus was on reducing the risk of violent death and hunger: 'We lived from day to day', people recalled, and they say did not think much about the future. Mr Kešo, a single electrotechnical engineer who had been a teenager at the time, said:

> We didn't hope for anything because everything was oriented towards day-to-day survival … get water, collect humanitarian aid, simply actions that would carry us from minute to minute, from hour to hour, and not being burdened by what would happen tomorrow, and what this – altogether – could mean. So, [not] where do I see myself, what will things be like in a year's time, which faculty will I enrol for, no normal thoughts at all.

However, after such initial statements, many of my interlocutors indicated they had desperately longed for an end to the violence and for much more beyond that. Such recollections now featured mainly as painful testaments to one's past naïveté and to the cruelty of history. Many bitterly remembered their initial expectation that the violence would be a short interruption of normal movement. Others went further. Asked whether he had any hopes during the war, Mr Uzunović, also in his teens during the siege, said, 'Of course, I still cry because I had them'. He referred to the lack of regularity of movement internal to days and weeks and to the need for rapid response to immediate needs (water, food, etc.), surrounded by boredom. Then Mr Uzunović recalled he had anxiously waited for a 'big party' suited to a 'proper liberation', and continued:

That's one thing that never happened. And then, I don't know, I had a feeling, probably like everyone because of the stories they told us, that we had potential for everything imaginable, that as soon as this would stop everything would start moving ... that the things I missed, which I longed for badly, would come and that everything would in that same second return to normal. It was like, okay, everything will stop and something will happen and we'll all be happy ... I still carried this image of the end of something, like a war, that it would be something great, spectacular, and that people would charge up with positive energy and everything would go as it should. Which, of course, didn't have any chance of actually happening, that things would return to normal, nothing exaggerated.

Men who had fought in the war also recalled thinking ahead, occasionally at least, about the moment when they would collectively pick up the pieces and move forward. Mr Mujić, a 47-year-old electrician, father of two sons, who lived in a house in Dobrinja's *mahala*, said:

It was day by day, hopefully survive today, and tomorrow we'll see. Tomorrow is a new day, new solutions to find, new fortunes [*nova nafaka*], I didn't think much about the future. Of course, I thought about the war ending, the killing ending, that work would begin, that construction would begin, building up. But I was sceptical about that.

The rhythms of peace negotiations served to emphasise non-fulfilment. Mr Tahirović, who also served in ARBiH:

We had no future at all. We didn't hope for anything. Whenever we could, when someone had a generator that worked, we watched our news on someone's TV, our fifteen minutes news bulletin. Actually, we did live in some hope: there were continuous promises by some foreigners, Americans, Europeans, that it would quickly, that it would last briefly, that our Alija Izetbegović and Karadžić and, what was he called, the Croatian president at the time, would come to an agreement. And all the time we hoped, we waited for some dates, that until 12 August, that it would be announced: 'That's it'. We were promised all kinds of things, but I never especially, I didn't believe it could stop, and when it did stop, I didn't believe it had stopped.

Similarly, the wartime entries of the Gimnazija Diary contained many references to peace talks, ceasefires and the reluctance of 'the World' to intervene. Occasional expressions of timid hope were always followed by bitter disappointment. In late 1995, when Dayton negotiations did actually end the violence, this did not merit a mention in the Diary.

Yet to understand the sense of inadequate current movement in the emic histories of yearning I gathered in Dobrinja, it is the immediate postwar period that is crucial. Of course, there was relief. Some recalled euphoric expectations and even most sceptics said they had believed things could, and would, only get better. As with references to wartime yearnings, the narrative structure of those recollections was almost uniform across the board: an initial statement of hope for movement (sometimes for 'catching up'), followed by the word 'however' [*međutim*], and then an evocation of crushing disappointment. 'However, nothing came of that', people said, 'however, it turned out completely differently', or 'however, none of that' [*međutim, niđe veze*]. It was along those lines that 55-year-old hairdresser Mrs Bašić provided me with one of those quotes that summarise entire chapter sections:

> 'It's over', I said, 'come on, let's move towards better things'. However, of that 'over' there isn't even an 'o'. [*Gotovo je, rekoh, hajmo, idemo bolje. Međutim od tog gotovo nema g.*]. ... So I honestly don't know, all this seems somewhat forced to me. Look at that end itself, there's something there that's not clean to me.

Those who detailed the immediate postwar situation in Dobrinja sometimes spoke of optimism and new beginnings, but more often they painted a picture of chaos, lawlessness and severe social problems. Dobrinja's infrastructure had been devastated. An additional reason for its postwar problems, many argued, was its location on the former siege line, now the boundary zone between the two BiH entities, which had become a node in black market traffic, particularly of heroin. Here, it seems to me, Dobrinja might be relatively specific within the Sarajevo agglomeration. Elsewhere in the city the immediate postwar period was often recalled more positively as a time of 'catching up' in terms of, for example, food and, for some, travel. This was especially so amongst the numerous people who had jobs with one of the many foreign organisations that were present in Sarajevo at the time. Joy and a degree of hyperactivity were common dimensions of much of their recollections of the first few years after the signing of the Dayton Agreement. Some Dobrinjci had worked for such organisations too, of course, but in retrospective narratives I collected in this apartment complex the optimism of the immediate postwar period was overshadowed by much bleaker assessments. Interestingly, then, if many Dobrinjci felt their wartime self-organisation cast them as superior to the rest of the city, the stories of postwar chaos, crime and especially drug abuse suggest that the hangover also seemed to be much more brutal.

Crucially, when discussing those years, most of my interlocutors focused on their growing realisation that the end of the war was not only less spectacular than expected ('It was just the shooting that stopped'), but that it seemed to be less and less deserving of being defined as an end at all. Mr Bučan recalled returning to Dobrinja from the front in late 1995:

> We returned to Sarajevo, a wonderful feeling. A year, perhaps two, after that was really beautiful, we socialised, it was really nice. We got rid of all that anger that had accumulated within us during the war. Luckily I had a crowd who really supported me in everything and I supported them. So we really lived as a whole [*k'o cjelina*]. However, of all those people, only I and one other man, who also has a wife and kids, remain. All the others left, all of them, to Canada, to the U.S., to Austria, to Germany ... Everything changed, my life totally changed. I got disappointed in all this. Now, when I think about it, I wish I had left the city in the 1990s, I'd have returned now with a few million marks on my account, I'd buy a job somewhere in some strong firm. I'd work, as opposed to the people who were here during the war. They are in a position of great advantage to people here, who were in the war, and who fought in the war for this homeland, but who got nothing. Nothing, literally nothing. So, simply, when the war ended. I'd have liked to be on another planet, not in Sarajevo, not in Bosnia, on a totally different planet. Because this will never again be the Sarajevo that was.

As we have seen, BiH's Dayton constitution consolidated the results of the war in a labyrinthine institutional structure that was considered both dysfunctional and far removed from the state people had fought for during the war. When asked how the war ended for him, electrician Mr Mujić, who also served in the BiH army for the full four years, said:

> It was stupid. I don't even know how it started, why it started. So many people were killed, so many wounded. I lost eight members of my close family, my brother lost both legs. Now when I think, it was all stupidity. All of it, in fact, is now as it was before the war: we have to live, to communicate, to talk, to socialise, we have to work. So some great stupidity ... For a time I didn't believe that the war had ended. Simply, you lived with that war, the war was present, it's like a stone in your shoe that bothers you for four years and one morning you wake up and it's gone and you can't believe it ... When I think of all that, it was a great stupidity. A time that passed in vain. A great emptiness in our lives.

For those who had spent the war in Dobrinja, the end of the war meant that adult male household members could return to civilian life. People counted their blessings in so far as their family had survived intact. Yet, increasingly, some felt a lingering suspicion that the 'end' was not quite as clear cut. Mrs Varešanović said: 'You think, the war has ended, everything will start anew, we'll catch up [*sve će se nadoknaditi*]. And then when you see that everything has been destroyed, the economy and everything, that everyone looked to earn their bread abroad [*trbuhom za kruhom*]'.

This lack of a clear ending, of a radical break between an abnormal past of violence and a future of 'normal' forward movement was also present in the narratives of those who had been teenagers during the war. They recalled scepticism due to repeated failed ceasefire agreements and, like Mr Uzunović, whose hopes for a big liberation party had not been fulfilled, they tended to emphasise that they had expected a much more spectacular end to the war than what they actually got. Ms Musić said she had always thought: 'that you would, I don't know myself what I thought. That you would know something, something. However, in fact it's only the shooting that stopped. So I don't know really'. The disappointment that followed initial expectation made the war period itself, in Mr Mujić's words, 'a time that passed in vain', in terms of forward movement. This took on a particular form amongst people who, like I, had been in their teens or early twenties when war broke out. They often took my presence as a point of comparison, focusing on academic trajectories. 'I only finished my university degree recently', said teacher Mr Kahriman, 'I lost eight years of my life because of the war'. While this was particularly prevalent amongst men, most of whom had been in ARBiH, women also spoke in those terms, and beyond academic trajectories too. Lejla, for example, felt that her generation had been just old enough to get a taste of life before the war, only to see it brutally cut off. She recalled the first rock concert she attended in the early 1990s, contrasting it to the isolation that had followed. Her generation, she said, really paid the price for the war. Just when the moment had come 'to live', the war had started. 'We totally missed out on everything', she said, 'and afterwards it was too late'. Strikingly, Lejla explained, her cohort was the only one that has no graduation photo on the school wall, for they never had a ceremony. Comparing this with the lives of friends who were about ten years older, she pointed out that this was only the first in a range of things they would have had, had life run its normal course, but missed out on. The immediate prewar period was central to such evocations amongst other thirty-somethings too. In the words of web developer Ms Musić:

> Just before the war … that remains perhaps, in a way, the happiest period of my life. So I was sixteen/seventeen, I'd just started in a way to, you know, to get to know the world, my surroundings, create something, feel part of something, discover things, etc. That was the happiest, most beautiful period of my life. And that's how the war caught me, dancing, joyous, I don't know. It hit

me with my eyes wide open and in fact I didn't understand what happened, I mean, today I realise that I wasn't aware what was happening. I assume that probably all others also say it was like that. I too thought that it couldn't happen to us … that this was some phase of passing madness, some hysteria, I don't know what, which would last ten days or so, and that would be the end. And even when the first victims fell, when it became terrible, cruel, I still thought it would last only briefly.

Pattering in Place at the Dead Point

I don't expect anything spectacular here. I think that simply too much. … I don't know, how many years have passed, twenty years, I don't know how many years since the war. The same things are happening to me. I talk with the same people, discuss the same problems. So I don't think that something specific can happen that would improve the situation … I am so desperate and embittered, I don't know what to say.

Ms Mušić spoke those words in 2008, almost thirteen years after the end of the war. What we find here is a sense of circularity, of non-progress in a life reduced to surviving through permanent chasing – itself seen to be the product of collective entrapment. In such emic diagnoses of Daytonitis – of people 'not moving well enough' and of BiH, collectively, 'going nowhere' – what were the currents in which Dobrinjci felt forced to 'swim' more than a decade after the end of the war? How can we understand the sense that the war had not properly ended? Emic histories of yearning for movement, I have shown, are key to address these questions. By the time of my research in 2008-10, people in Dobrinja had adapted their mundane practices to longlasting entrapment and most saw no end to it on the horizon. But while they accepted, reluctantly, that suspension had become usual for them (the 'is'), they did not consider it normal. Nor did they categorise the prosperity of their former 'normal lives' (the 'was') as an exceptional period of stability and predictability. A global view might show it to be an anomalous blip in history, but for them that period happened to be the first – and best – part of their lives, fondly remembered not as exceptional but as 'normal'. They felt robbed of 'normal lives' by the war, and, although average material conditions in Sarajevo had improved since war's end in 1995, they still felt they were 'pattering in place'. The recent financial crisis that preoccupied Western Europe and the U.S. did not feature much in such concerns. Positing Western European populations, who they thought were still moving pretty well, as the reference group,[4] my interlocutors thus attributed their predicament during the last two decades itself mainly to an extreme exception: war. While clearly also subject to global political–economic reconfigurations, their lives remained marked as Dayton; that is, not-quite-postwar, and therefore 'abnormal'.

This refusal to normalise occurred through contrasts with previous 'normal lives', but also through embedding one's predicament in the political impasse of BiH. Drawing on her research in the unrecognised Turkish Republic of Northern Cyprus (TRNC), Navaro-Yashin urges us to study how contexts where lives are kept 'on hold' are contingently 'carved out as "place" through specific historical agencies' (2003: 120). How did my Dobrinja interlocutors attempt to make political sense of the 'dead point' at which their lives were kept on hold? Which 'historical agencies' did they consider to be 'carving out' Dayton BiH as a 'place'? The economy of possibilities in which yearnings for 'normal lives' emerged in this Dayton Meantime did not just concern internal matters in BiH, but also its geopolitical position, which in Dayton BiH was sharply experienced as part and parcel of one's fate (Ćurak 2002). Thirty-something Iskra once compared Dayton BiH to a brutal football game where the referee had blown his whistle and everyone was magically fixed in their positions. Thirteen years later, she said, they were still standing there. The referee was still present too: as we saw, OHR retained considerable intervening powers in BiH, but now rarely used the whistle. The Dayton Agreement consolidated the results of the war, institutionalising national divisions in all polity organisation and thus facilitating nationalist organising at the expense of all other forms of politics. Those who had initially been most vocal against it, Serbian nationalist politicians, had by the time of my research become Dayton's staunchest defenders. Yet this was always presented as a solution for the time being: if BiH had to exist, they argued, it had to be 'Dayton BiH', whatever its faults. And its faults, everyone agreed, were many. In an interview, Milorad Dodik, then president of Republika Srpska, once said that BiH was 'in a position of endless temporariness'.[5] This resonated with how people in Dobrinja felt, but most would strongly dispute Dodik's preferred solution: further strengthening of the entities. While Dayton had 'stopped the shooting', as we saw, most of my interlocutors now considered it a major part of the problem, failing to deliver a proper end to the war and preventing the establishment of a 'normal state' as a platform for renewed collective movement. The referee did, however, relentlessly remind people in BiH of the need for such movement, or more precisely, of the only legitimate path to avoid reverse movement back to war: the process of EU accession, often referred to as *Put u Evropu* [The Road into Europe]. I now focus on the temporal dimension of this 'Road into Europe', which its politicians, its foreign supervisors and most of its 'ordinary people' projected as a normative future for BiH.

The Road into Europe

I should immediately note here that my Dobrinja interlocutors did not mention the EU much. I suggest this was due to the fact that the imperative of EU integration functioned largely as a meta-discourse that did not require explicitation. Opinion polls returned vast majorities in favour of EU membership and BiH's largely segregated public spheres were permeated by normative evocations of the 'Road into Europe'.[6] Ruling and opposition politicians, foreign intervention personnel and their EU and U.S. chiefs, all major media and almost all NGOs subscribed to this. I am not suggesting that there was mass support for concrete EU policies in BiH, but that hardly anyone projected desirable polity futures outside of this framework. Perhaps most strongly in Sarajevo, it set the terms of debate: policies were presented as steps forward on the 'Road into Europe' and opponents rejected them due to their perceived inadequacy in those same terms. This discourse seeped into everyday talk too: people would point out a problem in their surroundings and sarcastically sigh, 'Yeah, like that, we'll move into Europe!' [*Ovako ćemo u Evropu!*]. This relative hegemony was thickened by its multiple avatars: alongside the path to EU membership, there were requirements such as changing border controls as part of the 'Road Map' for visa liberalisation, bringing food safety standards in line with EU import regulations and refurbishing football stadiums along UEFA rules. The 'Road into Europe' was thus built around a normative model of progress, often with measurable performance indicators monitored by EU institutions, the Council of Europe, NGOs, etc (Bieber 2013; Coles 2007). Like in a computer game, every next 'level' could only be acceded cumulatively. Long before continuous assessment was introduced in BiH higher education – yes, as part of EU 'Bologna' reforms – the country itself was subject to it.

In principle, the 'Road into Europe' thus seemed to contain all the ingredients to serve as a remedy for the suspension of the Dayton BiH Meantime, structuring engagements with the 'near future' (Guyer 2007) around a set of milestones that could provide the yearned-for collective movement from the 'dead point'. On the above evidence, one would be tempted to think it worked. Yet I suggest that the

FIGURE 5.1. Playing on the acronym for the country's name, which also means 'I would like', many cars in Dobrinja carried this country sticker, in the blue-yellow EU colours: 'I too would like [to move] into Europe' (reproduced by author)

insistence on normative forward movement, and the ubiquitous EU campaigns promoting 'ordinary people's' role in it, did not make the 'Road into Europe' into an effective mobilising device in everyday terms. I now draw out three reasons for this.

Firstly, the 'Road into Europe' was structured around the ranking of polities, all on the move. League tables saturated media coverage. Due to their role in the war, Serbia and Croatia were particularly relevant points of comparison, but the EU accession of former Warsaw Pact states was also evoked as proof of BiH's humiliating inadequate movement. And the list went beyond that. Take an example from a Sarajevo daily.[7] The article was entitled 'BiH worse than Kenya, better than Fiji: According to a report by the Heritage Foundation and the Wall Street Journal, BiH comes 104th out of 179 countries'. Only in the body of the text did we learn that the table concerned 'levels of economic freedom'. There was no explanation as to how the neoconservative Heritage Foundation assessed this. Headed by Hong Kong, the top ten included only two European states (Switzerland and Ireland). Although Europe was always held up as BiH's reference group, this passed without comment. Then, noting that BiH came thirty-eighth out of forty-three European countries, the author sarcastically added: 'On this ladder, our country, with 57.3 points (0.2 point less than last year), comes under Kenya, Zambia, Cambodia, Honduras, Nicaragua, Egypt, and so on, but we are – look at that! – better than Fiji'. Ubiquitous commentary of this type showed that the key lay not in any substantial criteria for such tables but in the act of ranking itself. And since BiH always came out unsatisfactorily, this merely confirmed what people in BiH knew already: they were not moving well enough. A particularly eloquent outcry was provided in a magazine article by the musician Samir Šestan, subtitled 'Broken time-machine':

> While we move with the speed of a snail on Lexaurin, the world does not stand still. So that, while we are formally moving forward (although it is actually more that we are running in circles), the slowness of our movement in relation to all others means that we increasingly lag behind. In fact, instead of reducing it, this government increases the gap between us and the rest of the world. Only thus is it possible that even the countries who were behind us immediately after the war, meanwhile become unreachable exemplars, and that we are on the bottom of Europe. And in world terms in the category of notorious losers. ... In the meantime, children die, pensioners dig through rubbish containers, unemployment is dramatic, refugee centres are still active, the economy dies under crazy public spending, the state is falling apart, and we – hurt, maddened and instigated by mafia media – scream at Europe from whom we expect salvation. (Šestan 2010: 19)

This screaming at Europe for salvation leads us to a second reason for the weak grassroots mobilising capacity of the discourse of the 'Road into Europe'. While Šestan's image of Dayton BiH's disastrous rate of comparative movement mainly concerns obstacles within the country itself, there is a further factor at work, which is related to people's perceptions of EU enlargement itself. An analogy can be made here with chasing. Like the chasing that characterised people's everyday lives, the 'Road into Europe' suggested a future-oriented activity of moving forward in space and time, built on a degree of hope that the objective was reachable. Yet like with *ganjati*, there was great uncertainty. Crucially here, the objective was itself moving and threatened to escape one's grasp. Most people in BiH believed the sequential, progressive form of EU conditionality was undone by double standards, or at least ambiguity. Every inauguration of a new government in a 'big' western state elicited concerns about possible implications for BiH's forward movement. In Dobrinja, comparisons with Serbia were especially crucial, but, over time, suspicion grew that the EU might not take in new members for the foreseeable future, regardless of 'progress' in aspiring candidate states. The goal-posts, people thus felt, were being shifted, rendering the 'steps' of the 'Road into Europe' less than solid. Like everyday chasing, then, the Road into Europe suggested frenetic movement (tiring, demanding, targeted, coordinated etc.), but for most people in BiH it mainly implied waiting.[8]

This brings us to a third factor, concerning 'punctuation'. Guyer argues that the 'near future', the temporal horizon for the 'organisation and mid-term reasoning' of collective action, between an immediate present and a fantasy future, is becoming increasingly 'punctuated' by dates that are 'qualitatively different', rather than 'quantitatively cumulative … position[s] in a sequence or a cycle' (2007: 416). She gives examples of debt payments, temporal limits on legal claims, 'use by' dates, contract terms, commemoration events, peacekeeping forces and the inclusion of states in treaties. All these kinds of dates were relevant in Dobrinja lives, but not in a uniform manner. On the one hand, in household livelihood practices much chasing was punctuated by the interplay of date regimes of salary, pension or benefit payments with those of utility bills. The former were themselves often irregular due to their dependence on the date regimes of precarious state budgets, dependent, in turn, on IMF loans. Here people tried to coordinate their actions and yearnings with collective calendars. On the other hand, the polities of which they were citizens were governed by yearly cycles of commemorations – particularly of wartime events – but also by seemingly more 'cumulative' dates for government formation, budget approval, policy implementation, legal reform, etc. Many of the latter were anchored in the conditionality of the 'Road into Europe'. Yet, in a pattern that had already characterised the punctuation of the war period by negotiation deadlines, people in Dobrinja found that, time and again, such dates on the 'Road into Europe' did not hail an end to the Dayton Meantime.

In an earlier article (Jansen 2009), I have analysed geopolitical ranking as it emerged on the 'Road into Europe', emphasising the spatial dimension in the sense of entrapment through a study of affective engagements with documents of mobility regulation. In this book I focus on the temporal dimension, but I briefly summarise my argument on spatial confinement here. The 'everyday geopolitical discourse' I detected – a routine, nonofficial mode of representation of one's collective place in the contemporary world – functioned on the assumptions that all collectivities should occupy 'a place in the world' and that this matters, and that such collective places in the

world are ranked in a spatiotemporal hierarchy of forward movement. As a result of strict EU visa regimes, I found, Dayton BiH (and
Serbia) saw a process of subject formation relying on a double lack of
movement: the making, through documents, of citizens as entrapped
subjects in precarious collectivities in the shrinking EU's 'immediate outside' that were themselves seen as failing to catch up. During
my Dobrinja research, EU visa regimes were widely considered a
humiliating materialisation of the inversion of European geopolitical
hierarchies, including a sense of shamefully having to catch up with
Eastern Europeans, now EU citizens, who had until recently envied
Yugoslav's cross-border mobility with the 'red' SFRY passport. My
interlocutors often complained that they were imprisoned within
BiH and many of those who could, secured additional or alternative,
more desirable passports. Some had obtained documents from the
states in which they had resided as refugees, whereas others qualified for passports from neighbouring Croatia on the basis of place of
birth or ethnonational affinity.[3] This was seen as a matter of practical-
ity, of dignity, but also of security in case things turned for the worse
in Dayton BiH. As entrapment increased through the EU accession of
nearby states, the visa queues in front of Sarajevo EU embassies thus
increasingly cast their geopolitical shadow. With anti-Eurocentrism a
luxury that people in its 'immediate outside' could only afford at the
price of their own exclusion, I argued, in this historical conjuncture,
recursive Eurocentrism became the channel through which they were
able to prove their Europeanness in terms acceptable to that very EU.

After the publication of this article, in December 2010, Schengen
visa requirements for BiH passport holders were lifted. Given the
vehemence of resentment of restrictions on cross-border mobility
and of yearnings for visa-free travel prior to this decision, one could
expect this to be the harbinger of earth-shattering change. I was in
Sarajevo at the time and I kept my eyes and ears wide open. This is
what I found:

… silence …

Simply put, the yearned-for liberalisation of cross-border mobility
signified the end of its relevance as a topic in Sarajevo. There was
no celebratory atmosphere, no marked change in travelling practices,

no increase in flight connections with EU member states. In fact, the number of connections decreased over the next few years. Those who travelled with visas before, now travelled without them. Many of those who had not travelled before, still did not, often explaining this with regard to financial concerns. Crucially, there was no real change in everyday geopolitics: a sense of semiperipherality, marked by recursive Eurocentrism, still reigned. The issue of cross-border mobility now reappeared only in periodical outcry over calls by some EU governments to reintroduce visa restrictions. In Guyer's terms, this is one example of the way in which my Dobrinja interlocutors felt that what could be a 'next step' on the sequential, staged 'Road into Europe' failed to prove 'quantitatively cumulative'. Rather than 'starting to move things from the dead point', it was experienced as merely 'qualitatively different'.[10]

Waiting and the Refusal to Normalise

While insisting on the links between household and polity movement, Dobrinjci thus engaged with these scales in very different ways. In household projects the temporal reasoning of enforced presentism and a punctuated near future led them to continually engage in chasing (which included much waiting). Yet with regard to questions of polity, the same patterns facilitated a low level of reasoned engagement in collective action for the near future. Many distanced themselves from anything they considered 'politics' altogether. As we shall see in chapter 6, very few people were engaged in trade unions, citizens' associations, religious organisations or any other channel for collective action. Young teacher Aida:

> I hope I will earn a pension, that I will live through my life without health problems. So preserve my health. Earn a pension, perhaps broaden my group of close friends. Find some life partner perhaps, who will make me happy, and whom I will make happy. But generally, about the state, the city, I don't look at that at all. I only look at myself as an individual and I think everyone started to look at themselves as individuals.

As we saw in chapter 4, Aida located any collective hope in young people. As for the 'Road into Europe', most saw no point in trying to coordinate their actions and yearnings with its date regimes. In this figure of fantasy futurism the imperative of forward movement remained but its regime of temporal reasoning led 'ordinary people' to see their proper role as one of waiting. They yearned for forward movement and considered it conditional on a change in BiH power constellations.[11] But that would itself be movement. So while they had a diagnosis of the political impasse, they revealed no cure for it, let alone one 'ordinary people' could help bring about. Occasional references were made to SDP or to a 'boot'/'strong hand', but most people resorted to vague evocations of giving youth a chance and nurturing proper values regarding work, order and parenting. 'Politics' remained a domain reserved for immoral politicians. Most people referred to desired future trajectories in general terms, emphasising the need for decreasing unemployment, for rooting out corruption, for establishing discipline – embedded in the master trope of a 'functioning', 'normal state'. Occasional references to EU integration were directly anchored in this. Mr Zdravko Čelebić, a retired personnel officer and married father of two daughters, of whom one was abroad, said: 'I think that this process of joining the EU, that this could integrate BiH as a state and that it would strengthen it economically … I think it can, in the coming period, only be better than it has been until now'. Likewise, Mr Nikola Vujanović, a retired professor of around sixty, father of two sons, one of whom had been killed as an ARBiH soldier, said: 'I really don't know when things will get better. Perhaps, but only perhaps, things will get slightly better if we move towards the EU because then they will be forced to change certain things, to make a functioning system, and not just to think about how to fill their pockets'.

We thus come full circle. People in Dobrinja were deeply concerned with forward movement as a condition for 'normal lives'. They 'sensed the political' in their own experiences of 'not moving well enough', embedding it in collective polity movement. And in this way, they ended up disabling their potential political subjectivity. Which logic drives this paradoxically depoliticising effect of people's insistence on bringing politics into the equation?

As we saw in chapter 1, Hartman's research in Romania (2007) found that people's key reference point for 'transition' was Europe/ the West. Yet they did not project a unilinear development towards western-style liberal-democratic capitalism. Instead, they left open the definition of the yearned-for 'normality-to-come', which could not be measured by performance indicators but was projected as a flawless state of 'living decently' (ibid.: 208). Hartman found no evocations of past 'normal lives' but detected a comforting dimension in this fantasy futurism: the continuous deferral of the utopian object of normality placed it beyond proof or doubt and protected people against disappointment. Let us relate this back to questions of movement. Hage (2009) detects a generalisation and intensification of a sense of existential immobility in the 'permanent crisis' of the 2000s. He argues that contemporary Australian celebrations of endurance of 'stuckedness' serve as 'a governmental tool that encourages a mode of restraint, self-control and self-government' (ibid.: 102). In BiH, many sayings reflected this, from 'shut up and suffer/endure' [*šuti i trpi*], over 'don't make waves' [*ne talasaj*], to 'Mujo [the proverbial ordinary Bosnian] has weathered worse things than this' [*izdržao je Mujo i gore*]. The spectre of violence was crucial: 'just let there be no shooting' [*samo nek' ne puca*]. Yet, such exhortations to restraint coexisted with expressions of yearnings for forward movement and scorn for the 'politics' that prevented this. Since this critique was articulated through the evocation of movement of past 'normal lives', both discourses – one centred on endurance and one on the imperative of collective movement – functioned simultaneously as channels for the expression of exasperation, as vehicles for a refusal of normalisation and as tranquillising demobilisers. In chapter 6 I explain how this combination also informed peculiar forms of convivial engagements with 'politics'.

Most people who remembered the 1980s in Dobrinja seemed to approach the projected normative movement of the 'Road into Europe' in what we could call a 'knowing' way. It was as if they tried to show me that they knew very well what proper forward-looking movement ought to look like. They recalled a past that had a future – more precisely: a past in which gridded, collective movement was remembered to have facilitated a 'certain' household future. SFRY temporal reasoning was remembered as 'enduring', i.e., sequentially cumulative (Guyer 2007: 416). In particular, people's recollections of 'normal lives' evoked how movement was embodied in material products of collective labour that had allowed them to feel it: flats, workplaces, schools, hospitals, railways, bridges, etc. Living amongst such landmarks of Yugoslav socialist forward movement – many now ruined or incapacitated – they were caught in the interplay of the projected normative movement of the 'Road into Europe' and the actual suspension of Dayton BiH. This was illustrated by a 'Photo of the Day' in a Sarajevo daily, picturing a rusty crash barrier, roadside rubble and a tyre of passing truck.[12] The caption said:

Totally worn out car tyres, road shoulders falling apart, potholes in roads that are being 'repaired' and 'restructured' at least two times a year, which is, true, every time packaged into some new story about the 'revitalisation of the state'. However, concretely, on the ground, nothing changes since 1995. The same stories, the same potholes. Until when?

Sure, massive financial aid had flowed in for postwar construction, some of it invested in housing, schools, bridges and so on. Yet
Dobrinjci did not 'feel' those investments as part of a tangible collective future-oriented project. All over the country, billboards depict-
ing children under EU iconography, said, 'It is time for us to turn
towards the future'. But behind the children they portrayed EUFOR
soldiers, whose presence these billboards were meant to legitimise.
For people in BiH, this undermined the rhetoric of an incipient future
by reinforcing the sense that they still lived mainly not-quite-postwar
lives: lives in the Dayton BiH Meantime.

On Linearity

I conclude this chapter with a note on the uneasy position of conventional anthropology concerning the prominence of linearity in
temporal reasonings such as the ones I found in Dobrinja. As so often
in BiH, self-deprecating humour provides a good entry. So, a joke
about Mujo, who returns from a visit to Sweden:

> Mujo: 'Suljo, it's amazing, Sweden is twenty years behind us!'
> Suljo [*incredulously*]: 'What do you mean, mate, Sweden behind us!?'
> Mujo: 'Yes, twenty years behind! They're still living well!'

This joke crystallises out the normative valuation of linear forward
movement I found in yearnings for 'normal lives' and in critical diagnoses of the Dayton Meantime. Dobrinjci were concerned how well
they were equipped – as a household and as a polity – to inscribe
themselves, at least also, in movement towards rising living standards, towards the establishment of a 'functioning state' and towards
an ascendance to a dignified 'place in the world'. This is a classic
developmentalist conception of 'space as time' (Massey 2005: 5),
with some locations considered 'ahead' and some 'behind'. It is not,
however, a teleological model of 'transition' from 'totalitarianism' to
'freedom'. Instead, it is a domesticated modernist template bereft of
optimism, in which people yearned for 'normal lives', both remembered and projected. Any emancipatory political project in BiH, I
contend, will need to take such yearnings into account, despite their
nostalgic, modernist, petit bourgeois and Eurocentric dimensions.

How do we study such reasonings anthropologically? In a cultural
relativist tradition, often coupled with the libertarian paradigm I
have specified earlier, anthropologists tend to focus on the oppressive
workings of such modernist temporal reasoning, usually attributed

to elites, and to reve(a)l (in) resilient subaltern alternatives such as cyclical temporality (Connerton 1989; Munn 1992). Bewitching nonlinear temporality is a major feature in post-Yugoslav literature and films, but I found it to be largely absent from mundane formulations of critique or alternatives. For many Dobrinjci, its association with nationalism, therefore with war, and therefore with most of today's problems, made it an unlikely source of critical inspiration.[13] 'Running in circles', both at the Dayton dead point and as part of a representation of BiH as a place of recurring violence, was what my interlocutors yearned to escape from. For example, Mrs Redžić, director of one of Dobrinja's primary schools, repeated the common line that 'every fifty years we have war here'. Yet, minutes later, when critically diagnosing the situation in BiH, she complained, 'We are always late, always late!'

Confronted with such ubiquitous evocations of linear forward movement, I did not discern a subaltern culture of temporality. Instead, I traced people's attempts to reason their way through a predicament they themselves found disorienting. Studies of postsocialist transformations have noted that, in contrast to the space–time compression often associated with the end of the Cold War, the actual experience of what was projected as 'transition' altered people's temporal reasoning. Many experienced it as a period in which time was slowing down or even going backwards (e.g., Platz 2003). Suspended in the Dayton Meantime, my Dobrinja interlocutors relied on the imperative of forward movement to shift the attention away from cultural otherness to an economy of movement. How should anthropologists engage with this? Ferguson's report of an encounter with a Zambian man is inspiring in this respect (2006: 18). Charmed by the aesthetics and sustainability of Sesotho-style round mud, stone and grass houses, Ferguson asked this man why he wished to build an expensive 'European' house that lacked those qualities. 'What kind of house does your father have in the U.S.?' the man asked, 'Is it round? Does it have a grass roof? Does it have cattle dung on the floor?' No it did not. 'How many rooms does it have?' Here, Ferguson had to stop and think before he replied, 'About ten, I think'. Pausing to let this sink in, the man said, 'That is the direction we would like to move in'. Apart from the fact that I find Ferguson's inclusion of this story, exposing his own privilege, a refreshingly honest turn in anthropology, I also think he is right to follow the man's insistence to shift 'from the question of cultural difference to the question of material inequality', and to take seriously his 'aspiration to overcome categorical subordination' (ibid.: 20). Dayton BiH expressions of 'the direction in which we would like to move', I argue, should not be reduced to mere expressions of 'Westernisation' or 'imposed modernity'. This book argues that, just because of their location outside the western 'centre', such yearnings for forward movement, and the linear temporal reasoning in which they were embedded, should not be rejected as less authentic.

Emic diagnoses of Daytonitis constructed around the constitutional symptom of 'pattering in place' indexed a sense that lives in the Dayton BiH Meantime were considered not quite postwar and not quite on the road to the EU. My interlocutors systematically drew my attention to their social location: not to who they were, but to the 'when' and 'where' of their lives. It was living-in-Dayton BiH that constituted their predicament, they impressed on me, for it reduced people to 'surviving', entrapped in BiH's borders and suspended in the Meantime. As opposed to 'normal lives', which would entail spatiotemporal forward movement, it was living in a waiting room, without it being quite clear what the waiting was for and how long it would last. In Massey's terms, Dobrinjci felt that, for them, space really had become time, and that time had become space.

Notes

1. In a more extreme example, a couple that is finding it difficult to conceive is sometimes said to be chasing a child [*ganjati dijete*].
2. In a 2007 BiH-wide survey, only a third of all respondents expected things to get better on a personal level. Some 60 per cent thought they were unchanged from a year previously. These scores were strongly affected by income but bore no relation to national or religious affiliation. Asked about the situation in BiH more generally, almost 90 per cent assessed it as 'quite bad' or 'very bad', some 70 per cent saw no change compared to a year earlier and about half expected no change within the next year (UNDP 2007).
3. Much scholarly attention has been devoted to *jugonostalgija* (some recent work includes e.g., Kurtović 2012; Petrović 2012; Spasić 2013). In this book, rather than elaborating on post–Yugoslav remembering and forgetting per se (see e.g., Jansen 2005a, 2008b, 2009), I deliberately focus on dynamics of the temporality of 'gridded' forward movement in evocations of 'normal lives'.
4. In a survey (UNDP 2007), respondents were asked to suggest a country that could serve as a model for BiH's future development. Some 30.2 per cent said BiH needed no model, 21.7 per cent mentioned Switzerland, 10.6 per cent Germany, 10 per cent Slovenia and 7 per cent Sweden. The U.S. came way down in the ranking, and no one referred to any of the former Warsaw Pact states that had become EU members.
5. 'Dodik: Bosna je beskonačna privremenost' [Dodik: Bosnia is endless temporariness], *6yka*, 26 October 2010 [www.6yka.com].

6. In a 2009 BiH-wide survey, over 70 per cent of all respondents said they would vote for BiH membership in the EU in a referendum (over 80 per cent amongst Bosniaks) (Šalaj 2009: 54). Asked 'what or where will BiH be in twenty years' time?' over 70 per cent of respondents in a UNDP survey answered, 'in the EU' (UNDP 2007). Noting such unusually uniform answers to an open question, the study's authors were startled that 'respondents interpreted the question as virtually exclusively oriented towards "where" rather than "what"'. Leaving aside the poor wording of the question, I am surprised by their surprise.

7. 'BiH gora od Kenije, bolja od Fidžija: u izvještaju Heritage Foundation i Wall Street Journal, BiH 104. od 179 zemalja' [BiH worse than Kenya, better than Fiji: BiH 104th out of 179 countries in a report by the Heritage Foundation and the Wall Street Journal], *Oslobođenje*, 13 January 2012, 22.

8. Simić (2009) identified a similar sense of suspension in mid-2000s Serbia on its own 'Road into Europe'. Yet in Serbia at the time, note, even if state borders were still disputed, the existence of the polity itself was not.

9. This mainly concerned persons whose names suggested Croatian ethnonational heritage, but, due to specific wartime document policies by the government of neighbouring Croatia, it also included some others.

10. Another example concerned the 2008 arrest of Radovan Karadžić, fugitive wartime president of Republika Srpska. While it dominated media reporting for a while, people's comments suggested that this long-awaited event, gratifying as it might have been, was not only considered long overdue but, when it finally happened, did not represent a 'quantitatively cumulative' step.

11. A UNDP survey indicates that it was precisely because few people believed that BiH had internal political forces that were able and willing 'to move things from the dead point' that the discourse of the 'Road into Europe' appeared as a welcome reminder of the need and desire for forward movement, while also allowing a distance from politics (UNDP 2007).

12. 'Foto dana' [Photo of the Day], *Oslobođenje*, 10 June 2008, 24.

13. I am aware that my approach privileges reasonings of what Harvey calls 'secular spatiotemporalities' over the 'mythological timespace of religion and nationhood' (2000: 194). This book's focus on lives seeks to recover the significance of everyday practice in people's attempts to 'inhabit the world *again*' (Das 2007: 62), rather than tracing their 'ascent into the transcendent' (ibid.: 15). Transcendental alternatives (for example, those related to religion) were at play in Dobrinja and they did underlie some critiques of the current situation. Yet in my research they only appeared alongside 'secular' ones, and, most importantly, not one single person brought them up spontaneously to diagnose or criticise. When discussing hopes and fears for this research project, everyone, it turned out, privileged 'secular' forward movement, without ever engaging in other modes of temporal reasoning. This, of course, may have to do with my positioning as a highly educated Western European but I would be reluctant to attribute it only to that. Instead, I read it as an indication of the normative power of the trope of forward movement in people's attempts to make (political) sense of their predicament in the Dayton Meantime.

PART III

LIVING WITH DAYTONITIS

– Chapter 6 –

CONVIVIALITY IN THE MEANTIME
[or, Towards a Critique of Dayton Non-politics]

in which we address issues of politika, *detachment and complicity beyond Dobrinja ethnographic data to sketch, in dialogue with materialist versions of hegemony theory, a portrait of conviviality in the Dayton BiH Meantime*

February 2008. On a cold Dobrnja night, Iskra, Dado and I are having drinks in our local pub. As we walked in, a man handed me a flyer announcing a demonstration on Saturday, one in a row of events sparked by the stabbing of a teenager on a tram a few weeks ago:

> Let's gather again this Saturday to demand the RESIGNATIONS of those in the cantonal and the city authorities who have, with their non-work, not deserved that we continue to pay them with our money. PROTEST MEETING on SATURDAY 01.03.2008 in front of the CATHEDRAL. Your voice AGAINST NON-WORK, IRRESPONSIBILITY and TOO MANY PRIVILEGES must be heard too. Now you can move the situation from the dead point, now you have a chance to do something FOR THE FUTURE OF OUR CITY AND OUR CHILDREN. Now YOU ARE NOT ALONE anymore. WE DESERVE BETTER! CITIZENS OF SARAJEVO.

On the reverse side the flyer urges everyone to join the protest 'except if they believe that …', followed by a list of spurious suppositions that membership of any of the parliamentary political parties in Canton Sarajevo, including those from the opposition, could exempt one from stray bullets, knifing, the hazards of treatment in public health care, potholes in the road, ludicrous funding priorities, corruption, drugs, theft and poverty.

Maida and her brother Sejo join us. When I put the flyer on the table, Maida, one of the organisers of the demonstrations, breaks into an enthusiastic story. She is soon interrupted by Iskra, who has been unusually quiet until now. Iskra has just been informed that yet another job application was unsuccessful and she is pessimistic about another two she is waiting to hear about. Always one for irony at her own expense, today she is angry and depressed. Despite her own engagements in protest, education and consciousness raising, Iskra dismisses the Saturday protests. Maida, upset, replies that it is important to show 'them' that we will not just take anything. Of course, she argues, 'they' will say that they are democratically elected and that elections are the channel for expressing disagreement. In contrast, Maida says: 'These protests … finally, for the first time people have the courage to say "Enough! We won't be treated like that anymore!" To me this is a grain of hope. It's not so much about resignations or so, I mean, the political parties arrange all that anyway. That's not what it's about'. Rolling his eyes Dado suggests we stop talking about *politika*. A week later, when the five of us find ourselves in the same place, Maida asks us to join the next demonstration. Iskra is noncommittal now. Dado is in a dark mood and has no time for it at all. When Maida's brother encourages him to come and protest, he turns it into a joke, playing on his status as a disabled war veteran. 'So you're going to scream against the state that I fought for!' Sejo says: 'Exactly! That is exactly why you should come: it's the state you fought for. Look what they made of it. Are you satisfied? Come on, tell me, are you satisfied?' Dado does not take the bait.

Maida and Sejo convey what is also the predominant interpretation in sympathetic oppositional media reporting on the protests, converging around the idea that the arbitrary stabbing on the tram was the drop that made Sarajevans' bucket overflow. People have passively put up with politicians who only think about their privileges and their businesses/political empires, it is argued, but now they have decided enough is enough. The issue of safety and especially the bare life of 'our children' have emerged, it is suggested, as a lowest common denominator where people draw the line. They have woken up from years of apathy. When I join the demonstrations on a number of Saturdays, they gather a few hundred, and on a couple of occasions a few thousand people. Alongside criticism of various executive governments in Dayton BiH, some slogans thematise the contrast between this relatively low turnout and ubiquitous dissatisfaction. Parodying the apathy of fellow citizens, one says, *Nije do mene* ['It's not up to me']. Citing a common expression recently used in a song by the politically explicit band Dubioza Kolektiv, two others simply say *Trpim* [a combination of 'I suffer' and 'I endure']

and *Šutim* ['I remain silent', 'I shut up']. Reflecting this, and referring to Sarajevans' legendary ability to ignore what happens around
them in the city's numerous bars, demonstrators often point out a
dichotomy between 'us' and 'those who drink coffee'.

Kurtović (2012) offers a theoretically incisive exploration of the 2008
protests and of the ways in which subsequent citizen's engagements
were shaped by Dayton BiH's 'politics of impasse'. She focuses on
activists who decided that 'drinking coffee' was not enough. In contrast, this book does not focus on protest – although my epilogue will
partly revolve around a later set of demonstrations. With some exceptions – Maida, Sejo and Mr Uzunović, who were engaged in those
citizen's initiatives – very few people I knew in Dobrinja attended the
protests. Some did mention the murder on the tram as a symptom of
what I call Daytonitis and virtually everyone harshly criticised 'those
up there', the politicians I shall refer to as the 'Dayton ruling caste'.
But if their bucket was overflowing, it did not lead them to take to
the streets.
  This chapter deconstructs the presumed choice between coffee
drinking as apathy and protesting as political agency, seeking to
contribute to anthropological understandings of the reproduction
of domination without recourse to physical violence. We could ask:
if dissatisfaction with government was as widespread as this book
documents, how come the streets were not packed with more protesters, and more often? However, in line with my efforts to 'sense
the political' in Dobrinja yearnings for 'normal lives', I broaden the
scope of my analysis beyond protest. My interlocutors knew that
their dissatisfaction with the Dayton ruling caste was widely shared
across BiH. This knowledge also underlies the ways in which the
flyer above attempts to mobilise people for protest. I therefore ask:
if so many Bosnians blamed the ruling caste for being unable to lead
'normal lives', how did this caste retain, for two decades, its grip on
government in a country with a free and secret vote? How did ubiquitous scorn for governing politicians coexist with their institutional
longevity?
  This chapter addresses issues of legitimacy, complicity and the
reproduction of domination in dialogue with anthropological work
that goes beyond simple dichotomies of domination/resistance and
state/society. In line with my earlier critique of a powerful libertarian paradigm in anthropology, this requires a theorisation of
political agency that decouples it from automatic association with
subversion.

'Normal Lives', *Politika* and Limits of Nationalist Interpellation

Over and above any possible party-specific preferences, many Dobrinjci expressed generalised scepticism with regard to politics. Not mincing their words, they sweepingly characterised all or almost all politicians as cynical, power-hungry, greedy schemers, liars and thieves. Indeed, a common pastime in Dayton BiH, often while drinking coffee, was called 'barking' [*lajati*] at politicians. Some of the characteristics most widely attributed to politicians included *bahatost* [a brutish kind of arrogance], *nerad* [non-work], *lopovluk* [thievery] and *javašluk* [negligence, lack of care]. Reflecting ethnographic findings in various locations in Dayton BiH (e.g., Armakolas 2007; Bartulović 2013; Helms 2007; Jansen 2006b, 2013b; Kolind 2008; Sorabji 2006, 2007; Stefansson 2010), the blame for the affliction of Daytonitis was thus placed mainly in *politika* – widely used to denote an immoral sphere populated by self-interested politicians organised through parties (Kolind 2008: 123–34). In what follows I employ the emic term, to be distinguished from other uses of 'politics' as ideology or transformative collective practice. I maintain the distinction to be able to engage in 'sensing the political' in such conceptions, but it should be noted that many Bosnians suggested precisely that in Dayton BiH there was no politics outside of *politika*.

After having painted her predicament in dismal terms, contrasting this with her previous 'normal life', Mrs Varešanović, a retired sales manager and widowed mother of two sons who lived in the U.S., provided a concise summary of the widespread disgust with *politika*:

Q: Do you think that there are people for whom things are better today than before?

Sure, there definitely are! That's people who have connections [*veze*], who have stolen their fill in this war [*koji su se nakrali u ovom ratu*]. They live well. Their children live well. They have everything. Everything, they have. Especially politicians.

Far from being a 'hidden transcript' shared in 'private' spaces by the subordinate (Scott 1990), the image of *politika* as an immoral sphere was publicly ubiquitous. Even party members and aspiring politicians tended to inscribe themselves into it. Take Mr Hadžić, the president of one of the MZs in Dobrinja. He had been an active cadre of the League of Communists in his work organisation before the war. Unemployed for over a year, he now received a fee for his work in the MZ. He had been an SDP candidate in successive municipal elections but appeared too low on the ballot to stand any chance of being elected. Once he told me that another party had offered him a good place for the next elections and, in what I hope was a joke, he added, 'I said I'd only do it for 200,000 KM'. Mr Hadžić blamed his consecutive low positions on the ballot on his assertiveness and his sincerity: 'There is still something decent in me' [*U meni ima još nešto pošteno*], he said. The judgment on which this was based – that success in *politika* depended on the opposite of decency – was extremely widely shared. The way in which people exempted individual politicians as possibly uncontaminated and, precisely therefore, unable to exert any influence, further confirmed this. Mrs Varešanović, for example, said that there 'probably existed' some honest politicians but that, 'they didn't have the space to articulate that', or that, 'as individuals they couldn't do much with "those ones" working collectively' [*ako su ovi grupno*].

In line with other ethnographic findings, most of my Dobrinja interlocutors positioned themselves implicitly as representatives of 'the people' [*narod*], portrayed as powerless and victimised by the unscrupulous politicians that populated *politika*. Earlier chapters have shown how this generalised distancing from *politika* was an integral part of a broader shared concern with 'normal lives', in which diagnoses of Daytonitis identified two constitutional symptoms – the 'lack of a system' and 'pattering in place'. They posited self-proclaimed modest aspirations converging around the predictable, smooth everyday reproduction of forward movement of 'normal lives'. This presupposed physical safety, good and rising living standards, relative equality, 'freedom' of various kinds, and obliviousness to politics – all of which, my interlocutors believed, should be made possible by effective gridding by a 'normal' state that 'showed concern'. Such yearnings for 'normal lives' provided the most widely shared common framework for political reasoning and set aspirational standards.

How do we square this with the fact that the most commonly offered explanations for the longevity of the Dayton ruling caste in outside commentary on BiH revolve around nationalism? The idea here is that three nationalist elites secured ideological consent from their target populations by appealing to their sense of national belonging. In Sarajevo, this explanation was most relevant in relation to SDA, the largest party claiming to protect Bosniak national interests and the one with the longest record of government. SDA (and some smaller parties) did indeed seek to mobilise Sarajevans with Bosniak religious–nationalist rhetoric. Via media, schools and mosques they interpellated people with 'Bosniak names' through projections of a national renaissance after communist oppression. This had no doubt been an important dynamic in the early 1990s events in BiH, but almost two decades later I did not encounter such hopeful identification with an emancipatory Bosniak nationalist agenda in Dobrinja. As we saw, none of my interlocutors – not even activists of SDA or other parties with Bosniak nationalist profiles – formulated their political concerns in those terms. In fact, several practising Muslims, SDA members, spontaneously emphasised that they had never experienced their religious commitment as a basis for discrimination during their Yugoslav 'normal lives', thus disqualifying their own party's claims that it had freed them from the yoke of godless communism.

This does not mean that nationality was not a parameter in political reasonings in Dobrinja. As Mujkić (2007) argues, it was the formulation of fears in the national key that was central to the reproduction of the status quo in the Dayton BiH 'ethnopolis'. Mujkić describes the Dayton BiH ruling caste as a set of three mutually dependent groups of political entrepreneurs who secured long-term domination through the continuous production of crises around threats to national survival (see also Vlaisavljević 2006). Emphasising that the Dayton institutional setup itself – with its 'vital national interest' veto clause – constitutionally cemented such patterns, Mujkić embeds this argument in a version of the 'prisoner's dilemma', arguing that many BiH citizens voted for 'their' (nationally defined) politicians because they believed that national others would vote for 'theirs'. While none of my Dobrinja interlocutors with 'Bosniak names' explicitly referred to threats to national survival, we have seen that some – sometimes only by implication – did point the finger at some national others, such as RS prime minister Dodik, who did not 'love' the state of BiH, to explain their current inability to lead 'normal lives'. Yet even then, as we saw, they mainly raised concerns of functionality, that is, of statecraft.

The most important point of Mujkić's argument, I believe, is that it draws attention away from questions of ideological consent per se, highlighting instead the institutional reinforcement of voting along nationalist lines through Dayton channels of representation (see also Ćurak 2004). During my research, nationalist hope and, probably more so, fear, arguably retained the capacity to mobilise large numbers in BiH on sufficiently frequent occasions to contribute to the longevity of its triadic ruling caste. Yet while this explanation is most powerful when addressing politics in BiH as a whole, I propose a complementary emphasis on dynamics internal to its three largely nationally homogenised fiefdoms (recognising, nevertheless, that these need to be understood in the broader frame of Dayton BiH). If we focus there, that is, on the institutions where most actual statecraft occurred, I suggest, an understanding of the reproduction of the Dayton ruling caste a decade and a half after the war requires that we complement an eye for nationalist evocations of hope and fear with other arguments.

To start with, unsurprisingly, Dobrinja members or sympathisers of particular parties differentiated between politicians on the basis of their party affiliation, rather than nationality per se. SDP supporters – and they were most numerous amongst my interlocutors, as they were amongst the Dobrinja electorate – often mentioned the presence of people with different national backgrounds in this party as a plus. As we saw, in two consecutive elections it was the SDP candidate for the BiH presidency, a Croat, who swept the board here. SDP voters blamed what were widely called 'national parties' in government – Bosniak ones as well as Serbian and Croatian – for most ills, reasoning that support for such parties, concretely in Sarajevo for SDA, came from people other than themselves. While it foregrounded nationalist interpellation, this explanation did not necessarily attribute deeply felt national identification to any of those people. Instead, SDP sympathisers in Dobrinja often suggested that SDA's appeal, at least in the current period, was not based on belief or commitment as much as on opportunism or stupidity. Moreover, most SDA sympathisers themselves did not explain their engagement in terms of nationality issues either, emphasising commitment to BiH statecraft instead (see below).

If the relative success of hegemonising projects can be assessed by the degree of their successful transformation of a population's 'horizon of the taken-for-granted' (Hall 1988: 44; see also Comaroff and Comaroff 1992; Joseph and Nugent 1994), the fact that 'normal lives' were at the heart of shared concerns in Dobrinja thus points to the limits of any Bosniak nationalist hegemonic project by the Dayton ruling caste in this apartment complex. For, notwithstanding dramatic political changes in the early 1990s, the values and aspirations foregrounded by Dobrinjci displayed a remarkable degree of continuity: today's projections of 'normal lives' (the 'ought') were largely updated forms of the 'was', that is, of their communist-coloured version around which late Yugoslav self-management had formulated its hegemonic project (amongst Dobrinjci, to a large degree, successfully).[1] Crucially, despite their actual dismantling of

much SFRY gridding infrastructure and despite anticommunist statements by SDA politicians elsewhere, in Sarajevo the Dayton ruling
caste did not openly reject the legitimacy of yearnings for 'normal
lives' thus understood. On the contrary, when competing for broad
popular support, all politicians presented themselves as the actors
most likely to deliver the 'system' that would allow them to unfold.
In fact, with remarkable agility, some leading politicians even echoed
the generic dismissal of *politika* as a dirty business at the expense of
ordinary people.[2]

Common Ground for Interpellation:
The Fantasy of the Not-Yet-State

When asked what they themselves would do if they were in a position
to break out of the Dayton Meantime – admittedly a question invit-
ing fantasy futurism – my Dobrinja interlocutors tended to speak of
sudden, all-encompassing change to bring the state 'in order'. Some
said they would open workplaces and raise pensions; some that they
would 'erase nations'; some that they would install a one-person
presidency; some that they would root out corruption; some that they
would abolish the entities within BiH; and so on. But many did not
specify anything, simply expressing a desire for a working 'system'
in which 'normal lives' could unfold. In this way, as we saw, the
structural—moral diagnosis of the 'lack of a system' and of 'pattering
in place' entailed political criticism but in effect reinforced demobili-
sation. People placed the key responsibility for providing a 'normal
state' in … the state. The state, in other words, should institute itself.[3]
    In Dobrinja, 'the state' thus emerged as a fetish (Taussig 1992). This
was a potential ground for successful interpellation into a hegemonic project. We have seen how, amongst my interlocutors, rather
than revolving around 'sacred and erotic attraction, even thraldom,
combined with disgust' (ibid.: 111), evocations of the state more commonly emerged in a language of 'system' and 'movement'. Yet questions of the statehood of BiH and of statecraft in BiH remained deeply
entangled. All Sarajevo parties, including those, like SDA, that also
deployed Bosniak-nationalist rhetoric, sought to appeal to the shared
concern with 'normal lives' in a 'normal state'. Such commitment
was the lynchpin of legitimacy claims by SDP and of its *Država za
čovjeka* ['A State for People'] electoral campaign in 2010. While, unlike
SDA, it could not look back on almost two decades in government,
this party did enjoy its share of institutional influence. In the early

2000s it had been at the centre of the short-lived Alliance for Change government. During my Dobrinja research in 2008–10, it participated in governing coalitions in important municipal authorities (such as in Novi grad) and in some cantonal ones outside of Sarajevo. It also occupied one of the three seats in the BiH presidency. After the 2010 elections, SDP formed coalitions with SDA in a series of executive governments, including those of Canton Sarajevo and of the Federation. The behaviour of SDP politicians in the prolonged bargaining that preceded them, in their short existence and in their collapse soon after convinced many even amongst its voters that this party was no less a manifestation of *politika* than others, although its tentacles were not spread as broadly as those of SDA. For all those reasons, like the flyer for the protests that opened this chapter, I treat SDP as a faction of the 'ruling caste' in Sarajevo and I contend that my argument on the reproduction of this caste below applies, to a large extent, to this party too.

All major political parties vying for people's support in Sarajevo proclaimed a commitment to a 'normal', 'functioning' BiH state. Yet how could this contribute to the reproduction of their positions? After all, none of them could claim to have delivered much on this front. The answer, I suggest, lies in the temporal peculiarities of Dayton BiH. Namely, when the ruling caste mobilised the 'fantasy of the state' (Navaro-Yashin 2002), this was a projected reification of a not-yet-state. Of course, deferral is at the core of all state fetishism, which revolves precisely around the tension between the actual incompleteness and the projected completeness of the state. Roseberry calls for an analysis of 'state *projects* rather than state *achievement*' (Roseberry 1994: 365, italics in original), and he points out that the most promising entry points for such an analysis are provided by instances of failure or breakdown. In Dayton BiH, I found an intensified version of this deferral in state fetishism. As this book shows, even the ruling caste could not pretend that the 'actually existing' Dayton BiH state was a strong and unified entity. Instead, interpellation occurred through the projection of such characteristics on a 'normal' BiH not-yet-state.

Laments about the faults of the 'actually existing' state further reinforced the degree of hegemony that this state-centred discourse enjoyed, for it engaged in contestation precisely on those terms. So, it was not success that determined the extent to which this hegemonic project took hold. Many Dobrinjci classified party-political statements of commitment to instituting a proper state as empty promises amongst many other ones –to create thousands of jobs, to complete a motorway, to root out corruption and so on. But the institutional structure and the regime of temporal reasoning of Dayton BiH allowed politicians, even those who had ruled for almost two decades, to reject any responsibility for the absence of a 'normal state'. They blamed this failure on other politicians: those claiming to represent national others, but also those of other parties and foreign emissaries. What was crucial, I contend, is that against the background of the affliction of Daytonitis, stated commitments to a not-yet 'functioning BiH state' resonated with yearnings for 'normal lives'. In a psychoanalytically inflected understanding of hegemony, Salecl argues that the appeal of political discourse rests on the construction of 'a symbolic space in which we can appear likeable to ourselves', a discourse organised 'in such a way that it leaves space open to be filled by images of our ideal ego' (1992: 57). If people resented that Daytonitis had condemned them to 'survive' through endless 'chasing' – even for the most basic livelihood requirements – the discourse that emerged in this respect as the most appealing to my Dobrinja interlocutors was one that evoked a 'normal state' called BiH which 'showed concern'. For SDP sympathisers in particular, this included an explicitly stated desire to weaken or abolish its institutionalised national forms.

Yet we should note that most Dobrinjci did not feel that any party-political discourse in Dayton BiH allowed them to appear quite like-able enough to themselves. Instead, they often expressed a sense of abandonment and that, surely, is more a sign of *not* being mobilised (enough) by any hegemonic project. In this respect, even if we allow for the possibility of ambiguous combinations of Bosniak-nationalist and pro-BiH discourse, it is worth mentioning that 'disciplinary–symbolic power' (Wedeen 1999b) was less prominent in Dobrinja than one might expect in a constellation which teemed with potential for it. Clearly there were occasions on which people were interpellated through BiH state symbolism, particularly through Ideological State Apparatuses (Althusser 1971). War sacrifice in particular remained a crucial referent. We encountered examples of this in the discussion of schooling. It also emerged in street name changes and in annual commemorations of wartime massacres by VRS shelling, organised by MZs. To different degrees, some people inscribed themselves into this. Some waved Dayton BiH or RBiH flags at football games or at weddings. Some, as we saw, mobilised BiH state symbolism to underpin their claims to legitimacy as school teachers or as bus drivers. Yet during my research, such commemorations, for example, attracted very few people, of whom many were there out of profes-sional duty. I suggest that, in 2008–10, in Dobrinja, the Dayton ruling caste did not need to invest much in BiH state symbolism nor in

Bosniak nationalist symbolism. One reason was that, while threats posed by Serbian and Croatian nationalists were often rhetorically invoked, they posed no electoral competition to any of the leading parties in Sarajevo. The total pool of votes to be shared amongst the ruling caste was guaranteed. It was unimaginable that large numbers of Sarajevans would vote for Croatian or Serbian nationalist parties, who rarely sought to interpellate inhabitants of the capital anyway, largely ignoring even their fellow nationals there.

All in all, for a setting associated with war and nationalism, many dimensions of Dobrinja lives could unfold relatively oblivious to any nation or state symbolism in the service of the Dayton ruling caste. The only prominent iconography in the Dobrinja landscape consisted of the 1984 Olympics logo engraved in some apartment blocks.[4] Rather than being enticed to sing the BiH hymn, people sarcastically remarked on the fact that there were not even any approved lyrics to this tune.[5] And if TV Sarajevo always referred to Sarajevo as the 'capital city of BiH', everyone knew that this was only the case to a degree – with two parallel centres in Banja Luka and western Mostar. For most in Dobrinja, then, this was at best interpellation in the name of a not-yet-state. And with regard to this 'state fantasy', a peculiar pattern emerged in the appeals for popular support by the Dayton ruling caste. Leading Sarajevo politicians did emphasise their strength by expounding their wartime and postwar role in defending BiH statehood. But in terms of statecraft in 'actually existing' Dayton BiH, they often stressed their weakness. Evoking people's yearnings for 'normal lives', they sought to position themselves alongside them. They too, leading politicians said, were victims of Daytonitis, and, due to the pernicious *politika* of others, they could only hold out for a 'normal state' called BiH. As we saw, some of my Dobrinja interlocutors did sympathise with certain politicians along these lines when, as Mrs Varešanović said, 'those [other] ones [were] working collectively'.

Apathy and Engagement

In a study of young people in Serbia, Greenberg (2010) rejects normative qualifications of 'apathy' with regard to politics as signs of 'failure'. 'Non-participation', she says, also allows the fashioning of moral subjectivity around powerlessness, and, 'we should ask *what* people … are opting out of when they do not participate in politics' (ibid.: 63, italics in original). I agree, but in this chapter I approach such questions from another angle. When protesters on the streets of Sarajevo in the winter of 2008 criticised their fellow citizens for 'remaining silent' and for 'suffering/enduring', they saw apathy as support for the status quo. In this context, I think this is correct, but I would fine-tune both accusations. Firstly, protesters knew that people were hardly silent about politics: they were well aware that 'barking' at politicians was a widespread activity. What the protesters meant is that people did this amongst themselves while 'drinking coffee', instead of raising their voice directly at those politicians. Secondly, and most importantly, I qualify the idea that people who did not protest, but perhaps 'barked' over coffee, were always merely 'suffering/enduring' the Dayton status quo. If chapter 5 emphasised the demobilising, perhaps tranquillising tendencies of temporal reasonings that underlay waiting in the Dayton Meantime, here I propose that we insert, alongside the apathetic, nonresponsive stance this implies, the possibility of an active, responsive dimension in nonresistant engagements with *politika*. This second dimension too, I shall argue, contributed to the reproduction of the Dayton ruling caste.

I now first introduce this second dimension in terms of formal political participation. In the next section I will go beyond this. How did Dobrinjci, despite their aversion to *politika*, actively engage with it? Firstly, many voted in elections. Some of my interlocutors did not vote and justified this by saying they could not find a politician who deserved their support. Yet most did vote. Some emphasised that they and their families systematically voted for the same party; others, like Mrs Varešanović, had voted for candidates from different parties in different elections. Some hastened to qualify their participation in elections, saying they voted without illusions, and, in a few cases, putting it down to loyalty to friends. Novi grad in fact saw one of the lowest turnouts in all of BiH (under 40 per cent in 2008 local elections and 50 per cent in 2010), so my interlocutors contained an untypically low proportion of abstainees. Total BiH turnout (55 per cent in 2008 and 56 per cent in 2010) is low in European comparative perspective, but I find it still relatively substantial for a country where a survey (UNDP 2007: 13) found that political parties enjoyed the lowest degree of trust of all institutions (including for example, media, police, courts and foreign intervention agencies) and that, in an open question to name BiH's 'main weakness', 'politicians'/'politics' and 'corruption' followed hot on the heels of 'unemployment' (ibid.: 38).

The second element of engagement with *politika* is therefore even more striking: party membership. Like Mrs Varešanović, many of my older interlocutors, whether or not they had, like her, been party members, had been engaged in Yugoslav-era *društvenopolitički rad* ['societal-political work'] through local or workplace organisations. Many emphasised that, in Dayton BiH, they stayed clear of any such engagement. A countrywide survey (UNDP 2009: 62) found very low rates even of passive membership in any kind of associations, including veteran's organisations, trade unions, religious organisations, etc. The highest percentage (4 per cent) was for membership of leisure clubs. Yet 7 per cent of all respondents reported to be members of a political party. Since, two years earlier, 16 per cent said they had once joined a party (UNDP 2007: 26) and, one year earlier, 13 per cent in another BiH-wide study said they were currently party members (Puhalo 2008: 105), this may well be a case of serious under-reporting. In fact, in the 2007 study, the percentage of reported party membership was almost double that of those who said they had ever taken part in a demonstration (9 per cent).[6] Along with Serbia and Croatia, BiH has one of the highest rates of party membership in Europe (Van Biesen, Mair and Poguntke 2012). Quite a few of my Dobrinja respondents also said they were members of parties and some told me they had been members of different parties over the years. Here too, given the tendency to distance oneself from *politika* some under-reporting may have occurred.

A question thus emerges: if *politika* in BiH was widely considered nothing but a dirty business, how can we explain such relatively high rates of participation?

The Transformation of Material Channels to Pursue Life Projects

If my Dobrinja research found a shared concern with 'normal lives' in a 'normal state' – updated from its Yugoslav version – and if the Dayton ruling caste in Sarajevo did not really try to transform this framework of 'common sense' around 'normal lives', but to inscribe itself in it, can we even speak of any hegemonic project at all? I believe we can if we refrain from privileging questions of ideological consent or symbolism at the expense of material dimensions. To this aim, a productive conceptualisation of hegemony focuses on process and contestation in the kind of material–political understanding that Gramsci intended in the first place (Smith 2004: 104; 2011). Hegemony, then, refers to, 'a common material and meaningful framework for living through, talking about, and acting upon social orders characterised by domination' (Roseberry 1994: 361). So, people do not have to be categorised either as deluded by ideology or instead as autono-mous grid evaders. Hegemonic projects include attempts to enforce material regulation and the establishment of a shared 'language of contention' through the setting of 'central terms of contestation and struggle' (ibid.). One can speak of a successful hegemonic project to the extent that an elite establishes 'legitimate forms of procedure, ... prescribed forms for both acceptance and discontent' (ibid.: 364).

Largely along those lines, in their study of missionaries in early colonial southern Africa, Comaroff and Comaroff (1992) trace a 'conversation' along which 'the colonisation of consciousness' was conducted. Their argument against overly textual understandings of consciousness describes Tswana people's engagements with mis-sionaries as:

> [M]otivated by a desire to appropriate the cultural and technical power of the whites without losing their autonomy. In the effort to harness that power to their own ends, however, they joined the conversation. ... In so doing, they were indicted into the *forms* of European discourse. ... They could not but slowly begin to internalise the terms through which they were challenged. (ibid.: 245–46)

Analogous to this approach, in what follows I reconstruct a Dayton BiH 'conversation' on livelihood matters between the Sarajevo ruling caste and its potential electorate. Despite many differences, the anal-ogy lies in the structural inequality of this 'conversation': in the fact that it took place on the terrain of that ruling caste, which was largely able to set certain terms of engagement at the exclusion of others (see also Linger 1993; Woost 1993).

This brings me to a third and, I argue, crucial way in which Do-brinjci inserted themselves into *politika*: as potential recipients of clientelist allocation. Let's look at an example. Mrs Fejzić, a sixty-year-old widowed and retired teacher, shared a flat with one of her two adult sons, her daughter-in-law and two grandchildren. Asked if she believed there were honest politicians in BiH, she said:

> Well I think there are, there are. Only their surroundings, the society in which they find themselves, shackles them so much [*toliko ih sputavaju*], that their ideas can't be realised at all.

Q: If you had the power, what would you change?

> I would only do, that the police and the judiciary stand on its own legs, and to give them back their prewar socialist competences. Then things would be solved to a large extent.

During the war, a VRS shell hit the entrance of Mrs Fejzić's building, killing her husband and wounding her two sons. Later her oldest son was seriously wounded again while on ARBiH duty. Disabled, he continued army service as an administrator. Then he completed his last university exams and his dissertation. At the graduation ceremony, Mrs Fejzić recalled, professors declared, 'Young ladies and gentlemen, whichever workplace you find us in, turn to us for employment or anything else'. So soon after she told her son to call on his former dissertation supervisor, who had taken up a leading political position in Sarajevo: 'Go see him. He's in that position now. Ask if he can do anything'. And, sure enough, 'he helped him, through his connections, I don't know how' to a job in a public institution. In 2008 Mrs Fejzić's son was still employed in the same institution.

Extrapolating from Mrs Fejzić's example, I now try to outline how the Dayton ruling caste successfully reproduced its domination by monopolising the 'terrain of contention' (Roseberry 1994: 362). If people lamented the 'lack of a system', then, this did not mean there currently was not any system at all. Regardless of ideological consent, the ruling caste had transformed possibilities for the pragmatic pursuit of life projects, from the basic reproduction of livelihoods to grander ambitions. To sketch the contours of an 'actually existing' system of gridding in Dayton BiH, I turn to Bojičić-Dželilović's (2013) analysis of the role of informal practices in the longevity of the country's ruling caste.[7] In the 1992–95 war, Bojičić-Dželilović explains, three political elites – legitimising themselves, to different degrees, in nationality terms and with regard to statehood – criminally and violently engineered a political and economic reconfiguration. Afterwards, in Dayton BiH, these elites continued to rule through 'a tacit agreement on "the rules of the game", … lodged in a political settlement lacking a shared vision of BiH's statehood' (ibid.: 218), allowing them to consolidate and expand on the wealth and influence gained during war. Yet if the privileges of this Dayton ruling caste were based on the expropriation of, amongst others, its own electorate, how did it persist now that the direct coercion of wartime had become less acceptable? Bojičić-Dželilović shows that this was achieved through the recruitment of broad layers of the population into informal channels of allocation. Emphasising its pervasiveness across the social hierarchy in Dayton BiH, she argues that, while informality allows temporary individual escape from social exclusion, the unequal relationship on which it depends produces, at best, 'adverse inclusion' (ibid.: 221) and ultimately reproduces domination (ibid.: 220).[8]

In a process of what many in BiH referred to as 'primitive accumulation', and in line with Gramscian understandings of hegemonic process (Smith 2004; 2011), the Dayton ruling caste ruthlessly continued to appropriate public resources, thus transforming the material base and state institutions. Since the infrastructure within which such resources existed (and sometimes, those resources themselves) had been 'socially owned' before, built up with people's contributions through Yugoslav socialist self-management, this involved a radical redistribution of wealth through dispossession of the large majority. Social property had mostly first been converted into state property. As such, it was placed under the direct control of particular ruling political parties. Some of it was then transferred to private ownership – this, often crooked, process was also steered by political parties. Importantly, at the top end this occurred in conjunction with capital flows originating from, amongst others, EU states, the U.S., Russia, Turkey, Iran and the Gulf. These dynamics allowed a thin layer of BiH citizens to profit handsomely from the country's particular insertion into global finance capitalism, while they encouraged many others to continue to aspire to material standards associated with 'normal lives', which were now only accessible through loans from foreign banks (unlike most other sectors, banking in Dayton BiH had long been largely privatised and foreign-owned). Yet the hegemonic project we can detect here, as I argued before, was 'selective' (Smith 2011).

Here it is important to remind the reader of some harsh figures for June 2008 (unless specified otherwise, figures concern Novi grad municipality).[9] The registered employment rate was 16 per cent. The average net wage was 807 KM (€412) plus a (federal) average of 262 KM (€134) for meals and transport. The registered unemployment rate was 14 per cent and only very few received benefits on this basis (ca. 300 KM [€153]), and this for a maximum of two years (usually for a much shorter period). Around 20 per cent of all BiH households received some (non means-tested) war-related allowances, for example, for war disability (at 100 per cent disability, 805 KM [€411]) or for civilian victims of war (at 100 per cent disability, 300 KM [€153]). The distribution of such payments was extremely top-heavy. Around 16 per cent of people in Novi grad drew pensions. The average (federal) pension was 340 KM (€173) and half of all pensioners received the minimum pension of 282 KM (€144). Other (means-tested) welfare payments amounted to a maximum of a few hundred KM altogether. The official four-member household 'basket' was calculated at 528 KM (€270), covering only food and hygiene. A rival 'syndical' basket was set at around 1500 KM (€767). With mass unemployment and an aging population, many Bosnians were thus not even exploited through surplus extraction of the value they produced through their labour. Competition for jobs was fierce. Moreover, very large numbers of people were dependent on allowances and pensions (often in addition to remittances). Crucially, therefore, dispossession was accompanied by targeted allocation, especially of public sector jobs and war-related allowances.

I argue that in Sarajevo, a decade and a half after the war, it was in these practices of allocation, more so than in nationalist appeals to ideological consent, that we can detect the most effective mechanisms of a hegemonic project by the ruling caste (see also Kurtović 2012: 50–65). It is here, I contend, in the realm of statecraft in BiH, that the most intensive interpellation took place, and it is here that the central terms of contestation were most systematically enforced. Clearly, party clientelism is hardly unique to Dayton BiH. I could tell a tale or two from Belgium, where I grew up. Yet this is not a comparative analysis of forms of clientelism, nor a detailed analysis of its functioning in Dayton BiH per se. Instead, I now propose to contribute to the conceptualisation of hegemony, analysing people's enmeshment with the ruling caste through the notion of 'conviviality' and emphasising, once again, the specific temporal dynamics at work in the Dayton Meantime.

Conviviality: Invitations That Are Hard to Decline

My use of the term 'conviviality' is inspired by Mbembe's attempt to overcome dichotomous analyses of domination/resistance in sub-Saharan Africa through a focus on complicity (1992). Politics in postcolonial Africa, he argues, is best seen as 'a promiscuous relationship': a 'convivial tension' between rulers and ruled, converging in a 'logic of familiarity and domesticity' (ibid.: 5). Coexisting in the same cultural space, Mbembe says, the dominant and the dominated then mimic each other's styles, mixing majesticity and vulgarity. Widely cited, Mbembe's analysis has also been criticised for privileging stylistics over interests (Cohen 1992: 59; Olaniyan 1992: 51) and for his neglect of material livelihoods (Weate 2003: 38), both preventing a more subtle understanding of stratified complicity in practice. To be fair, Mbembe does mention material interests, stating, for example, that: 'flattery is not just produced to please the despot; it is manufactured in a quest for profit or favours. The aim is to share the table of the autocrat, to "eat from his hands"' (1992: 21).

Mbembe also notes that, ultimately, despite its potential grating and erosive effects, the convivial ridicule on which he focuses leaves untouched the 'material base' of the dominant (ibid.: 15). Yet he does not develop this much, focusing instead on symbolic representations. In contrast, I propose a predominantly materialist conceptualisation of conviviality in Dayton BiH. We have already encountered a pattern of conviviality in my interlocutors' expressions of sympathy for politicians' claims that, with regard to the making of a 'normal BiH state', they inhabited a shared space of equivalent weakness due to the intransigence of 'other' politicians. While this could be expressed in the register of nationality, and it often was elsewhere, in Dobrinja I mainly encountered it in nationality-neutral form, like in Mrs Varešanović's words above. Yet it is another pattern of conviviality, signalled by Mrs Fejzić's story about her son, that I want to address here. With regard to the 'actually existing' state of Dayton BiH, namely, politicians did not only project weakness but also strength. While the offer of employment favours at the graduation ceremony provided an example, this was less present in their slogans and speeches, and more in their attitude with regard to their influence and their wealth. Here I would include luxury cars, suits, sunglasses and watches; arrogant and careless behaviour (recall the key characteristics attributed to top politicians in Dayton BiH); blatant lies; and, crucially, invitations extended to a potential client base. In bare material terms the ruling caste could successfully project itself as powerful because: (a) it successfully monopolised the appropriation of public resources; (b) it openly enjoyed the fruits of this appropriation; and (c) it could shrug off any attempts to be called to account for it. The latter point was important: even when some top politicians and their tycoon allies in other post-Yugoslav states were being imprisoned, in Dayton BiH the ruling caste's grip on the relevant parts of the dispersed judiciary still provided them with impunity.

All these issues were common topics in widespread 'barking' at politicians, and, unsurprisingly, leading politicians' attempts to evoke resonances with yearnings for 'normal lives' were often met with scorn. Yet, despite their stated disgust with *politika*, in terms of the pragmatics of their everyday lives, everyone in Dayton BiH did inhabit spaces shaped by the Dayton ruling caste. One's social location – the mere fact of living in Dayton BiH – left precious few alternatives. The ruling caste provided pragmatic routes to secure bare lives and to transcend them in the direction of 'normal lives'.

Sometimes through capillary networks of middlemen, its representatives then extended invitations to people to insert themselves into those channels. Such invitations existed in parallel forms in the different Dayton BiH fiefdoms, sometimes more and sometimes less articulated with nationality. A generic Sarajevo version would look something like this:

> Dear people. We know you just want 'normal lives'. You deserve it and we're doing everything to make this possible. Unfortunately our efforts are frustrated by those who don't love this state and by toothless foreigners who equalise victims and aggressors We feel your pain! But don't despair, we're holding out for a proper solution, a functioning BiH state, which we know you and your loved ones sacrificed so much for, just like we did. Then we'll complete our Road into Europe, which we're working on day and night. Please calmly wait. After all, we're in this together! In the meantime, we invite you to join us. In return for your support, we'll help you in the pursuit of your livelihoods (and, in some cases, much beyond that!). Unfortunately, for most of you, due to the fault of all the others mentioned above, this won't amount to conditions for a 'normal life', but it's the best we can offer you. Please sign here!

While such invitations sometimes involved explicit calls for people to enter through the front door and take up (subordinate) places in the party-controlled machinery of allocation, much of it emerged more implicitly in the form of backdoors left ajar.[10] The key factor in the reproduction of the Dayton ruling caste, I argue, was that it had made those explicit 'front door' and implicit 'backdoor' invitations hard to decline. Its strength lay in its capacity to exclude or at least make unattractive most alternative routes to pursue life projects, for most people at most times. Moreover, people reasoned that, if they declined invitations, there were plenty of others waiting to accept. In such a constellation, many, regardless of their views on party politics, considered themselves lucky to be invited via the front door; and more still felt that finding themselves within reach of an open backdoor was preferable to not finding themselves there. Mrs Fejzić's son was one of them.

In that way, the Dayton ruling caste, I argue, did more or less successfully compel large layers of the population to pursue life projects through material channels controlled by their parties, benefitting them and individuals within them, and reproducing their influence and wealth. To a large extent it determined the 'terrain of contention'. The flyer with which I opened this chapter attempted to mobilise people for anti-government protests based on the premise that three forms of knowledge were widely shared amongst citizens: (1) that the basics of life in Dayton BiH were threatened by abandonment and mismanagement by privileged, lazy and cynical politicians; (2) that membership of or support for leading parties was a way in which people sought shelter from such threats; and (3) that problems were so all-encompassing that even that could not be considered a fully effective insurance strategy. Most people, like Mrs Fejzić, saw this as an unchangeable situation beyond their control. And my Dobrinja interlocutors did indeed broadly agree that it was impossible to pursue even the most basic life projects, let alone to 'get on', without an informal connection, usually called *štela* (pl. *štele*, a 'connection', see chapter 4).

This reflected BiH-wide survey findings which returned massive majorities of respondents who believed that a *štela* could facilitate access to education, health care treatments, visa applications and so on (UNDP 2009: 75). The highest score concerned finding employment. Unemployed and young people (more likely to be unemployed too) attached the greatest importance to *štele* in their depiction of Dayton BiH (ibid.: 76). Sarajevan respondents were on average slightly less convinced of the use of a *štela*, but in follow-up focus groups many argued that in the capital too they were in fact indispensable for most pursuits (ibid.: 77–78). They also refracted the use of *štele* by 'ordinary people' against setup privatisations, contracts and tenders. The somewhat lower Sarajevo score in this survey could be explained by the fact that the capital offered at least some routes to pursue life projects that were less directly embedded in party structures, especially through employment in foreign intervention agencies and NGOs.[11] By no means can we conclude that *štele* were irrelevant in these institutions, but the party-political ruling caste did exercise less control over them.[12]

Ethnographic studies in Dayton BiH have pointed out the proliferation of *štele* in a broad spectre of spheres (e.g., Brković 2010, 2012a, 2012b; Čelebičić 2013). In my experience of life in Sarajevo, an extremely widespread form, which very few people could or wanted to circumvent, concerned public health care. But the work of connections also pertained, for example, to disability allowances and pensions, permits of various kinds, education, building maintenance and so on. In many of those cases there was no direct entanglement with political parties, although there sometimes was.[13] Mrs Fejzić did not mention political parties, but, given their grip on public institutions, it is likely that her son's employment did involve party links.

While *štele* were crucial dimensions of the pursuit of life projects in Dayton BiH in many different ways, their meshing with political party structures was perhaps considered most important of all in regulating access to jobs. With staggering unemployment rates and a very large (semi-)public sector, the most coveted prizes in the pursuit of life projects were relatively secure jobs in public institutions (see Bourdieu 1979: 71). Here, political parties, who directly controlled those institutions, were at the core of the mobilisation of *štele*. Note that party membership and connections were not always sufficient to secure such employment. The pressure on public-sector jobs was such that it was not uncommon for them to be bought: candidates paid members of a commission or a director well over a year's salary in order to be appointed over other candidates. Rumours about unofficial pricelists circulated and some people took loans to buy a job. Joining a party was thus often a small part of a larger chase.

This is an appropriate point at which to ask: is this conviviality simply a multiparty version of the mode of political domination that existed in the SFRY? Mrs Varešanović said absolutely everything had been better 'before':

> Everything is worse [now]. At that time, nothing interested me. Not *politika* either. I had everything. And today, on TV, you watch their fights, their disputes, some problems. I'm included in everything, although I don't need that. I'm old already, retired, but I'm nonstop included, through TV, in stories. Nonstop. Even with friends, they only talk about what this one did, what that one did. I'm permanently included, even if I don't want it. I don't even have to watch TV for it, friends talk about it. *Politika* is permanently present, on TV, when socialising, in the trolleybus, on the street. That story is never-ending.

Q: And that was not the case before?

> No, it wasn't.

As we saw in chapter 5, many Dobrinjci – including former members of the League of Communists such as Mrs Varešanović – remembered their lives during late Yugoslav socialism as largely oblivious to politics. They did not mention either ideological interpellation or conviviality, although it is well known that chasing a *štela* had been an important ingredient of life in Yugoslav self-management socialism too, just like the tendency to declare detachment from *politika* (see e.g., Anđelić 2003; Goati 1989). How, then, were my Dobrinja interlocutors able to unanimously evoke such lives as referents for a far superior 'normality'? How could they argue that everything had changed for the worse? No doubt, in Yugoslav times many had 'barked at' politics too, yet in comparison with today's circumstances they recalled the reproduction of 'normal lives' made possible by state gridding. People remembered a 'system'. Not a perfect system, many hastened to add, but one that had been much more effective in its facilitating of 'normal lives' for most. If my Dobrinja interlocutors did recall party clientelism at all, they stressed that it had been possible to live 'normal lives' without it. Invitations had been extended, and backdoors had been left ajar, but both my interlocutors who had been members of the League of Communists and those who had not remembered it had not been so hard to decline or ignore them.

Such narratives suggest that the threshold of clientelism had been shifted downwards: if in the SFRY, it was recalled, declining front door invitations and ignoring open backdoors would hinder the realisation of ambitious life projects beyond 'normal lives', today this could block even the most modest reproduction ('surviving'). Contrary to any interpretations of Yugoslav socialist self-management as totalitarian, my interlocutors argued that it was with the establishment of a parliamentary multiparty democracy and a form of capitalism that a ruling caste had come to monopolise livelihood paths to a greater degree than ever before. In Dayton BiH (as anywhere and anytime), some people accepted invitations in order to pursue luxury and grand ambitions. Whichever criteria we use to assess necessity, it is clear that, while sometimes mobilising the opportunities offered by conviviality because they felt they had to, some people no doubt also used them simply because they felt they could. Yet regardless of any precise definition of survival, my interlocutors in Dobrinja resented that the threshold at which one could only or almost only proceed through accepting explicit and implicit invitations to share in the clientelist allocation of public resources lay very low in comparison with the two points of reference: former Yugoslav lives and current Western European lives. With towering unemployment, very low salaries, pensions and allowances, and consumer prices that were only marginally lower than in most Western European countries,[14] accepting party-political invitations and slipping in through backdoors became a way for some to meet basic requirements of not-even-normal lives.

Recalling Mbembe's linking of conviviality and commensality ('the aim is to share the table of the autocrat' [1992: 21]), we can thus picture every Dayton BiH fiefdom as a publicly funded refectory. Unlike in autocracy, we see a set of tables presided over and supplied by leading figures of different parties in the Dayton ruling caste, who bickered over the precise boundaries between their tables, but agreed on the principle of divvying up the monopoly on the appropriation and allocation of scarce public resources. They then extended invitations to people to join them at their table, and left some backdoors open for others to slip in. In Dayton BiH, I contend, to different degrees, some 'ordinary people' had already joined the banquet. Others were queuing up. Clearly, one could sit at the centre of a table on a daily basis, or only once at the very end of one. Even sitting under it might be considered good enough in the circumstances, for at least it allowed access to the banquet's crumbs. In this way, the notion of 'conviviality' sheds a light on how survival, life projects and routines were in fact 'gridded' in Dayton BiH, but in ways that people considered a far cry from the 'system' that featured so centrally in their yearnings for 'normal lives'.

Brother, Cards on the Table?

Q: What do you most frequently talk about and with whom?

With friends and family about the thievery that reigns in this state.

Q: What do you expect for your future?

To find some politician with plenty of money and to marry him.
— A seamstress from Bijeljina (Helsinški parlament građana 2005)

So how did people in Dobrinja respond to these explicit and implicit invitations? As we saw, in their conversations with me and while 'drinking coffee', 'the people' [*narod*] were largely presented as non-complicit. Daily 'barking at politicians' over coffee ritually confirmed this: they mostly portrayed themselves and the majority of their fellow citizens as uncontaminated by immoral *politika*. In such verbal performances, most ignored the invitations extended to them by the Dayton ruling caste. Party members, as we saw, largely exempted their own party from the evils of *politika*. Virtually everyone, thus, sought to show they inhabited an alternative sphere. As this book has shown, people felt they paid a heavy price for that: abandonment.

How do we interpret this? The difficulties I encounter here are well known to ethnographers: how can an approach based on trust get to the murky entanglements that might, in some cases, under-lie people's continual distancing from *politika* (see Kurtović 2012: 58–65)? Let me be frank about the limitations of my data. People shared with me their engagement in the formal arena of politics – whether as party activists, MZ councillors and/or voters. But, because of their insistence on the gap between *politika* and their everyday lives, my insight into any possible informal engagements with it, such as Mrs Fejzić's, was limited. My research interests lay mainly elsewhere anyway. Still, I do not want to shy away from the truth claims I make in this chapter. They are based on inference from my data, on insights from other studies and on my own experiences over many years in Sarajevo. Despite my methodological conundrum, I insist on addressing this issue, to add what I consider a necessary critical edge to my attempts to 'sense the political' in Dobrinja yearnings for 'normal lives'.

Let me approach possible complicity with a typical imagination of a radical break. Asked what she would do to improve lives in the country if she had the power to do so, Mrs Bašić, a married retired hairdresser in her mid fifties said:

> First, fairly [*pošteno*]. I would distribute fairly however much I had. First jobs for people ... Actually, first I would carry out a revision of everything. No apologies, let nobody get angry, but this is chaos what is being done now. The kind of flats they have, I don't know how many, what kind!? So, brother, cards on the table, fairly! [*brate karte na sto, pošteno!*]

Mrs Bašić's fantasy scenario would, no doubt, lead some high-up members of the Dayton ruling caste to seek exile in countries where they would be welcomed by their business/political allies. The scale of enrichment of many leading politicians, their impunity and the cynical blatancy with which they flaunted the fruits of their shady dealings was indeed disturbing. It is certainly not my aim to absolve them here. Yet I approach the issue from the other end. After all, many Dobrinjci pointed out that the real gravity point of party politics lay not in ideology or in care for a common good, but in unscrupulous struggles for wealth. Moreover, resonating with the flyer for the protests, they complained that it was impossible to get by without a *štela* and that political parties were central to this. How then did they themselves get by?

I propose we relate this back to concerns with 'messed-up values' and, beyond that, to the 'lingering doubts' about 'our people' being somehow immature for democracy (see chapter 4). Both were largely attributed to others and usually characterised as further entrenching the symptoms of Daytonitis. In these worries, I contend, we can make out contours of an awareness that conviviality did indeed implicate 'ordinary people'. For what would happen if Mrs Bašić's call for 'cards on the table' did not stop at the luxurious flats of the Dayton ruling caste to which she referred? What if not only Mrs Fejzić but all my Dobrinja interlocutors put their cards on the table? Ultimately, some might blame politicians for thievery and, given the circumstances, hope to marry one. Yet we do not need to address this issue on that scale. Some people in Dobrinja, we saw, admitted to riding city transport without paying and to not paying maintenance and heating bills. Some frowned at this but these practices were so widespread, and the dissatisfaction with GRAS, the *upravitelji* and energy providers so great, that many thought it legitimate in the given circumstances. By extrapolation, if they would be called to account for using party-political *štele*, I believe some would have one or two autobiographical tales to tell: a child employed, perhaps, or a war-related allowance approved. It is not and cannot be my intention here to try to expose my interlocutors in Dobrinja as crafty dissimulators. Yet nor would it be realistic to assume that I ran into a selection of people who, without exception, could afford and were willing to pursue their life projects outside of *politika* in a Dayton BiH constellation where, they themselves argued, mechanisms of clientelist allocation were crucial to the reproduction of lives. In the absence of a 'normal state', they themselves portrayed political parties as multi-tentacled menaces permeating all sectors of such lives. They lived in Dayton BiH and acted within spaces available to them, so it is unrealistic to imagine them all as inhabiting a pristine zone, opposed to *politika*. I therefore understand widespread expressions of detachment from *politika* as rhetorical strategies in the formation of moral subjectivity (Kolind 2008: 135–48; Spasić 2013: 123–31). I suggest that the very knowledge about the reach of conviviality further encouraged the use of such strategies to remove *politika* from everyday lives that might in fact – I say might! – include acceptances of the invitations by the ruling caste in attempts to overcome abandonment. I now relate this to the question of cynicism.

Yurchak's work on political subjectivity in Leningrad (1997; 2005) shows that most people in the late socialist Soviet Union were aware that official ideology bore little relation to actual life experiences. Yet they also believed it was there to stay and they pretended to go along with it – for example by taking part in parades organised by the Communist Party. Yurchak argues that 'cynical reason', then, allowed the reconciliation of one's disbelief in official ideology with one's own participation in its reproduction (1997: 171). And people used political jokes to release the anxiety about such incongruities. In that way, Yurchak states, late Soviet socialism persisted, and saw little explicit contestation from citizens because most people considered it 'omnipresent and immutable, even if largely false' (ibid.: 183–84; 2005: 32). Even the government did not pretend to believe in it any longer, but it still had the means to secure mass compliance, which, Yurchak says, people saw as the 'only possible way of having a normal and full life under these conditions' (1997: 186). Claims by Mrs Varešanović, and so many other Dobrinjci, that they wanted nothing to do with *politika* resonate with Yurchak's notion of a 'normal life', understood to be a life as oblivious as possible to politics (2005: 118–21). Yet there are major differences. In the Soviet Union, living such a life required outward compliance within what Yurchak calls a 'hegemony of form' (ibid: chapter 2), based on the feeling that everyone else was also obliged to routinely engage with the official order of signification (see also Wedeen 1999b: 152). As we saw, such requirements were relatively low key in Dobrinja. Moreover, while many political jokes existed, the exposure of the faults of *politika* I detail in this book was channelled mainly through what Yurchak calls 'analytical discourse' (1997: 184). He associates this with the glasnost period, when jokes were replaced with explicit, public discussions of the incongruity between ideology and experience. Since a sense of immutability was central to its perpetuation, the Soviet 'hegemony of form' thus disintegrated and cynical reason ceased to play its reproductive role. This book has shown how such 'analytical discourse' – often in rudimentary diagnoses – flourished in the Dayton BiH Meantime, whether in the form of academic texts, news reports, rants at the *okretaljka*, jeremiads at the MZ, or 'barking' over coffee.

Yet there is more to hegemony than signification. Yurchak mentions in passing how the 'hegemony of form' was also embedded in, 'tightly structured events of daily public life', referring to city transport, employment, schooling and consumption (ibid.: 167). While his focus lies elsewhere, this comment indicates that people's lives were 'gridded', and that the very pursuit of material reproduction in his interlocutors' everyday lives in Leningrad was likely to sometimes enmesh them with the Party. I have shown how this worked for Dobrinjci in the multiparty environment of Dayton BiH. Could cynicism function alongside 'analytical discourse' in such entanglements? Navaro-Yashin, in a study of 1990s 'public life' in Istanbul, has argued that 'mundane cynicism' was 'the most common sort of relationship with the state in contemporary Turkey' (2002: 170). Deploying the Lacanian term of 'fantasy' to theorise affective investments in the state, she recounts how people displayed awareness of the falsity of state ideology but nevertheless engaged in, 'everyday activities *as if* the state were there to deliver justice, *as if* it were an institution, a person, something tangible, *as if* it were a wholesome entity' (ibid.: 171). Since the state imposed itself on everyday lives in a variety of material manifestations, people inevitably encountered those in practical ways. Their mundane cynicism, Navaro-Yashin says, rested on 'worldly necessity', it was about 'an income, about bread and butter' (ibid.: 165), and in that way pragmatic pursuits of livelihood reproduction contributed to the reproduction of the state as fantasy.

In Dayton BiH, I contend, this logic was complicated by an ambiguity between the 'actually existing' state and the 'not-yet-state'. The latter, the projected 'normal BiH state', did enjoy much appeal in Dobrinja, so no mundane cynicism was apparent here. But nor did that projected state provide much bread or butter. The former, actually existing Dayton BiH, could do this: accepting ruling caste invitations could facilitate the pursuit of life projects, thus enmeshing people in *politika* through capillary networks of conviviality. As for politicians of the Dayton ruling caste: everyone assumed that cynicism structured their strategies. As for my Dobrinja interlocutors: any number may have accepted their invitations to conviviality at any point in time. Yet I would argue that no cynicism – mundane or otherwise – with regard to the state was required to deal with this, for the *'actually existing' state of Dayton BiH did not rely on any ideology or fantasy to be publicly upheld*. Its sovereignty status relied on geopolitics and its structure of domination, I contend, on the appropriation and allocation of public resources. Within their de facto closed pool of potential voters, political parties did not really try very much to interpellate many people through ideology (if mentioned at all, they all tended to pay lip service to some form of social democracy). Instead, as we saw in Mujkić's analysis above, they used pre-political nationalist fear mongering on the scale of inter-national competition, and, as I argue in this chapter, invitations to nonpolitical conviviality within their fiefdoms. One of the ways in which my interlocutors, whether they were ensnared in clientelism or not, could handle the latter was through 'barking' at politicians – a very rudimentary form of what Yurchak calls 'analytical discourse'. They could also engage in more rigorous, recognisably critical analysis. In any case, even if they had slipped through some backdoor or other, they could deflect this and deny conviviality with the Dayton ruling caste by removing *politika* from the portraits of their lives. And those who did acknowledge having accepted invitations, like Mrs Fejzić, were unlikely, I believe, to see this as in any way related to *politika*. Like her, I expect, they would see such claims to their little share from the banquet as a separate and insignificant issue. In particular, I suggest, they would not perceive any link between such acts and the reproduction of the

Dayton ruling caste. Like Bojičić-Dželilović, I contend that such links exist.

Conviviality in the Meantime

To close this chapter, I link the issue of conviviality back to the specific temporal framework that structured Dayton BiH. This interface, in my view, represented a key factor in the reproduction of the Dayton ruling caste. In Yurchak's Soviet Union and Navaro-Yashin's Turkey, the government projected stability, and this was largely accepted by citizens, regardless of ideological consent. For all intents and purposes, to most people involved, the political order was there to stay. In contrast, my Dobrinja interlocutors could not possibly harbour illusions of stability. They had only recently lived through a period in which the order they had been accustomed to had, to general shock, proven all too mutable. Moreover, the 'actually existing' state of which they were now citizens bore all the hallmarks of instability: Dayton BiH was considered makeshift and continually disputed. Crucially, in the view of my Dobrinja interlocutors, in the rhetoric of the Sarajevo politicians vying for their votes, and in the exhortations by foreign emissaries, it was never supposed to last in this form. Instead, they all agreed, this 'actually existing' state, afflicted by Daytonitis, should be modified into a 'functioning' one. Stability, then, was meant to be reached at the end of such modifications, which were presented as embedded in the 'Road into Europe'.

In chapter 5 I showed how this 'Road into Europe' was largely engaged with as belonging to the realm of fantasy futurism, removed from the immediate concerns of everyday lives. It was sometimes hoped that steps in the direction of EU membership would facilitate the making of a 'normal state' in BiH, yet in practice my Dobrinja interlocutors detected little evidence of collective forward movement from the 'dead point'. So they did in fact share a certain experience of immutability, namely one of forced 'pattering in place'. This continuous sense that lives were stuck in an 'exceptional' period of which no one saw the end was reinforced by both rhetoric and practices of members of the Dayton ruling caste. In Sarajevo, politicians could and did explain any conceivable problem with reference to the blockage of the establishment of a 'functioning BiH' by others. Rather than accounting for the ills of actually existing statecraft in BiH, they shifted the rhetoric to challenges to the statehood of BiH by those 'who did not love the state'. In disputes between ruling politicians from different, largely nationally homogenised fiefdoms, as we saw, all roads led to Dayton. The ruling caste then called upon their respective electorates to 'hold out' with them, that is, to wait, until they would deliver the grand solution they promised. Any discomfort currently experienced, those politicians argued, was of a temporary nature in two ways. Firstly, they said, it would not last. Secondly, they claimed, the fact that they had not been able to solve it was explained precisely by Dayton BiH's temporariness.

A conception of lives in Dayton BiH as lives in the Meantime was widely shared – and I contend this further entrenched the patterns of conviviality identified above. I have shown how, eliciting some conviviality in temporal entrapment seen to be imposed by various others, politicians relied on alternative projections of strength: through the clientelist machines of their parties they 'invited' people to support them in exchange for access to channels to pursue life projects. My argument is that, regardless of any levels of ideological consent, precisely because everything in Dayton BiH was presented as existing in the Meantime, this reproduced the ruling caste in the face of enormous dissatisfaction with *politika*. The problems, politicians claimed, were temporary. Acceptance of any invitations, and the entanglements they entailed, people could therefore reason, were also temporary: they allowed the reproduction of not-even-normal lives in a Meantime not of their own choosing.

Hage (2009), as we saw in chapter 5, has argued that waiting serves as a neoliberal disciplinary governmental tool to produce docile and (if possible and/or necessary) productive bodies. Auyero (2012) ethnographically shows how this works in practice in welfare policies in Argentina that teach poor people to be not citizens, but 'patients of the state', condemned to wait. Both authors emphasise the impact of neoliberalisation and both conceive of waiting not as a straightforward, consciously deployed instrument of rule by elites, but as an example of Bourdieusian 'strategies (of domination) without strategists' (ibid.: 61). In Dayton BiH, as we have seen in chapter 4, the label of 'neoliberal statecraft' does not apply to the same degree as in Argentina or Australia. Crucially, since the preferred channel for the reproduction of livelihoods consisted of salaried jobs in the large public sector, and 'employing one's children' was a major concern for many of my interlocutors, there was not much need for the Dayton ruling caste to demobilise 'the masses' inside their fiefdom through control over their time (i.e., to render them docile by making them wait). At least for the time being, simmering and almost universal dissatisfaction with *politika* had not led to collective political action.

Most of my Dobrinja interlocutors did want a 'normal state' and, in the Meantime – while there was not one yet – they made do in the 'actually existing' state of Dayton BiH. Rather than counteracting any existing outright resistance, then, the Dayton ruling caste could prevent its inception by keeping any ideological contention out of *politika*. They successfully set the terms of the 'conversation' in entirely nonpolitical terms, keeping the country in limbo and forcing large numbers of people to spend much time chasing some *štela* or other. Monopolising the public resources amongst them, they extended 'invitations that were hard to decline', and counted on there being sufficient numbers of people who would not be able or willing to turn them down, whether for a seat of honour at the banquet or, more commonly, for the crumbs that were left.

Crucially, relative complicity was not dependent on consciousness – on how people understood it. It existed to the extent that they accepted invitations to facilitate or enhance the pursuit of life projects by entering the 'conversation' on the terrain of the Dayton ruling caste. No ideological consent was required for this. If I am right in this assessment, the common emphasis of foreign and domestic campaigns on education or consciousness raising can only yield limited results. Some such work is definitely worthwhile, in my view, especially to point out the degree to which small acceptances of conviviality contribute to the reproduction of the Dayton ruling caste. Yet, ultimately, I contend that people in Dayton BiH do not need to be enlightened about the criminality of their ruling caste. They know about it, often first hand. It is here that the most difficult challenge lies. On the side of the Dayton ruling caste, I believe its *bahatost* (brutish arrogance) can be reduced only by interventions into the criminal material practices that sustain it. If we are condemned to stay within the bounds of liberal democracy, this means at least ending impunity through coercive judiciary means. On the side of 'ordinary people' in Dayton BiH, I believe only the provision of alternative channels to pursue livelihoods could make it possible for sufficient numbers to decline invitations of conviviality.

In Dayton BiH, through incorporation – heavily stratified – waiting thus emerged as part of a more encompassing governmental tool: the imposition of the Meantime as a framework for the pursuit of life projects. And while I do not believe there were strategists in Sarajevo party headquarters explicitly designing schemes that would keep people living in the Meantime, I do believe that a degree of instrumentality can and should be attributed to the Dayton ruling caste for having enshrined it and for not doing anything to change this. I have not worked either with leading figures in BiH political parties or with foreign emissaries stationed in the country, but I contend we need to state outright that the Meantime was – and unfortunately still is as I write this – their time.[15] An affliction for many, Daytonitis, for them, was a blessing that allowed them to cynically reproduce their privileges. In the case of the domestic Dayton ruling caste, this occurred through electoral parliamentary democracy. I have shown that both symptoms of Daytonitis worked in its advantage: the 'lack of a system' strengthened its control over livelihood channels through the exclusion of alternatives, and 'pattering in place' disqualified the application of any 'normal' criteria to its actions by declaring everything to be temporary. In addition to referring to difficulties to scrape by for bodily reproduction, people's qualifications of life in Dayton BiH as 'surviving' thus draw attention to the peculiar drawn-out temporal structure within which it unfolds. Lives afflicted by Daytonitis were lives in the Meantime. And, for most, that Meantime was a mean time indeed.

Notes

1. I focus on Dobrinja here, but note that a BiH-wide survey confirmed that voters of all major parties in BiH tended to express the largest support for ideological statements that are usually associated with 'social democracy' (Puhalo 2008: 98).
2. Indeed, on a 2013 SDA rally in Mostar, Bakir Izetbegović said, without a trace of irony, 'BiH is a rich country and its citizens are born rich, but between them and that wealth stand politicians' (www.slobodnaevropa.org). Izetbegović was the Bosniak member of the BiH presidency, strongman of SDA, a party that had been in government almost without interruption since 1990, and main representative of the dynastical political-business empire founded by his late father, the first president of BiH.
3. As we have seen in chapter 5, the emphasis on movement displayed a similar tautological structure: providing the conditions of forward movement would represent movement in itself. Road and destination were one.
4. After my research, a new roundabout in Dobrinja was decorated with the official BiH state crest.
5. I could not have invented it myself: the proposed lyrics, co-written by an author from Republika Srpska and one from the Federation (one would have thought a contributor from Western Herzegovina would have been imperative to comply with Dayton 'trivision') languished in a parliamentary drawer under the working title *Intermeco*. An intermezzo for the Dayton meantime.
6. In contrast, while 20 per cent said they might join a political party one day, 22 per cent of respondents said they might join a demonstration one day (UNDP 2007: 26).
7. See also, for example, *Problems of Post-Communism* 2004; Andreas 2008; Divjak and Pugh 2008; Donais 2005; Pugh 2005.

8. Bojičić-Dželilović writes about 'ethnic elites'. Focusing within the Sarajevo fiefdom, I use the more generic 'ruling caste', which included parties that also tried to mobilise people with nationalist rhetoric. Bojičić-Dželilović herself argues against what she calls 'myopic' readings of Dayton BiH, pointing out that informality 'in the economic foundations of the local "elite bargain" struck against the disaccord over the future of the Bosnian state, operates as a parallel mechanism of exclusion which extends across discrimination and inequities associated with the primacy of the ethnic principle' (2013: 219).

9. Figures taken from *Mjesečni statistički pregled Federacije BiH* [Monthly statistical overview Federation BiH] August 2008; *Statistički Bilten za Mjesec Juli* 2008 [Statistical bulletin July 2008].

10. I thank one of the anonymous reviewers for encouraging me to differentiate my earlier, less precise argument along these lines.

11. Many foreign intervention institutions and NGOs based in Sarajevo offered relatively high salaries and/or honoraria. Yet the combination of fixed-term or casual contracts and the volatility of foreign funding priorities meant that their employees, who could and often did consider themselves lucky, were still exposed to the Meantime logic of Dayton BiH (e.g., Baker 2012).

12. In an earlier BiH-wide survey, 87 per cent of all respondents stated that half or more of all functionaries were corrupt. The foreign intervention agencies did better, but they too were widely perceived as corrupt (UNDP 2007: 15).

13. Questions in the UNDP focus groups were constructed such that the role of political parties did not emerge as a central theme, which could mean it was more or less understood, as suggested by some other focus group results on 'political participation' (UNDP 2009: 78).

14. In 2007, on aggregate, some 35.21 per cent of household expenses went on food and drink (amongst the highest proportions in Europe), 22.15 per cent on accommodation, 11.25 per cent on transport, 5.44 per cent on household equipment, 5.28 per cent on clothing, 4.03 per cent on health care, 3.28 per cent on communications and 0.53 per cent on education. This left only 12.83 per cent for other expenses (3.64 per cent for recreation and culture, 2.02 per cent for tobacco, and 7.17 per cent for miscellaneous). All figures taken from the website of Federal Office of Statistics [www.fzs.ba].

15. And, let me acknowledge that, to the extent that it facilitates academic trajectories of those who write studies of Dayton BiH, it can be considered *our* time too. A disturbing thought.

EPILOGUE
Shovelling and Numbering for 'Normal Lives'

✑

in which we return to yearnings for 'normal lives' and the projected role of the state therein from the perspective of Sarajevo at two later moments in the Dayton Meantime – winter 2012 and early summer 2013

Early February 2012. I arrive in Sarajevo some fourteen hours later than scheduled, which is not itself unusual in winter months, when snow and fog decimate the already limited number of flights that land or take off at the city's airport. The plane from München makes a U-turn just before Sarajevo and lands in Zagreb, Croatia, instead. After a verbal tussle with the flight attendants and the pilots, who first tell us we must all return to our city of departure in Germany, we are allowed off the plane. Zagreb Airport is heavily affected by the snow too. On the coach for Sarajevo, chartered by the airline company, the camaraderie amongst the passengers is strengthened by a shared awareness that we may not make it to Sarajevo anytime soon. Already on the straight stretch of the former 'Motorway of Brotherhood and Unity', traffic is reduced to one lane only. Weather reports from all over BiH, delivered by relatives and friends over mobile phones, are transmitted from row to row. When we turn south, across the border into BiH, we know that both the snow and the quality of the roads will only get worse. Yet, proceeding very slowly, we keep on driving. After midnight, we enter the only stretch of motorway completed in BiH so far – Mr Fazlagić's example in chapter 4 is still as relevant as four years earlier, and his own party, SDP, is now co-responsible. Driving on the heels of a snow plough, we miraculously bridge the last forty kilometres to the outskirts of Sarajevo. It takes us another hour to make our way to the coach station, with a helpful Sarajevan sitting in front with the (Croatian) drivers, pointing out where, approximately, the carriageway may be located under the massive layer of snow that stretches between buildings on either side. We literally slide towards our destination: the Sarajevo coach station. Frantic phone calls have already established that the city's streets have not been cleaned yet. Indeed the snowfall is so ferocious that it would hardly help. No taxis, usually awaiting arriving coaches, are to be seen. Passengers whose final destination lies elsewhere are organising to stay the night with friends or relatives. A few courageous drivers have somehow fought their way through the snow in order to pick up some people, and lifts are organised. I am lucky to find a place in a van going to the centre, a few kilometres away. In return for directions to their hostel, a group of tourists will drop me off at the point nearest to my destination. Yet after a spectacular ride/slide on the main street along the river, the only one where even a van can break through the snow, we all disembark to continue on foot. This requires carrying our luggage above our heads and wading through the snow. Delivering the tourists to their hostel, I continue on my own, past the Serbian Orthodox church and the Catholic cathedral, where I cross paths with a pair of snowboarders. A few hundred metres further, and at least fifteen minutes later, covered in snow from head to toe, I am ready to climb the six floors to the most deserved glass of *rakija* I have ever savoured. Finally, after more than a decade in anthropology, I have an arrival story that can remotely start to match those of colleagues working in Melanesia.

The next day is a Saturday and, to me, Sarajevo has never looked more beautiful. There is virtually no traffic. Most shops are closed. Pedestrians take over the normally car-clogged streets. Rubbish is invisible due to the snow. It is eerily quiet. I have never seen so much snow in my life. Born and bred Sarajevans tell me they cannot remember such an amount either. Homemade film clips almost instantly appear on the internet, with particularly popular ones showing people jumping off the first floor of their houses. Yet life in a snowbound city is also a challenge. Dangerous icicles are forming rapidly on roofs and, for this reason, schools remain closed until the end of the month. Civil Protection (CZ) organs start coordinating emergency measures, cantonal maintenance services work overtime and municipal authorities call on people to shovel snow in front of their houses and buildings while also offering small fees to volunteers in work teams. However, partly given the labyrinthine anatomy of government and partly due to people's longstanding dissatisfaction with public services, these efforts are widely considered too little and too late. Tired of photo shoots of politicians in work outfits, their ties set off by fluorescent protective gear, many roll up their sleeves themselves. Snow shovels are soon sold out on the markets, but new batches arrive quickly. And people shovel. Some do so as part of organised groups – some students, for example, shovel in front of public buildings – and others on their own. For three days I do nothing else myself.

What is striking in those shovelling days is that the snow becomes a vehicle for conversation amongst neighbours and amongst strangers. We find ourselves in an exceptional situation and, for once, that exception is of a 'natural' rather than of a 'Dayton' kind. A force of nature brings people together, not just around complaints and jokes – there is never any shortage of either in Sarajevo – but around concrete work to be done. This is not a generalised effort shared by all, nor does it last long. It is momentary and superficial. Some immediately incorporate the problems caused by the snowfall as just one more element into their laments about the inefficiency of provision of utilities and about the incompetence and carelessness of politicians. When media report the story of an unemployed man, desperate to feed his family, who travelled from a small town to offer shovelling services in Sarajevo, the outcome reminds us that we are still in Dayton BiH: he is briefly employed by an embassy. And even many of those who do shovel as if their lives depend on it, return to the default position of yearning, after a flurry of activity. Yet there is a moment where things are different, and, perhaps more importantly still, where it seems that things really could be different.

In light of this book, two things emerge as crucial. Firstly, for many, the sight of a (threatened) breakdown of basic material conditions for 'normal lives' conjures up memories of wartime survival. During those days, it becomes clear just how a concern with the basic reproduction of lives lies immediately under the skin of many who lived through the siege of Sarajevo. Yet partly for the same reason, it is also a moment to muse on the relative togetherness of the war period, recalled by many, as we saw, as a time when, in the face of destitution, danger and loss, inequality was much smaller and solidarity much stronger than in Dayton BiH.

Secondly, these shovelling days also elicit recollections of an episode in Sarajevo history that are couched in much more idyllic terms: the Olympic Winter Games of 1984. Although organised in a period of large unemployment and occasional shortages, the *Olimpijada* features very prominently in people's positive recollections of life 'before'. Many recall February 1984 as the glory days of their city: a time when the world had come to them and when they had proudly opened themselves up for the entire world to see. Then too snow had come very suddenly. In fact, there had been no snow until just before the opening of the Games, and then, miraculously, enormous amounts fell just when they were needed most. Recruits of the Yugoslav People's Army were sent up the ski slopes to flatten the snow with their boots – their commander was a man who later played a major role in the siege of Sarajevo by the Serbianised 'inheritor' of that army. Yet others too rolled up their sleeves. Countless numbers of people, in Dobrinja and elsewhere in Sarajevo, have told me how, at the time, they shovelled for days to make their city shine. They often used this as a counterexample to highlight the first constitutional symptom of Daytonitis along the lines of both its structural and its value dimension. For example, discussing civic engagement, a sense of duty and the need for 'a system' in 2008, Saša, an employee of a foreign intervention agency, told me:

> I remember when I was eleven, I voluntarily cleared snow in the city for the Olympics. Nobody told me to, nobody forced me. I did it and I, I felt part of something that was going on in this city. It was a big project and I was somehow part of it. ... And now the entrance to my building is iced up and I almost break my neck every day. So imagine older people in the building. But have I gone and grabbed a shovel to clean it up? No I haven't. And if I *would*, I'm sure that the neighbours would look from behind their curtains and say 'Look at that idiot shovelling snow'. So my neighbour, who herself breaks her legs on her high heels every morning, would look at me and, I'm sure, she would think I was a total idiot. But before, we did those things. There was a shared storage space downstairs with some tools, and ... people would take a shovel and clean it up. Always. I don't remember it ever being iced over. But now nobody will do it for fear of being branded an idiot.

It is, of course, rather common for people to compare a past sense of order, responsibility, civic duty and solidarity favourably to their current situation, particularly when it concerns neighbourly relations. Yet the question of whether the entrance to Saša's building had really always been so much better taken care of at the time need not concern us here. What I want to reemphasise here is that, during my research in Dobrinja from 2008 to 2010, many recollections and projections of 'a system' that would allow 'normal lives' to unfold implied some active engagement by citizens themselves. Exasperation at the lack of such upward and outward gridding was a core theme in the dissatisfaction I found and snow shovelling was a particularly frequent marker in both memories of such engagement and calls for it. In the extraordinary month of February 2012, it is precisely snow shovelling that provides a brief glimpse of its potential revival.

June 2013. I am in front of the building of the BiH parliament. I am waiting. Around me there are several thousand people, carrying flags, banners and signs, and blowing whistles. We are all waiting, but have decided to transcend our 'barking' at politicians over coffee and make our impatience known. I have never seen so many people on any demonstration in BiH. Like my friends, I am pleasantly surprised that something is happening, finally. It is worth pointing out that the demonstrations also moved the writing of this book from an umpteenth 'dead point'. This is due to the concrete case that sparked the protests and the ways in which demands are articulated. I cannot claim that this outburst of what is after all a relatively small crowd, mobilised by a self-selected set of educated, urban organisers, faithfully represents broad popular dissatisfaction, but the protests do revolve in remarkably systematic fashion around shared concerns that I identify and analyse in this book. There are no two ways about it: I feel childishly vindicated and take to my writing with renewed vigour.

The protest's core demand is summarised in four letters that many wear on a white ribbon around their arm: JMBG. This acronym stands for *jedinstveni matični broj građana* [unique master citizen's number], introduced in Yugoslavia in 1976 and current in most of its successor states. Officially, the term in BiH is now JMB and a few days into the demonstrations many media outlets drop the G. Yet the protesters stick to JMBG, precisely because this G is short for 'citizens'. The JMBG makes one bureaucratically legible and embeds people as rights-bearing and claim-making citizens into the BiH polity. It is the most basic route of the inscription of individual bodies into 'a system'. Required for many routine procedures, it is a number combination that identifies every citizen of BiH from birth.

Or at least, it should do. For over three months now, no JMBGs have been issued. In May 2011, over a year ago, the Constitutional Court instructed the BiH parliament to bring the names of some territories of registration in line with the constitution. As in so many other cases, parliamentarians have been unable to come to an agreement. Yet another Dayton stalemate. A few days ago, Sarajevo media reported on the case of a baby girl, Belmina, who needed urgent medical treatment abroad but who could not be issued with a passport, or added to that of her parents, since she had no JMBG. On the initiative of a small group of people who coordinated their activities over social network media, a protest was organised. The BiH parliament offered a temporary solution and the parents took their girl abroad. However, dissatisfied with such a makeshift solution – built yet again on a form of conviviality that positioned the ruling caste as charitable patrons – the demonstrators blocked the exits of the building during a session of the BiH parliament. They vowed not to leave before a permanent solution was reached. After an intervention by the High Representative in BiH, who was primarily concerned with 'liberating' foreign bankers attending a convention in the same building, the demonstrators did eventually disperse, but returned soon after. The JMBG protests were born and eventually last for weeks, from vigils involving small groups of people to mass-attended concerts by BiH performers. Fears that a temporary solution was not good enough proved correct: a few days later, another baby, called Berina, died in a Beograd hospital, having lost crucial hours at the border because she had no travel documents. She had no JMBG: there was no proof of her existence as a citizen.

On this particular day there are middle-aged couples, students, pensioners and a conspicuous contingent of parents with small children. Some of the latter are in pushchairs and others are drawing and playing under an improvised shelter with the sign 'Terrorist camp'. This is a response to claims by politicians from Serbian nationalist parties based in Republika Srpska and from Croatian nationalist ones in Western Herzegovina that the blockade on the first day of the protest was a 'hostage crisis' orchestrated by 'Bosniak' parties and by 'foreign embassies'. Their delegates have since refused to turn up for work, with the president of the Assembly of Republika Srpska using a speech to trawl through the names of protesters on social network media in an attempt to prove that the demonstrations are a Bosniak attack on Serbs dressed up as civic activism. Parliamentarians and ministers from Serbian and Croatian nationalist parties claim they are therefore not safe in Sarajevo and in that way justify their absence over the next few weeks. Nothing new there then. Nor is there anything original in the fact that some of the parties who appeal mainly to Bosniaks, on their part, have been trying to align themselves with the protests. This is vehemently rejected by the organisers. During the blockade, parliamentarians of all parties were caught in the building and over the course of the demonstrations I never see any sign of party affiliation or any ethnonational symbolry. Today, I notice two flags of Dayton BiH and one of the SFRY. Later, on the internet, I see one woman with the lily flag of the Republic of BiH, associated by Serbian and Croatian nationalists – and to a degree, by some Bosniak nationalists too – as a specifically Bosniak symbol. Most slogans harshly criticise the ruling caste in its entirety for its incompetence, arrogance, greed, carelessness, selfishness and especially for its 'non-work' [*nerad*]. Politicians of all the different ruling parties, including SDP, which is now part of many ruling coalitions, are targeted.

The hasty and hopeful declarations by some that these protests constitute an all-inclusive trans-BiH political uprising, the first of its kind since the antiwar demonstrations of 1992, are wide off the mark. Support from Western Herzegovina and from Republika Srpska is minimal. Moreover, the JMBG protests could be seen as deeply apolitical, both in the ways they seek to circumvent the Dayton conundrum of BiH's territorial setup – which directly concerns its statehood – and in their formal, bureaucratic character. We find no ideological content here, no crystallisation of interests, no formulation of a desirable collective future, let alone of ways to organise it. Yet, for many, there is a hopeful dimension to these demonstrations.[1] Unlike what outside commentators suggest during those days, I believe their specificity does not lie so much in the generalised criticism of the ruling caste or in the rejection of nationalism. Instead, it lies in the peculiar minimalist ways in which demands are framed through an extremely elementary, drily bureaucratic register of citizenship. And the political significance of this framing must be understood in its conditions of existence: the Dayton BiH Meantime. To conclude this book, I offer an interpretation of the spark contained in the protests' gesture towards a break with conviviality in the Meantime. I argue that, in the historical conjuncture of Dayton BiH, in this geopolitical 'here' and 'now', this was conceived of as a necessary first step.

At the end of the blockade on the first night, the small group of organisers formulate demands that remain the same throughout. First, they demand an immediate and permanent deal on the issuing of JMBG, that is, implementation of the order by the Constitutional Court. Second, the creation of a state solidarity fund for medical treatment abroad of children who cannot be taken care of within BiH.[2] Third, compulsory contributions into this fund of 30 per cent of the salaries of BiH parliamentarians and ministers until the end of their mandate. Fourth, guarantees that there will be no criminal prosecution of protesters who took part in the 'blockade', as has been threatened by some politicians. After a few days, some demonstrators and media commentators take the opportunity to air their views on the territorial implementation of the first demand. They thus enter the question of the Dayton territorial setup itself and thereby inevitably position themselves with regard to the competing parties in the parliamentary debate. Concretely, they argue in favour of an arrangement for the issuing of JMBG which will strengthen the competences of the 'central' BiH state organs. I do not doubt that, if the question was posed in this manner, this would be the preference of most demonstrators. Yet, significantly, the parents of the girls concerned and the organisers of the protest immediately distance themselves from any such statements. Over the next few weeks they largely successfully call on those who join the protests to refrain from such demands. Here is what one organiser wrote about it a few days ago:

> It is important to note that to each and every one of the initial seven citizens who started this, it is all the same whether these numbers [JMBG] will be distributed on the state level, on the entity level, on the district level, on the level of cantons, municipalities, local communes [MZs], or house councils. Later, some groups appeared who declared in the media that it is only acceptable that everything would be on the state level. That's not us. We simply want JMBG for children. We want elementary human rights and elementary services from the state we pay for. How this will be done, that's none of our concern.[3]

This statement echoes the concerns of many people on the protests around me: they explicitly distance the JMBG issue from questions of the state's territorial anatomy. They are aware that, as with virtually every other political issue in Dayton BiH, a proper, lasting solution that could satisfy anyone's preferences would require intervening in the constitutional structure itself. All roads lead to Dayton. Yet this is a one-way, dead-end road, because, once a political discussion arrives at the country's constitutional setup, and it almost always does, it becomes unsolvable. This setup, namely, is itself sacrosanct in the Dayton Meantime. As we saw, OHR is there to guarantee that this remains the case until domestic politicians reach an alternative consensus, which is extremely unlikely given their diametrically opposed perspectives on BiH statehood and given the exclusively national channels for representation written into that very Dayton constitution itself. In that way the stalemate is reproduced time and again. Some well-known examples at this stage include the population census (not held in 2011, 'pending'), revision of the electoral law (judged to be discriminatory by the European Court of Human Rights, 'pending') and of course JMBG.

In response, the organisers of the protest refuse to frame their concerns in the terms set by the Dayton structure and insist that their demands should not be mobilised to address those terms either. In the terms of this book, they refuse to shift the debate to questions of the statehood of BiH, stubbornly retaining their focus on the most elementary forms of statecraft in BiH. Wary of widespread scepticism towards any interest groups, political parties or even NGOs, they continue to present the JMBG issue in the most direct (and apolitical) way possible. Their demands are phrased as those of individuals who self-consciously occupy the position of citizens with a strictly formal – decidedly not convivial – relationship to their elected representatives. They want 'JMBG for children', nothing less and nothing more. They want 'elementary human rights and elementary services from the state we pay for' and they do not want this to become yet another case where the debate shifts immediately from these rights and services to the question of 'which (part of the) state'? Baby girl Berina, they will argue, died because the latter question was allowed to weigh more than the former. Indeed, to underline their refusal to enter the fray on the question of statehood, the blog entry above rattles off the entire spectre of 'vertical encompassment' in Dayton BiH. Humorously, it even includes the possibility that JMBG be issued by 'house councils', meaning it would be on the whole done by the people (usually pensioners) who communicate between residents and *upravitelji*. In any case, three key terms in this commentary allow us to embed the specificity of the protests in their Dayton conditions of existence: 'children', 'the state we pay for', and, crucially, bringing it all together, 'elementary'.

First, children. Protests in front of various government institutions in BiH are common. Most of them revolve around the demands of particular groups of workers, farmers, pensioners or veterans to access or maintain certain salaries or allowances. They rarely succeed in mobilising more than a few hundred people. As we saw, the only other major postwar demonstrations in Sarajevo took place in 2008, when a teenager had been stabbed to death on a tram. At the time, I joined hundreds, and on a few occasions thousands, of protesters who demanded more security in the city, a better-organised system of youth criminal justice and the resignation of several functionaries. This grew into a broader campaign for political *odgovornost*, that is, accountability/responsibility/answerability (for an insightful analysis, see Kurtović 2012: 119ff). Strikingly, five years later it is again the fate of minors that has brought people out on the street. Many of the same protesters are here now, some of the same organisers are involved and some rhetorical strategies and artistic interventions are identical. Yet the message is more specific and more universal at the same time. Both the 2008 and the 2013 protests converged around the physical security of human bodies, i.e., naked survival. Both used a rhetoric of care and images of parenting to shame the ruling caste for what was seen as their prioritisation of their privileges over basic human responsibility. The focus on children also denotes a concern with forward movement and temporal frameworks that allow predictability, conceived of as the minimal reproduction of life. Yet this time newborn babies serve as even more powerful icons of innocence and unmarked humanity. It is precisely in this way that they allow the articulation of an apolitical link between survival and bureaucratic routines of statecraft.

Second, 'the state we pay for'. The protests abound with criticisms of politicians' large salaries (at this point, BiH parliamentarians earn up to ten times the average wage in BiH). Everyone knows that these salaries are only a minor part of their incomes, but a focus on them, and on the fact that they eat up a good part of the enormous costs of the BiH administrative apparatus, allows the phrasing of demands as reasonable and minimalist. People, it suggested, just want 'normal lives', and they have taken to the street because they cannot even count on the most modest conditions to achieve this. Indeed, an invitation to a mass JMBG demonstration on 1 July states, 'It is our duty to demand a normal life for all children in BiH'. Alongside calls for resignations, the 2008 protests too called on politicians to 'do their jobs', yet its core activists relied on humorous strategies of over-identification, sharply exposing the absurdity of institutional politics in Dayton BiH and the obscene behaviour of the ruling caste. Five years later, the JMBG demonstrations contain much humour too but at the core they are deadly serious in their minimalism: they want their demands to be taken literally. If the classic scenario of popular mobilisation entails a crowd with maximalist demands pressuring politicians to refrain from minimalist compromises, here we witness the opposite. Crucially, instead of seeking resignations, protesters consistently emphasise that they want politicians to do their jobs. Over-identification is used as a rhetorical strategy, but at the core of the demonstrations lays an earnest call for representation. The protesters, of course, have at most voted for a few of the current BiH parliamentarians and, unlike the majority of the BiH electorate, many, we can safely assume, never voted for any of the ones that have been elected. Yet rather than rejecting to be represented by them, they actually demand such representation. You have been elected by us, they say, you receive a very high salary from us, we are not asking much from you: the very least you can do is to come to your workplace, to negotiate and to provide us with a solution for the issuing of JMBG. This is your job and a legal requirement following from the decision of the Constitutional Court. The demonstrators thus resolutely turn down the invitation that is so hard to decline: they reject conviviality.

In this way, the protests can be seen as a culmination of 'waiting': as a strategy conceived of specifically in the Dayton BiH Meantime and addressing suspension itself. In Dayton BiH, criticism of politicians as cynical merely states the obvious, and, with SDP grabbing a much larger share of the pie since the 2010 elections, hesitant hopes that this party could serve as the least of several evils have largely dissipated. The core threat of the protests, then, consists of a willingness to earnestly wait for elected politicians – all of them – to get to work and to refuse to refrain from that waiting despite one's conviction that they are scheming operators. The stark simplicity of this 'threat' is, I believe, key to the confused reactions by some of the ruling caste: they are used to acerbic commentary, they know they are held beyond contempt by the vast majority of the population, but they have no immediate riposte to a minimalist demand that suddenly takes them seriously. For weeks, small vigils – labelled 'Coffee at Five to Twelve' – are held outside the parliament building, waiting for elected representatives to turn up and demonstratively asking passers-by to be quiet so that 'the government can do its work'.[4] It is thus, paradoxically, through an earnest, insistent and theatrical enactment of waiting – even over coffee – that the protesters seek to usher their lives out of the Dayton Meantime.

This brings us to the third term: 'elementary'. Focusing on the fate of politically innocent children and demanding minimal professional responsibility from those who populate the institutions of 'the state we pay for', these protests revolve around a bottom line of administrative inclusion in the polity. While the demonstrators have much to complain about, mobilisation has congealed around the zero phase of statecraft: Dayton BiH now even lacks a system that bureaucratically recognises the very existence of the people born in its 'embrace'. This embrace, here, is not even conceived of as one of care – although the second demand of the demonstrations, for a solidarity fund to help sick children, touches upon this. Yet the lowest common denominator is not about care, nor even about rights and interests, but it is about legibility, about the registration of one's existence by the state. If my Dobrinja interlocutors kept on telling me, 'we need a system', on these demonstrations it is the skeleton of 'a system' that is sought. Even if it does nothing else, the protesters argue, the 'state that we pay for' should at least 'see like a state', it should engage in this minimal form of interpellation and render its people legible as citizens. As Vetters (2007) has argued, with a focus on labels such as 'refugees', 'DPs' and 'returnees' in Mostar, such 'administrative categorisation practices' constitute a source of shared experience for citizens in BiH. In the concrete case of the baby girls, such legibility is not even sought in order to make claims on that state as biological citizens (Petryna 2002), but to overcome entrapment and go abroad to seek medical care unavailable in BiH's health institutions. The shared concern that underlies the JMBG protests, then, is one with the most elementary dimension of the state, the absolute bottom line of 'a system', without which the forward movement of 'normal lives' in BiH, it turns out, cannot be imagined to unfold.

Notes

1. At least two friends emphasise spontaneously that they have not been to any demonstration since early 1992 (when very large demonstrations against nationalism and against the rising risk of war were held in the same place, only to be dispersed by SDS militia sniper fire), but that they feel that, 'if they were there then, they should be here now too'.
2. This should be seen against the background of the exceptionally high wages of most BiH politicians, relative to average living standards, and of a very widespread form of 'humanitarian actions', relying on vast numbers of small contributions to collect money for treatment abroad (Brković 2012a).
3. http://www.kontrapress.com/clanak.php?rub=Dru%C5%A1tvoandurl=Dnev nik-aktiviste-Kako-smo-poceli-pobunu-u-BiH
4. On 30 June, a small party with a non-nationalist programme, led by members of a business family from Western Herzegovina, organises a protest in front of the BiH parliament. About one hundred party sympathisers attend. Distancing themselves from this event, the organisers of the JMBG demonstrations cancel their coffee session on this day. At the same time, they announce a new campaign of civil obedience, consisting of a boycott of payments of utility bills to show political functionaries that 'citizens are their management board [*upravni odbor*], who reward success and punish failure' (www.jmbg.org).

REFERENCES

Adkins, L. 2011. 'Bourdieu and Economic Crisis', in S. Susen and B. Turner (eds), *The Legacy of Pierre Bourdieu: Critical Essays*. London: Anthem Press, pp. 347–65.

Agamben, G. 1998. *Homo Sacer: Sovereign Power and Bare Life*, trans. D. Heller-Roazen. Stanford: Stanford University Press.

Alexander, C. 2007. 'Soviet and Post-Soviet Planning in Almaty, Kazachstan', *Critique of Anthropology* 27(2): 165–81.

Allen, L. 2008. 'Getting by the Occupation: How Violence Became Normal during the Second Palestinian Intifada', *Cultural Anthropology* 23(3): 453–87.

Althusser, L. 1971 (1969). 'Ideology and Ideological State Apparatuses (Notes Towards an Investigation)', in *Lenin and Philosophy, and Other Essays*, trans. B. Brewster. New York: Monthly Review Press, pp. 127–86.

American Anthropologist 2005, 107(3). Special Issue: Moral Economies, State Spaces and Categorical Violence.

Anđelić, N. 2003. *Bosnia and Herzegovina: the End of a Legacy*. London: Frank Cass.

Anderson, B. 2006. 'Becoming and Being Hopeful: Towards a Theory of Affect', *Environment and Planning D: Society and Space* 24(5): 733–52.

———. 2007. 'Hope for Nanotechnology: Anticipatory Knowledge and the Governance of Affect', *Area* 39(2): 156–65.

Andreas, P. 2008. *Blue Helmets and Black Markets: The Business of Survival in the Siege of Sarajevo*. Ithaca: Cornell University Press.

Appadurai, A. 2000. 'Spectral Housing and Urban Cleansing: Notes on Millennial Mumbai', *Public Culture* 12: 627–51.

———. 2004. 'The Capacity to Aspire: Culture and the Terms of Recognition', in V. Rao and M. Walton (eds), *Culture and Public Action*. Stanford: Stanford University Press, pp. 58–84.

Aretxaga, B. 2003. 'Maddening States', *Annual Review of Anthropology* 32: 393–410.

Armakolas, I. 2007. 'Sarajevo No More? Identity and the Sense of Place among Bosnian Serb Sarajevans in Republika Srpska', in X. Bougarel, E. Helms and G. Duijzings (eds), *The New Bosnian Mosaic*. Aldershot: Ashgate, pp. 79–100.

Auyero, J. 2012. *Patients of the State: The Politics of Waiting in Argentina*. Durham: Duke University Press.

Badiou, A. 2009. *Pocket Pantheon: Figures of Postwar Philosophy*, trans. D. Macey. London: Verso.

Baker, C. 2011. 'Tito's Children? Educational Resources, Language Learning and Cultural Capital in the Life Histories of Interpreters Working in Bosnia-Herzegovina', *Südosteuropa* 59(4): 478–502.

———. 2012. 'Prosperity Without Security: The Precarity of Interpreters in Postsocialist, Post-Conflict Bosnia-Herzegovina', *Slavic Review* 71(4): 849–72.

Bartulović, A. 2013. *'Nismo vaši!': Antinacionalizem v povojnem Sarajevu*. Ljubljana: Znanstvena založba Filozofske fakultete

Bećirović, H. 2003. *Dobrinjska Ratna Drama*. Sarajevo: JOB BiH "Unija veterana".

Berman, D.M. 2007. *The War Schools of Dobrinja*. San Francisco: Caddo Gap Press.

Bieber, F. (ed.). 2013. *EU Conditionality in the Western Balkans*. London: Routledge.

Biehl, J. and P. Locke. 2010. 'Deleuze and the Anthropology of Becoming', *Current Anthropology* 51(3): 317–51.

Bloch, E. 1986 (1959). *The Principle of Hope*, trans. N. Plaice, S. Plaice, P. Knight. Oxford: Blackwell.

Bodnár, J. 1998. 'Assembling the Square: Social Transformation in Public Space and the Broken Mirage of the Second Economy in Postsocialist Budapest', *Slavic Review* 57(3): 489–515.

Bojičić-Dželilović, V. 2013. 'Informality, Inequality and Social Reintegration in Post-War Transition', *Studies in Social Justice* 7(2): 211–28.

Bougarel, X. 1996a. *Bosnie: Anatomie d'un Conflit*. Paris: La Découverte.

———. 1996b. 'Bosnia and Hercegovina: State and Communitarianism', in A.D. Dyker and I. Vejvoda (eds), *Yugoslavia and After*. Harlow: Longman, pp. 87–115.

———. 2005. 'Dayton, Dix Ans Après: la Leurre des Bilans', *Critique Internationale* 29: 9–24.

Bougarel, X., E. Helms and G. Duijzings (eds). 2007. *The New Bosnian Mosaic: Memories, Identities and Moral Claims in a Post-War Society*. Aldershot: Ashgate.

Bourdieu, P. 1979 (1963). *Algeria 1960*, trans. R. Nice. Cambridge: Cambridge University Press.

———. 1982. *Ce Que Parler Veut Dire: l'Économie des Échanges Linguistiques*. Paris: Fayard.

———. 1990 (1984). *Homo Academicus*, trans. P. Collier. Cambridge: Polity.

———. 1998. 'La Main Gauche et la Main Droite de l'État', in *Contre-Feux: Propos pour Servir à la Résistance contre l'Invasion Néo-libérale*. Paris: Raisons d'Agir, pp. 9–17.

———. 1999. 'Rethinking the State: Genesis and Structure of the Bureaucratic Field (trans. L. Wacquant and S. Farage)', in G. Steinmetz (ed.), *State/Culture: State Formation after the Cultural Turn*. Ithaca: Cornell University Press, pp. 53–75.

———. 2003 (1997). *Méditations Pascaliennes*. Paris: Seuil.

Bridger, S. and F. Pine (eds). 1997. *Surviving Post-Socialism: Local Strategies and Regional Responses in Eastern Europe and the Former Soviet Union*. London: Routledge.

Brković, Č. 2010. '"Šta Drugi Misle o Meni?": Protivljenje Feminizmu, Menopauza i Javnost u Post-socijalističkom Kontekstu', *Genero* 14: 3–23.

———. 2012a. 'Navigating Rules and Wills: Healthcare and Social Protection in a Bosnian Border Town', Ph.D. dissertation. Manchester: University of Manchester.

———. 2012b. 'Potraga za Vezama kao Konstitutivni Element Biološkog Aspekta Državljanstva u Bosanskom Gradu na Granici', *Antropologija* 2: 123–44.

Brubaker, R. 2002. 'Ethnicity without Groups', *Archives européennes de sociologie* 4(2): 163–89.

Buck-Morss, S. 2000. *Dreamworld and Catastrophe: The Passing of Mass Utopia in East and West*. Cambridge: MIT Press.

Burg, S. and P. Shoup. 1999. *Ethnic Conflict and International Intervention: Crisis in Bosnia and Herzegovina 1990–93*. Armonk: ME Sharpe.

Camus, A. 1985 (1951). *L'Homme Revolté*. Paris: Gallimard.

Čelebičić, V. 2013. 'Waiting is Hoping: Youth and Future in a Bosnian Border Town', Ph.D. dissertation. Manchester: University of Manchester.

Čengić, N.N. 2008. 'Život Poslije Smrti', *Odjek* 4: 93–96.

Clastres, P. 1974. *La Societé contre l'État*. Paris: Minuit.

Cohen, D.W. 1992. 'The Banalities of Interpretation', *Public Culture* 5(1): 57–59.

Coles, K. 2007. *Democratic Designs: International Intervention and Electoral Practices in Post-War Bosnia-Herzegovina*. Ann Arbor: Michigan University Press.

Collier, S.J. 2004. 'Pipes', in S. Harrison, S. Pile and N. Thrift (eds), *Patterned Ground: Entanglements of Nature and Culture*. London: Reaktion Books, pp. 50–52.

Comaroff, J. and J. Comaroff. 1992. 'The Colonisation of Consciousness in South Africa', in *Ethnography and the Historical Imagination*. Boulder: Westview, pp. 235–63.

Connerton, P. 1989. *How Societies Remember*. Cambridge: Cambridge University Press.

Corbridge, S., G. Williams, M. Srivastava and R. Véron. 2005. *Seeing the State: Governance and Governmentality in India*. Cambridge: Cambridge University Press.

Cowan, J.K. 2007. 'The Supervised State', *Identities: Global Studies in Culture and Power* 14(5): 545–78.

Crapanzano, V. 1985. *Waiting: The Whites of South Africa*. New York: Random House.

―――. 2003. 'Reflections on Hope as a Category of Social and Psychological Analysis', *Cultural Anthropology* 18(1): 3–32.

Critique of Anthropology 2012, 32(2). Special Issue: Anthropology and Anarchy.

Ćurak, N. 2002. *Geopolitika kao Sudbina: Slučaj Bosna*. Sarajevo: Fakultet političkih nauka.

―――. 2004. *Dejtonski Nacionalizam*. Sarajevo: Buybook.

Das, V. 2007. *Life and Words: Violence and the Descent into the Ordinary*. Berkeley: California University Press.

Das, V. and D. Poole (eds). 2004. *Anthropology in the Margins of the State*. Santa Fe: School of American Research Press.

de Certeau, M. 1990 (1980). *L'Invention du Quotidien: 1. Arts de Faire*. Paris: Gallimard Folio Essais.

Delpla, I. 2010. 'Catégories Juridiques et Cartographie des Jugements Moraux: le TPIY Évalué par Victimes, Témoins et Condamnés', in I. Delpla and M. Bessone (eds), *Peines de Guerre: la Justice Pénale Internationale et l'ex-Yougoslavie*. Paris: EHESS, pp. 267–85.

Divjak, B. and M. Pugh. 2008. 'The Political Economy of Corruption in Bosnia-Herzegovina', *International Peacekeeping* 15(3): 373–86.

Donais, T. 2005. *Political Economy of Peacebuilding in Post-Dayton Bosnia*. London: Routledge.

Donia, R.J. 2006. *Sarajevo: a biography*. London: Hurst.

Dunn, E. 2008. 'Postsocialist Spores: Disease, Bodies and the State in the Republic of Georgia', *American Ethnologist* 35(2): 243–58.

Erdei, I. 2012. *Čekajući Ikeu: Potrošačka Kultura u Postsocijalizmu i pre Njega*. Beograd: Etnološka biblioteka.

Fabian, J. 1983. *Time and the Other: How Anthropology Makes its Object*. New York: Columbia University Press.

Fehérváry, K. 2002. 'American Kitchens, Luxury Bathrooms, and the Search for a 'Normal' Life in Postsocialist Hungary', *Ethnos* 67(3): 369–400.

Ferguson, J. 1999. *Expectations of Modernity: Myths and Meanings of Urban Life on the Zambian Copperbelt*. Berkeley: California University Press.

―――. 2006. *Global Shadows: Africa in the New World Order*. Durham: Duke University Press.

Ferguson, J. and A. Gupta. 2002. 'Spatialising States: Toward an Ethnography of Neoliberal Governmentality', *American Ethnologist* 29(4): 981–1002.

Foucault, M. 1975. *Surveillir et Punir*. Paris: Tel Gallimard.

―――. 1991. 'Governmentality', in G. Burchell, C. Gordon and P. Miller (eds) *The Foucault Effect: Studies in Governmentality*. London: Harvester Wheatsheaf, pp. 73–86.

―――. 1994 (1973). 'Truth and Judicial Forms (trans. R Hurley)', in J.D. Faubion (ed.), *Power: Essential Works of Foucault 1954–1984, Volume 3*. New York: The New Press, pp. 1–89.

―――. 2010. *The Birth of Biopolitics: Lectures at the College de France, 1978–1979*, trans. G. Burchell. New York: Picador.

Fuller, C.J. and V. Bénéï (eds). 2001. *The Everyday State and Society in Modern India*. London: Hurst.

Gagnon, V.P. 2004. *The Myth of Ethnic War: Serbia and Croatia in the 1990s*. Ithaca: Cornell University Press.

Galbraith, M. 2003. '"We Just Want to Live Normally": Intersecting Discourses of Public, Private, Poland, and the West', *Journal of the Society for the Anthropology of Europe* 3(1): 2–13.

Galijaš, A. 2011. *Eine bosnische Stadt im Zeichen des Krieges: Ethnopolitik und Alltag in Banja Luka (1990–1995)*. München: Oldenburg Verlag.

Gavrić, S., D. Banović and M. Barreiro. 2013. *The Political System of Bosnia and Herzegovina: Institutions -Actors -Processes*. Sarajevo: Sarajevski otvoreni centar.

Gekle, H. 1998. 'The Wish and the Phenomenology of the Wish in *The Principle of Hope*', *New German Critique* 45: 55–80.

Gilbert, A. 2012. 'Legitimacy Matters: Managing the Democratisation Paradox of Foreign State-Building in Bosnia and Herzegovina', *SüdostEuropa* 60(4): 483–96.

Gilbert, A., J. Greenberg, E. Helms and S. Jansen. 2008. 'Reconsidering Postsocialism from the Margins of Europe: Hope, Time and Normalcy in Post-Yugoslav Societies', *Anthropology News* 49(8): 10–11.

Gilliland, M.K., S. Špoljar-Vržina and V. Rudan. 1995. 'Reclaiming Lives: Variable Effects of War on Gender and Ethnic Identities in the Narratives of Bosnian and Croatian Refugees', *Anthropology of East Europe Review* 13(1): 30–39.

Glennie, N. and N. Thrift. 1996. 'Reworking E.P. Thompson's "Time, Work-Discipline and Industrial Capitalism"', *Time and Society* 5(3): 275–99.

Goati, V. 1989. *Politička Anatomija Jugoslovenskog Društva*. Zagreb: Naprijed.

Goldman, J.A. 1997. *Building New York's Sewers: Developing Mechanisms of Urban Management*. West Lafayette: Purdue University Press.

Graeber, D. 2007. *Possibilities: Essays on Hierarchy, Rebellion and Desire*. Oakland: AK Press.

Green, S. 2005. *Notes from the Balkans: Locating Marginality and Ambiguity on the Greek-Albanian Border*. Princeton: Princeton University Press.

Greenberg, J. 2010. '"There's Nothing Anyone Can Do About It": Participation, Apathy and "Successful" Democratic Transition in Postsocialist Serbia', *Slavic Review* 69(1): 41–64.

——. 2011. 'On the Road to Normal: Negotiating Agency and State Sovereignty in Postsocialist Serbia', *American Anthropologist* 113(1): 88–100.

Guyer, J.I. 2007. 'Prophecy and the Near Future: Thoughts on Macroeconomic, Evangelical and Punctuated Time', *American Ethnologist* 34(3): 409–21.

Hage, G. 2002. '"On the Side of Life" – Joy and the Capacity of Being', in M. Zournazi (ed.), *Hope: New Philosophies for Change*. London: Routledge, pp. 150–71.

——. 2003. *Against Paranoid Nationalism: Searching for Hope in a Shrinking Society*. Annandale: Pluto / Merlin.

——. 2009. 'Waiting Out the Crisis: On Stuckedness and Governmentality', in G. Hage (ed.), *Waiting*. Melbourne: Melbourne University Press, pp. 97–106.

Hall, S. 1988. 'The Toad in the Garden: Thatcherism among the Theorists', in C. Nelson and L. Grossberg (eds), *Marxism and the Interpretation of Culture*. Urbana: Illinois University Press, pp. 35–57.

Hamzić, M. 2004. *Dobrinjska Tvrđava*. Sarajevo: Općina Novi grad.

Han, C. 2011. 'Symptoms of Another Life: Time, Possibility, and Domestic Relations in Chile's Credit Economy', *Cultural Anthropology* 26(1): 7–32.

Hansen, T.B. and F. Stepputat. 2001. 'Introduction', in T.B. Hansen and F. Stepputat (eds), *States of Imagination: Ethnographic Explorations of the Postcolonial State*. Durham: Duke University Press, pp. 1–38.

Hardt, M. and A. Negri. 2000. *Empire*. Cambridge, MA: Harvard University Press.

Hartman, T. 2007. 'Moral Vectors, Transitional Time and a "Utopian Project of Impossible Fullness"', *Social Anthropology* 15(2): 187–203.

Harvey, D. 2000. *Spaces of Hope*. Berkeley: California University Press.

Harvey, P. 2005. 'The Materiality of State-Effects: An Ethnography of a Road in the Peruvian Andes', in C. Krohn-Hansen and K.G. Nustad (eds), *State Formation: Anthropological Perspectives*. London: Pluto, pp. 123–41.

Hayden, R.M. 2007. 'Moral Vision and Impaired Insight: Or the Imagination of Other People's Communities in Bosnia', *Current Anthropology* 48(1): 105–31.

Helms, E. 2007. '"Politics is a Whore": Women, Morality and Victimhood in Post-War Bosnia-Herzegovina', in X. Bougarel, E. Helms and G. Duijzings (eds), *The New Bosnian Mosaic*. Aldershot: Ashgate, pp. 235–54.

———. 2010. 'The Gender of Coffee: Women and Reconciliation Initiatives in Post-War Bosnia and Herzegovina', *Focaal* 57: 17–32.

Helsinški parlament građana. 2005. *Hvala Što Ste Me Pitali Kako Sam*. Banja Luka: Helsinški parlament građana.

Henig, D. 2012. 'Knocking on my Neighbour's Door: On Metamorphoses of Sociality in Rural Bosnia', *Critique of Anthropology* 32(1): 3–19.

Herzfeld, M. 1996. *Cultural Intimacy: Social Poetics in the Nation-State*. London: Routledge.

hooks, b. 1990. *Yearning: Race, Gender, and Cultural Politics*. London: Turnaround.

Hromadžić, A. 2012. 'Once We Had a House: Invisible Citizens and Consociational Democracy in Postwar Mostar, Bosnia and Herzegovina', *Social Analysis* 56(3): 30–43.

International Crisis Group (ICG). 1998. *Minority Return or Mass Relocation?* Sarajevo: ICG.

Istraživačko-dokumentacioni centar (IDC). 2013. *Bosanska Knjiga Mrtvih / The Bosnian Book of the Dead*. Sarajevo: IDC.

Jansen, S. 2005a. *Antinacionalizam: Etnografija Otpora u Zagrebu i Beogradu*, trans. A Bajazetov. Beograd: XX Vek.

———. 2005b. 'National Numbers in Context: Maps and Stats in Representations of the Post-Yugoslav Wars', *Identities: Global Studies in Culture and Power* 12(1): 45–68.

———. 2005c. 'Who's Afraid of White Socks? Towards a Critical Understanding of Post-Yugoslav Urban Self-Perceptions', *Ethnologia Balkanica* 9: 151–67.

———. 2006a. 'The Privatisation of Home and Hope: Return, Reforms and the Foreign Intervention in Bosnia-Herzegovina', *Dialectical Anthropology* 30(3–4): 177–99.

———. 2006b. 'The (Dis)Comfort of Conformism: Post-War Nationalism and Coping with Powerlessness in Croatian Villages', in T. Otto, H. Thrane and H. Vandkilde (eds), *Warfare and Society*. Aarhus: Aarhus University Press, pp. 433–46.

———. 2008a. 'Troubled Locations: Return, the Life Course and Transformations of "Home" in Bosnia-Herzegovina', in S. Jansen and S. Löfving (eds), *Struggles for Home*. Oxford: Berghahn, pp. 43–64.

———. 2008b. 'Cosmopolitan Openings and Closures in Post-Yugoslav Antinationalism', in M. Nowicka and M. Rovisco (eds), *Cosmopolitanism in Practice*. Aldershot: Ashgate, pp. 75–92.

———. 2009. 'After the Red Passport: Towards an Anthropology of the Everyday Geopolitics of Entrapment in the EU's Immediate Outside', *Journal of the Royal Anthropological Institute* 15(4): 815–32.

———. 2010. 'Of Wolves and Men: Postwar Reconciliation and the Gender of Inter-National Encounters', *Focaal* 57: 33–49.

———. 2013a. 'People and Things in the Ethnography of Borders: Materialising the Division of Sarajevo', *Social Anthropology* 21(1): 23–37.

———. 2013b. 'If Reconciliation Is the Answer, Are We Asking the Right Questions?', *Studies in Social Justice* 7(2): 229–43.

Jansen, S. and E. Helms 2009. 'The White Plague: National-Demographic Rhetoric and its Gendered Resonance after the Post-Yugoslav Wars', in C. Eifler and R. Seifert (eds), *Gender Dynamics and Post-Conflict Reconstruction*. Frankfurt: Lang, pp. 219–43.

Jansen, S. and S. Löfving (eds). 2008. *Struggles for Home: Violence, Hope and the Movement of People*. Oxford: Berghahn.

Jašarević, L. 2012. 'Pouring Out Postsocialist Fears: Practical Metaphysics of a Therapy at a Distance', *Comparative Studies in Society and History* 54(4): 1–28.

Jean-Klein, I. 2000. 'Mothercraft, Statecraft and Subjectivity in the Palestinian Intifada', *American Ethnologist* 27(1): 100–27.

_____. 2001. 'Nationalism and Resistance: The Two Faces of Everyday Activism in Palestine during the Intifada', *Cultural Anthropology* 16(1): 83–126.

Joseph, G.M. and D. Nugent (eds). 1994. *Everyday Forms of State Formation: Revolution and the Negotiation of Rule in Modern Mexico*. Durham: Duke University Press.

Jouhanneau, C. 2013. 'La Résistance des Témoins: Mémoires de Guerre, Nationalisme et Vie Quotidienne en Bosnie-Herzégovine', Ph.D. dissertation. Paris: CERI, Université de Paris.

Kalb, D. 2012. 'Thinking about Neoliberalism as if the Crisis was Actually Happening', *Social Anthropology* 20(3): 318–30.

Kelly, T. 2008. 'The Attractions of Accountancy: Living an Ordinary Life during the Second Palestinian Intifada', *Ethnography* 9(3): 351–76.

Kolind, T. 2008. *Post-War Identification: Everyday Muslim Counterdiscourse in Bosnia Herzegovina*. Aarhus: Aarhus University Press.

Kosseleck, R. 1985 (1979). *Futures Past: On the Semantics of Historical Time*, trans. K. Tribe. Cambridge: MIT Press.

Kurtović, L. 2012. 'Politics of Impasse: Specters of Socialism and the Struggles for the Future in Postwar Bosnia-Herzegovina', Ph.D. dissertation. Berkeley: University of California.

Latour, B. 2005. *Reassembling the Social: An Introduction to Actor-Network Theory*. Oxford: Oxford University Press.

Lemon, A. 2000. 'Talking Transit and Spectating Transition: the Moscow Metro', in D. Berdahl, M. Bunzl and M. Lampland (eds), *Altering States: Ethnographies of Transition in Eastern Europe and the Former Soviet Union*. Ann Arbor: University of Michigan Press, pp. 14–39.

Li, T.M. 2005. 'Beyond "the State" and Failed Schemes', *American Anthropologist* 107(3): 383–94.

_____. 2007. *The Will to Improve: Governmentality, Development and the Practice of Politics*. Durham: Duke University Press.

Linger, D.T. 1993. 'The Hegemony of Discontent', *American Ethnologist* 20(1): 3–24.

Lubkemann, S.C. 2008. *Culture in Chaos: An Anthropology of the Social Condition of War*. Chicago: Chicago University Press.

Maček, I. 2009. *Sarajevo under Siege: Anthropology in Wartime*. University Park: Pennsylvania University Press.

Malkki, L. 1994. 'Citizens of Humanity: Internationalisms and the Imagined Community of Nations', *Diaspora* 3(1): 41–67.

_____. 2001. 'Figures of the Future: Dystopia and Subjectivity in the Social Imagination of the Future', in D. Holland and J. Lave (eds), *History in Person*. Santa Fe: School of American Research Press, pp. 325–48.

Mar, P. 2005. 'Unsettling Potentialities: Topographies of Hope in Transnational Migration', *Journal of Intercultural Studies* 26(4): 361–78.

Markowitz, F. 2010. *Sarajevo: A Bosnian Kaleidoscope*. Urbana: Illinois University Press.

Massey, D. 2005. *For Space*. London: Sage.

Mbembe, A. 1992. 'The Banality of Power and the Aesthetics of Vulgarity in the Postcolony (trans. J Roitman)', *Public Culture* 4(2): 1–30.

Meyer, J.W. 1999. 'The Changing Cultural Content of the Nation-State: A World Society Perspective', in G. Steinmetz (ed.), *State/Culture: State Formation after the Cultural Turn*. Ithaca: Cornell University Press, pp. 123–43.

Mitchell, T. 1999. 'Society, Economy, and the State Effect', in G. Steinmetz (ed.), *State/Culture: State Formation after the Cultural Turn*. Ithaca: Cornell University Press, pp. 76–97.

Miyazaki, H. 2004. *The Method of Hope: Anthropology, Philosophy and Fijian Knowledge*. Stanford: Stanford University Press.

_____. 2006. 'Economy of Dreams: Hope in Global Capitalism and its Critiques', *Cultural Anthropology* 21(2): 147–72.

_____. 2010. 'The Temporality of No Hope', in C.J. Greenhouse (ed.), *Ethnographies of Neo-liberalism*. Berkeley: California University Press, pp. 238–50.

Mjesečni Statistički Pregled Federacije BiH August 2008 (XII/8). Sarajevo: Federalni zavod za statistiku.

Mujkić, A. 2007. *Mi Građani Etnopolisa*. Sarajevo: Šahinpašić.

Mulić-Bušatlija, S. 2000. 'O "Zelenoj Aždahi", "Šejtanu" i Vozilu Koje je Letjelo kao da je Popilo *Red Bull*', *Dani*, 1 December, 14–15.

Munn, N. 1992. 'The Cultural Anthropology of Time: A Critical Essay', *Annual Review of Anthropology* 21: 93–123.

Musić, A. (ed.). 1998. *OŠ Skender Kulenović*. Sarajevo: OŠ Skender Kulenović.

Mustajbegović, S. 2003. 'Rat za Sarajevske Putnike', *Dani*, 12 December, 30.

Navaro-Yashin, Y. 2002. *Faces of the State: Secularism and Public Life in Turkey*. Princeton: Princeton University Press.

_____. 2003. '"Life Is Dead Here": Sensing the Political in No-Man's Land', *Anthropological Theory* 3(1): 107–25.

Novas, C. 2006. 'The Political Economy of Hope: Patients' Organizations, Science and Biovalue', *BioSocieties* 1(3): 289–305.

Novo, D. 1992. 'Novi Krug Trojkom', in *I Oni Brane Sarajevo*. Sarajevo: Informativni centar Večernjih novina, pp. 101–4.

Nuijten, M. 2003. *Power, Community and the State: The Political Anthropology of Organisation in Mexico*. London: Pluto.

Obeid, M. 2010. 'Searching for the "Ideal Face of the State" in a Lebanese Border Town', *Journal of the Royal Anthropological Institute* 16(2): 330–46.

Olaniyan, T. 1992. 'Narrativising Postcoloniality: Responsibilities', *Public Culture* 5(1): 47–55.

Ong, A. and S.J. Collier (eds). 2005. *Global Assemblages: Technology, Politics, and Ethics as Anthropological Problems*. Oxford: Blackwell.

Palmberger, M. 2013. 'Practices of Border Crossing in Post-War Bosnia and Herzegovina: The Case of Mostar', *Identites: Global Studies in Culture and Power* 20(5): 544–60.

Pančić, T. 2006. *Osobeni Znaci*. Beograd: Beopolis.

Patico, J. 2009. 'For Love, Money, or Normalcy: Meanings of Strategy and Sentiment in the Russian-American Matchmaking Industry', *Ethnos* 74(3): 307–30.

Patterson, P.H. 2011. *Bought and Sold: Living and Losing the Good Life in Socialist Yugoslavia*. Ithaca: Cornell University Press.

Pejanović, M. 2002. *Through Bosnian Eyes: The Political Memoirs of a Bosnian Serb*, trans. M. Bowder. Sarajevo: Šahinpašić.

Petrović, T. 2012. *YUROPA: Jugoslovensko Nasleđe i Politike Budućnosti u Postjugoslovenskim Društvama*. Beograd: Fabrika knjiga.

Petryna, A. 2002. *Life Exposed: Biological Citizens after Chernobyl*. Princeton: Princeton University Press.

Plakans, A. 2009. 'Latvia: Normality and Disappointment', *East European Politics and Societies* 23(4): 518–25.

Platz, S. 2003. 'The Shape of National Time: Daily Life, History, and Identity during Armenia's Transition to Independence 1991–1994', in D. Berdahl, M. Bunzl and M. Lampland (eds), *Altering States: Ethnographies of Transition in Eastern Europe and the Former Soviet Union*. Ann Arbor: Michigan University Press, pp. 114–38.

Povrzanović Frykman, M. 2002. 'Violence and the Re-discovery of Place', *Ethnologia Europaea* 32(2): 69–88.

_____. 2008. 'Staying Behind: Civilians in the Post-Yugoslav Wars 1991-95', in N. Atkin (ed.), *Daily Lives of Civilians in Wartime Twentieth-Century Europe*. Westport: Greenwood, pp. 163–93.

_____. 2012. 'Anthropology of War and Recovery: Lived Experiences', in U. Kockel, M. Nic Craith & J. Frykman (eds), *A Companion to the Anthropology of Europe*. Oxford: Blackwell, pp. 253–74.

Problems of Post-Communism 2004, 52(3). Special Issue: Criminalised Legacies of War.

Pugh, M. 2005. 'Transformation of the Political Economy of Bosnia since Dayton', *International Peacekeeping* 12(3): 448–62.

Puhalo, S. (ed.). 2008. *Ideološki Profil Glasača i Apstinenata u Bosni i Hercegovini*. Banja Luka: Friedrich Ebert Stiftung.

Radcliffe, S. 2001. 'Imagining the State as a Space: Territoriality and the Formation of the State in Ecuador', in T.B. Hansen and F. Stepputat (eds), *States of Imagination*. Durham: Duke University Press, pp. 123–45.

Rausing, S. 2002. 'Re-constructing the Normal: Identity and the Consumption of Western Goods in Estonia', in R. Mandel and C. Humphrey (eds), *Markets and Moralities: Ethnographies of Postsocialism*. London: Berg, pp. 127–42.

Reeves, M. 2011. 'Fixing the Border: On the Affective Life of the State in Southern Kyrgyzstan', *Environment and Planning D: Society and Space* 29(5): 905–23.

Ringel, F. 2012. 'Knowledge in Time: An Ethnography of Hope and the Future in Germany's Fastest Shrinking City', Ph.D. dissertation. Cambridge: University of Cambridge.

Rizzo, M. 2002. 'Being Taken for a Ride: Privatisation of the Dar es Salaam Transport System 1983–1998', *Journal of Modern African Studies* 40(1): 133–57.

Rockwell, E. 1994. 'Schools of the Revolution: Enacting and Consenting State Forms in Tlaxcala, 1910–1930', in G.M. Joseph and D. Nugent (eds), *Everyday Forms of State Formation*. Durham: Duke University Press, pp. 170–208.

Rofel, L. 1999. *Other Modernities: Gendered Yearnings in China after Socialism*. Berkeley: California University Press.

Rorty, R. 1999. *Philosophy and Social Hope*. London: Penguin.

Roseberry, W. 1994. 'Hegemony and the Language of Contention', in G.M. Joseph and D. Nugent (eds), *Everyday Forms of State Formation*. Durham: Duke University Press, pp. 355–66.

Šalaj, B. 2009. *Socijalno Povjerenje u BiH*. Sarajevo: FES.

Salecl, R. 1992. 'Nationalism, Anti-Semitism and Anti-Feminism in Eastern Europe', *New German Critique* 57: 51–65.

Sartre, J.-P. 1985 (1960). *Critique de la Raison Dialectique. Tome 1: Théorie des Ensembles Pratiques*. Paris: Gallimard.

Scott, J.C. 1985. *Weapons of the Weak: Everyday Forms of Peasant Resistance*. New Haven: Yale University Press.

_____. 1990. *Domination and the Arts of Resistance: Hidden Transcripts*. New Haven: Yale University Press.

_____. 1998. *Seeing like a State: How Certain Schemes to Improve the Human Condition Have Failed*. New Haven: Yale University Press.

_____. 2005. 'Afterword to "Moral Economies, State Spaces, and Categorical Violence"', *American Anthropologist* 107(3): 395–402.

_____. 2009. *The Art of Not Being Governed: An Anarchist History of Upland Southeast Asia*. Yale: Yale University Press.

Scott, J.C., J. Tehranian and J. Mathias. 2002. 'The Production of Legal Identities Proper to States: the Case of the Permanent Family Surname', *Comparative Studies in Society and History* 44(1): 4–44.

Šestan, S. 2010. 'Građani BiH kao Žrtve Bešćutne Vlasti', *Start*, 13 April 2010, 18–19.

Simić, M. 2009. 'Exit to Europe: State, Popular Music and "Normal Life" in a Serbian Town', Ph.D. dissertation. Manchester: University of Manchester.

Šimko, D. 2006. 'Sarajevo: Isolation in a Country Falling Apart', in R. Schneider-Sliwa (ed.), *Cities in Transition: Globalisation, Political Change and Urban Development*. Leiden: Springer, pp. 95–123.

Smith, G. 2004. 'Hegemony: Critical Interpretations in Anthropology and Beyond', *Focaal* 43: 99–120.

———. 2011. 'Selective Hegemony and Beyond-Populations with "No Productive Function": a Framework for Enquiry', *Identities: Global Studies in Culture and Power* 18(1): 2–38.

Sorabji, C. 2006. 'Managing Memories in Post-War Sarajevo: Individuals, Bad Memories, and New Wars', *Journal of the Royal Anthropological Institute* 12(1): 1–18.

———. 2007. 'Bosnian Neighbourhoods Revisited: Tolerance, Commitment and *Komšiluk* in Sarajevo', in J. de Pina Cabral and F. Pine (eds), *On the Margins of Religion*. Oxford: Berghahn, pp. 97–112.

Spasić, I. 2013. *Kultura na Delu: Društvena Transformacija Srbije iz Burdijeovske Perspektive*. Beograd: Fabrika knjiga.

Spasić, I. and A. Birešev. 2012. 'The State as the Great Classifier', in P. Cvetičanin and A. Birešev (eds), *Social and Cultural Capital in Western Balkan societies*. Niš: Centre for Empirical Cultural Studies of South-East Europe, pp. 145–59.

Spencer, J. 2007. *Anthropology, Politics and the State: Democracy and Violence in South Asia*. Cambridge: Cambridge University Press.

Ssorin-Chaikov, N. 2003. *The Social Life of the State in Subarctic Siberia*. Stanford: Stanford University Press.

Statistički Bilten za Mjesec Juli 2008 (IX/7). Sarajevo: Zavod za informatiku i statistiku Kantona Sarajevo.

Stefansson, A. 2007. 'Urban Exile: Locals, Newcomers and the Cultural Transformation of Sarajevo', in X. Bougarel, E. Helms and G. Duijzings (eds), *The New Bosnian Mosaic*. Aldershot: Ashgate, pp. 59–78.

———. 2010. 'Coffee after Cleansing? Co-existence, Co-operation, and Communication in Post-Conflict Bosnia and Herzegovina', *Focaal* 57: 62–76.

Šurković, Z. (ed.). 2003. *Gimnazija Dobrinja*. Sarajevo: Gimnazija Dobrinja.

Taussig, M. 1992. *The Nervous System*. London: Routledge.

Thompson, E.P. 1967. 'Time, Work-Discipline, and Industrial Capitalism', *Past and Present* 38, 56–97.

Thrift, N. 2006. 'Re-inventing Invention: New Tendencies in Capitalist Commodification', *Economy and Society* 35(2): 279–306.

Torpey, J. 1998. 'Coming and Going: On the State Monopolization of the Legitimate "Means of Movement"', *Sociological Theory* 16(3): 239–59.

Trouillot, M.-R. 2001. 'The Anthropology of the State in the Age of Globalisation: Close Encounters of the Deceptive Kind', *Current Anthropology* 42(1): 125–38.

UNDP (United Nations Development Programme). 2007. *Glas Tihe Većine*. Sarajevo: UNDP.

———. 2009. *The Ties That Bind: Social Capital in Bosnia and Herzegovina*. Sarajevo: UNDP.

Van Biesen, I., P. Mair and T. Poguntke. 2012. 'Going, Going, Gone… The Decline of Party Membership in Contemporary Europe', *European Journal of Political Research* 51(1): 24–56.

Vetters, L. 2007. 'The Power of Administrative Categories: Emerging Notions of Citizenship in the Divided City of Mostar', *Ethnopolitics* 6(2): 187–209.

Vlaisavljević, U. 2006. *Etnopolitika i Građanstvo*. Mostar: Dijalog.

Weate, J. 2003. 'Achille Mbembe and the Postcolony: Going beyond the Text', *Research in African Literatures* 34(4): 27–41.

Wedeen, L. 1999a. 'Seeing like a Citizen, Acting like a State: Exemplary Events in Unified Yemen', *Comparative Studies in Society and History* 45(4): 680–713.

———. 1999b. *Ambiguities of Domination: Politics, Rhetoric and Symbols in Contemporary Syria*. Chicago: Chicago University Press.

Wilson, F. 2001. 'In the Name of the State? Schools and Teachers in an Andean Province', in T.B. Hansen and F. Stepputat (eds), *States of Imagination*. Durham: Duke University Press, pp. 313–44.

Woodward, S.L. 1995. *Socialist Unemployment: Political Economy of Yugoslavia, 1945–90.* Princeton: Princeton University Press.

Woost, M.D. 1993. 'Nationalising the Local Past in Sri Lanka: Histories of Nation and Development in a Sinhalese Village', *American Ethnologist* 20(3): 502–21.

Yurchak, A. 1997. 'The Cynical Reason of Late Socialism: Power, Pretense and the *Anekdot*', *Public Culture* 9: 161–88.

———. 2005. *Everything Was Forever, Until It Was No More: The Last Soviet Generation.* Princeton: Princeton University Press.

INDEX

multiculturalism, 9–11, 99
muslims, 25–27, 64, 97, 99, 135, 194

names, 25, 85n1, 226
national homogenisation of
    population, 5, 10, 27, 133–34
national identification
    identitarianism, 10–14, 20–21
    identity categories in census, 5, 27
    relative intensity of, 25, 27–28
    and statehood, 132–35, 192–95
nationalism 10, 39, 110, 132–35, 184,
    192–99, 226–27
    ambiguity of Bosniak-cum-BiH
        nationalism, 99, 133–35,
        193–96, 226–28
    Bosniak nationalism, 22–28, 97–99,
        110, 132, 193–95 (*see also*
        SDA)
    Croatian nationalism, 22–28, 131–
        32, 155n5, 195, 199, 226 (*see
        also* HDZ)
    Serbian nationalism, 22–28, 92–93,
        174, 199, 226 (*see also* SDS)
Navaro-Yashin, Yael, 52–53, 131, 174,
    197, 214–15
nekultura, 66-69, 147–49
neoliberalisation, 52, 144, 217
newcomers, 147–48, 152
'normal lives'
    how to study yearnings for, 54–55
    the 'lives' in, 40–43
    as shared concern, 1–2, 8–9, 20–22,
        38–40
normality and abnormality
    anthropology of, 16–17, 20, 23–40,
        53
    of the Dayton BiH state, 143–45
    during BiH war, 79–82, 92–103
Nuijten, Monique, 136–37

OHR (Office of the High
    Representative), 76–77, 143–44,
    174, 228. *See also* foreign
    supervision
Olympic Games, 3, 78–79, 99, 151, 199,
    223–24
optimism, 43–44, 105, 170

order
    city transport as framework for,
        81, 83
    ordered/orderly state, 129-130, 144,
        153, 196
    schooling as framework for, 103
    and survival during war, 108–11
    yearning for, 66, 71–72
    See also gridding, system
ordinariness, 33–36, 42–43
'ordinary people', 176, 180–81, 196,
    208, 211–12, 218
organigram of BiH state institutions,
    5–6, 140–41

paramilitary formations, 24–25, 92–93,
    111
parenting, 115, 137–38, 148–49, 164–
    66, 181, 203, 217, 226, 229. *See
    also* children
pathologies, 18–20
pattering in place, 157–86, 216, 219
pensioner clubs, 124–25
pensions, 7, 103, 166, 178, 130
planning lives, 35, 50, 159
political parties, 4–5, 22–28, 123, 131,
    135, 167, 189–219, 225–27. *See
    also* HDZ, SDA, SDS, SDP
politicians
    appropriation of wealth, 203–6,
        212–13
    bahatost (brutish arrogance), 192,
        218
    'barking' at, 192, 200, 206, 209, 211,
        214–15, 225
    exasperation with, 129, 161, 190–93
    exceptions amongst, 135, 181,
        192–93
    impunity of, 206, 212, 218
    nerad (non-work), 75, 84, 189, 192,
        227
    projecting strength and weakness,
        199, 206–7
    reactions to JMBG protests, 230–31
    See also politika, ruling caste
politika (politics), 40, 143, 180–82,
    190–93, 196–97

www.ingramcontent.com/pod-product-compliance
Lightning Source LLC
Chambersburg PA
CBHW062107040426
42336CB00042B/2449